AGING
in Canada

AGING
in Canada

NEENA L. CHAPPELL
MARCUS J. HOLLANDER

ISSUES IN CANADA

OXFORD

UNIVERSITY PRESS

OXFORD
UNIVERSITY PRESS

Oxford University Press is a department of the University of Oxford.
It furthers the University's objective of excellence in research, scholarship,
and education by publishing worldwide. Oxford is a registered trade mark of
Oxford University Press in the UK and in certain other countries.

Published in Canada by
Oxford University Press
8 Sampson Mews, Suite 204,
Don Mills, Ontario M3C 0H5 Canada

www.oupcanada.com

Library and Archives Canada Cataloguing in Publication

Chappell, Neena L.
Aging in Canada / Neena L. Chappell, Marcus J. Hollander.

(Issues in Canada)
Includes bibliographical references and index.
ISBN 978-0-19-544766-8

1. Aging—Health aspects—Canada. 2. Aging—Economic aspects—
Canada. 3. Older people—Hospital care—Canada. 4. Older people—
Services for—Canada. 5. Medical care, Cost of—Canada—Forecasting.
6. Medical care—Canada—Forecasting. I. Hollander, Marcus J., 1946–
II. Title. III. Series: Issues in Canada

RA413.7.A4 C53 2013   305.260971   C2012-907873-5

Cover image: Yaromir/Shutterstock

Printed and bound in the United States of America

1 2 3 4 — 16 15 14 13

Contents

List of Illustrations

FIGURES

Figure 1-1: Percentages of Population Age 65+ in Selected Countries, 2011 and 2030

Figure 2-1: Dependency Ratios in Canada, 1971 to 2056

Figure 2-2: Percentage of Canadian Adults Reporting One or More Chronic Conditions

Figure 3-1: Who Receives the Care?

Figure 3-2: Sources of Support to Informal Caregivers for Seniors

Figure 4-1: The Origins and Current Status of the Continuing Care System

Figure 4-2: The British Columbia Continuing Care System in 1993

Figure 5-1: Substituting Home Care for Residential Care over Time

Figure 6-1: The PRISMA Model

Figure 6-2: The Chronic Care Model

Figure 6-3: The Enhanced Continuing Care Framework

Figure 6-4: Application of the Enhanced Continuing Care Framework to Older Persons

Figure 6-5: A Schematic of Client Flow through the System of Care for Older Persons

TABLES

Table 2-1: Life Expectancy at Birth in Selected Countries, 2007

Table 2-2: Percentage of Population Age 65+ in Selected Countries, 2010 and 2050

Table 2-3: Chronic Conditions among Canadians Age 45+, 2009

Acknowledgements

Neena L. Chappell thanks her family and friends for their support. Marcus J. Hollander thanks his wife for her support. In addition, we would like to recognize the contributions of Carren Dujela and Nancy Davis at the Centre on Aging, University of Victoria, and Nicole Littlejohn at Hollander Analytical Services Ltd.

Abbreviations

ADL	activities of daily living
AFC	Age-Friendly Cities (Communities)
ALC	alternate level of care
CAP	Canada Assistance Plan
CARMEN	Care and Management Services for Older People in Europe Network
CCAC	Community Care Access Centre
CCF	Co-operative Commonwealth Federation
CCM	chronic care model
CHA	Canadian Hospital Association
CHC	community health centre
CHSRF	Canadian Health Services Research Foundation
CHST	Canada Health and Social Transfer
CIHI	Canadian Institute for Health Information
CLHIA	Canadian Life and Health Insurance Association
CMA	Canadian Medical Association
COPD	Chronic Obstructive Pulmonary Disease
CPP	Canada Pension Plan
CSHA	Canadian Study of Health and Aging
ECCF	Enhanced Continuing Care Framework
ECCM	enhanced chronic care model
EHCS	extended health care services

EPF   Federal–Provincial Fiscal Arrangements and Established Programs Financing Act

GDP   gross domestic product

GIS   Guaranteed Income Supplement

HARP   Hospital Admission Risk Program

HTF   Health Transition Fund

IADL   instrumental activities of daily living

ISD   Integrated Services Delivery

OAS   Old Age Security

OECD   Organisation for Economic Cooperation and Development

PACE   Program for All-Inclusive Care for the Elderly

PHAC   Public Health Agency of Canada

PRISMA   Program of Research to Integrate Services for the Maintenance of Autonomy Model

QALY   Quality Adjusted Life Year

RCT   randomized controlled trial

SAIL   Strategies and Actions for Independent Living

SIPA   System of Integrated Care for Older Persons

SMAF   *Système de measure des l'autonome functionnelle /* Functional Autonomy Measurement System

SUFA   Social Union Framework Agreement

WHO   World Health Organization

Chapter 1

Introduction

As Canada's baby boom generation[1] begins to turn 65, attention from many quarters is focusing on the demographic trends that gerontologists have been discussing for years. These trends are most often discussed in terms of Canada's looming older adult population resulting from the aging of the baby boom generation. Just as relevant, but less often recognized, is the fact that this baby boom generation is currently the primary caregiving cohort to those who are already living in old age. That is, the significance of the baby boomers extends beyond the fact that they will constitute a large cohort of older adults in the near future and includes their caregiving role at present.

Canada, like other countries, is aging. Life expectancy—the length of time that we live—has been rising since the early 1900s. In 2006, we could expect to live to 81; in 1981, the average life expectancy was only 76. In 2006, those who reached the age of 65 could expect to live for another 20 years—that is, to 85. Compare this to 1981, when those who had reached 65 could have expected to live only to 82 (Statistics Canada 2010c). We are living longer, and there will be more of us who are elderly. This new demographic results from the large cohort of baby boomers in old age, increasing both the numbers and percentages of older adults within our population. In 2010, 15.3 percent of Canada's population was 65 years of age or older (65+) representing 4,386,969 older adults. In 2030 it will be 24.1 percent (7,844,309 older adults) (Denton and Spencer 2010).

Canada is not alone. Many European countries including the United Kingdom (UK), France, Germany, Sweden, Belgium, Spain, Italy, and Greece have higher proportions of older adults than does Canada. Japan's proportion is even higher. Some 23.1 percent of that country's population was 65+ in 2010, the highest percentage in the world and equaling 29.29 million persons (United Nations, Statistics Bureau 2008). And China—with a smaller percentage of older adults—nevertheless has the largest number, totaling 110 million older adults in 2010. This amounts to just over 8 percent of the population. (See Figure 1-1.)

Concerns about the rising tide of older adults centre around declining health and meeting the needs that consequently arise. Chronic conditions and disability increase in old age. It is estimated that between 81 percent (Gilmour and Park 2006) and 90 percent (Denton and Spencer 2010) of those 65+ living in the community live with such health problems. If we include those who live in nursing homes, this percentage would be higher. Common ailments include arthritis and rheumatism, high blood pressure, heart disease, diabetes, and bronchitis and emphysema (Ramage-Morin 2008; Turcotte and Schellenberg 2006). Society, though, is also evolving. More women are in the labour force, fertility rates have dropped, and children are geographically mobile—in other words, there are concerns about the availability of family members to provide care. Last but not

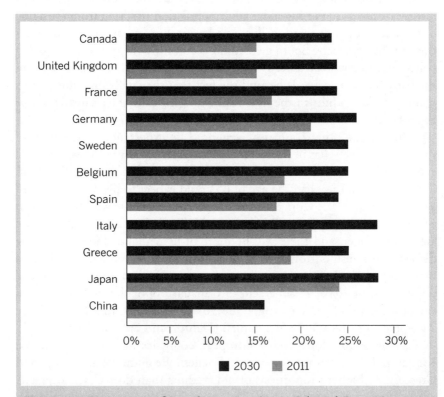

Figure 1-1 Percentages of Population Age 65+ in Selected Countries, 2011 and 2030

Sources: CIA World Factbooks 2011; United Nations 1999; Kinsella and Velkoff 2001; Mamulo and Scherbov 2009

least, the continually rising cost of the formal health care system is also an important issue.

These concerns are not new, but have become heightened in recent years. It is not uncommon to hear about the impending crisis in the Canadian health care system in terms of a "grey tsunami." This metaphor, for example, was used in the title of a 2008 article by ModernHealthcare.com: "A gray tsunami cometh. Long-term care is challenged by the on-slaught of the Baby Boomers, but concern is muted by a lack of im-mediacy" (Kirchheimer 2008). In the same year, the Ontario Professional Planners Institute hosted a symposium on "The Grey Tsunami, Aging Communities and Planning." By January 2010, the BC (British Columbia) Care Providers Association posted an article on their Care Online website entitled "Silver Tsunami No Longer in the Forecast—the Grey Wave is Here." In 2010 the Alzheimer Society of Canada released its report, "Rising Tide: The Impact of Dementia on Canadian Society," projecting the health burden of the disease from 2008 to 2038, and the economic costs of care, estimated to double every decade, to $158 billion in 2038. Due in part to this kind of coverage in Canadian and international reports, a gloomy picture of the future sustainability of the Canadian health care system has been painted. These reports note that costs are inexorably rising, and that caring for a growing elderly population may eventually bankrupt our health care system. As we discuss later, it does not have to be this way. People, including decision makers, have choices. Past choices got us into our current predicament. Better choices, more sophisticated analyses and political will can get us out of it.

Reports from many large national and private sector organizations also ignore the potential of increasing value for money in the Canadian health care sector that can be, and has been, achieved by developing integrated models of care delivery. An influential paper prepared for the CD Howe Institute by David Dodge, the former Governor of the Bank of Canada, and Deputy Minister of Finance, and Richard Dion (Dodge and Dion 2011a), estimates increases in health care expenditures. Their prescription for addressing such costs is as follows: sharply reduce public services; in-crease taxes; institute more co-payments by individuals; reduce the qual-ity of publicly funded health care; and develop a parallel privately funded system, i.e., two-tier health care. The TD Economics report "Charting a Path to Health Care in Ontario" also paints a gloomy picture about future policy options (Drummond and Burleton 2010). The solutions suggested in the TD Economics report include changes to the funding of doctors and hospitals, scaling back benefits, and increasing taxes. Other options include expanding information technology, focusing on quality care, and promot-ing healthier lifestyles.

It should be noted that concern over these issues is a universal phenomenon, not limited to Canada. A 2011 Organisation for Economic Cooperation and Development (OECD) report suggests the contours of this issue: "How to balance home and institutional care settings is at the core of long-term care policy initiatives in nearly all OECD countries" (Colombo et al. 2011, 33). The report provides a review of long-term care models in key OECD countries; however, regrettably, it fails to provide a framework for the organization of integrated systems of care delivery.

Our age of information overload can exacerbate understanding the issues involved. The views expressed on the extent and severity of the issues, as well as the solutions to the impending "crisis," are contradictory and often complex. These views range from one extreme (the claim that medicare and old age pensions will lead to certain bankruptcy) to the other (the claim that there is no issue). While the analysis of the problem is usually competent, many authors propose excessively dismal solutions, such as dismantling medicare. Such solutions typically fail to consider alternative ways to organize the overall system of care delivery to increase value for money.

Despite the sometimes extremist views, there are legitimate questions regarding the social and economic implications of the aging baby boom generation. Our view is that considerable potential exists for cost avoidance by more intelligent management as well as implementing efficient and effective care delivery systems, while continuing to provide the same (or indeed better) quality of care. Other writers have also argued that our health care system is sustainable. Our interest here is not whether costs will rise, but rather the extent to which rising costs are attributable to the increasing number and proportion of older adults. In terms of the aging baby boomers, we consider how to meet needs without runaway costs.

As a counter to negative perceptions such as those noted above, a variety of organizations have offered alternative opinions on how to meet the increased demand. The Canadian Health Services Research Foundation (CHSRF) published "Myth: Canada's System of Healthcare Financing Is Unsustainable" in 2007 and more recently their 2011 report "Research Synthesis on Cost Drivers in the Health Sector and Proposed Policy Options." Similarly the OECD regularly publishes reports on health care, such as *Achieving Better Value for Money in Health Care* (2009a). In 2010, the Canadian Federation of Nurses Unions released "The Sustainability of Medicare." The Canadian Medical Association recently issued a news release entitled "Canada's Doctors and Nurses Come Together to Urge Politicians to Act Now for the Future of Health Care" and "Voices into Action. Health Care Transformation" (which was the focus of their 144th annual meeting). The Canadian Healthcare Association includes among its publications "Change and Continuity in Canada's Health Care System" and "Continuum of Care: The Issues and Challenges for Long-Term Care." Much information is available.

Canadian Doctors for Medicare (2011) also maintain that our health care system is sustainable. They point out that the costs of medicare (doctors and hospitals) have not grown substantially. In 2009, such costs were 4.25 percent of gross domestic product (GDP) compared to 3.63 percent in 1981. They note that overall health spending as a percentage of GDP has grown, but is manageable. The growth in the elderly population only increases overall costs by one percent per year, and the increase in health care spending as a percentage of provincial budgets is the result of decreases in spending elsewhere to accommodate tax cuts. Thus, the authors argue, the health care system is sustainable on economic grounds. Similar arguments are made by the Caledon Institute (Ruggeri 2002).

Even economists who are concerned about rising health care costs recognize that aging per se will only add one percent or less per year to the costs of health care (Dodge and Dion 2011b). The factors that drive up cost are high technology, labour costs, and increased service utilization across all ages. However, these factors are not driven by uncontrollable external factors such as population growth. Furthermore, there should be future offsets in education costs as a result of the decreasing proportion of young people in our population over time. The perceived crisis in the sustainability of our health care system should be framed not in relation to demographic determinism, but rather in terms of challenges related to the organization and management of health services, particularly for older adults.

This leads us to apocalyptic demography, which refers to the oversimplified belief that a demographic trend, such as population aging, inevitably has dire consequences. An example of this is the assumption that because of the impending growth in the number of seniors and their higher-than-average use of health and social services, the country cannot sustain these public programs (Gee and Gutman 2000). This, we believe, is an overly alarmist view of our aging society.

Canadians recognize that our health care system is under stress and that the care of the elderly population is a major challenge, and Canadians are looking for solutions. There are many questions about the consequences of the aging of the baby boomers. What are the care needs of an aging society? How are our needs met now? What gaps exist between current care provision and the care that is required? What type of care system is both appropriate and cost-effective for an aging society? Is such a system feasible for Canada at this time? How do we establish such a system?

In order to consider the issues fully, we must challenge strongly held but erroneous assumptions and oversimplified answers. Contrary to current beliefs, the growing percentage of provincial budgets consumed by health care is not a reflection of a health care system in crisis. Rather, it is more likely an artifact of tax policy and federal/provincial transfers. A look at the broader picture reveals that there have only been modest increases in the percentage of GDP consumed by health care in Canada. For example, health care spending as a percentage of GDP increased from 10 percent to 10.5 percent in the 15 years from 1992 to 2007 (before the recent financial crisis) (CIHI 2011d). No cost crisis is reflected in these national numbers.

We argue here that, with good policy, it is possible to both provide better care and reduce costs. This can be accomplished, for example, by developing improved, integrated systems of care delivery for older adults and people with disabilities.

This book looks for answers. We summarize current knowledge. We look at the available facts, drawing on over 30 years of gerontological research in Canada and other western nations. We first examine the care needs of an aging Canadian society. We then discuss care provision as it currently exists for older adults in Canada, focusing first on unpaid/informal caregivers—the dominant care system in all societies. We go on to assess the formal health care system and its appropriateness for an aging society and then present a model that can be both appropriate for older adults as well as cost-effective. The concluding chapter offers our view of how to move forward.

In a nutshell, we argue that the increased numbers and proportions of older adults is cause for attention but not for alarm. There will likely be both an increase in demand as well as some change in the nature of demand. These will require action sooner rather than later. However, we know much about how best to provide care as we age, and how to do so in a cost-effective manner. We know, for example, that informal caregivers, primarily family members, are and always have been the mainstay of care when we become ill or disabled. This remains the case today, although increased longevity and the prolongation of complex conditions mean the demands on these caregivers cannot be minimized. Caregivers require support. Failing to support them leads to higher costs for the formal system. Furthermore, we argue that the underdeveloped continuing care system, including home care, has left this country with an unnecessarily high-cost medical care system plus inadequate services for its older population. Alternative models of care, notably integrated care models, offer potentially more cost-effective and appropriate care. Furthermore, investment in prevention offers a means to reduce the demand for care in the future.

Drawing on over 30 years each of international gerontological and health services research, as well as our own research and policy experience, we argue that while Canada has not "got it right" thus far, it can. This will require forward planning, redrawing boundaries within and between sectors, and collaboration and co-operation toward the goal of establishing a truly appropriate and cost-effective care delivery system for an aging society. As we see it, government has an essential role to play in the creation of such a system. The current gloom about the sustainability of our health care system is premature. There is now clear evidence of the potential for cost-effective alternative approaches that allow for significantly enhanced value in our health care system. This would involve moving from a framework of discussion in which more money is constantly requested to one in which value for money is carefully considered. "Getting it right" in regard to caring appropriately for older adults is possible. This book provides a blueprint for doing so.

Chapter 2

A Profile of Our Aging Population

Introduction

This chapter considers the health needs of older Canadians before later chapters examine how those needs are currently met and how they might be better met. First, we consider the increasing size of the 65+ population in Canada. While it is clear that the numbers and proportions of older adults are increasing, it is less clear that rising health care costs are a result of this unalterable demographic fact. Physical health does decline with age, but the changes that we may experience with a variety of chronic conditions and in disability (functioning) as we age are less straightforward than they may appear. And chronic conditions do not always lead to functional disability or activity restrictions. Furthermore, it is not necessarily the case that baby boomers will enjoy the same health in older age as the current elderly population. Health promotion potentially has an important role here: if we can decrease needs, we can begin to think about decreasing demands for care.

Some additional considerations include the facts that health is not only physical and that the aging population is not homogenous. It is interesting that subjective (psychological and emotional) health does not decline with age in the same way as physical health does. How do we explain this? And what are the implications for the quality of life in old age? Aging is associated with health issues, but the onset of these health problems tends to be gradual. Moreover, all older adults do not have high care needs. Subpopulations might be defined by age or by other factors. For example, Neugarten (1974) first distinguished between the young-old and the old-old over 35 years ago. Since that time, some have added the middle-old and the oldest-old or "fourth age" (Laslett 1996; Baltes and Smith 2003) using varying age ranges attached to these categories. ("Young-old" can encompass, for example, 55–75, 60–69, or 65–74; "middle-old" can be 70–79 or 75–84; and "old-old" might be 75+, 80+, 85+, or 90+.) The literature is replete with different age demarcations, but the terms are used to convey the diversity by age. Recognizing the heterogeneity of the older population is a starting point for adapting our health care system.

More Older Canadians

It is the increasing numbers and proportions of older adults (usually taken to be those 65+) that raise concern. More people are living longer. In Canada, life expectancy has been increasing since the early 1900s. We saw above that in 2006 overall life expectancy was 81 years (compared with 76 years in 1981); this is similar to France but lower than the life expectancy of Japan (82.6). It is higher than the US (78.1) or the UK (79.5) (see Table 2-1). Life expectancy at 65 has also been increasing. It was 85 in 2006, up from 82 in 1981 (Statistics Canada 2010c; Wilkins et al. 2008). By 2015, Statistics Canada (2008a) projects that for the first time in history there will be more persons who are 65+ than there are children (those below the age of 15), and that there could be twice as many older adults as there are children by the mid-twenty-first century.

**Table 2-1   Life Expectancy at Birth
in Selected Countries, 2007**

Canada	80.7
France	80.9
Japan	82.6
UK	79.5
US	78.1

Source: OECD 2011

Increased life expectancy raises the proportion of older adults in the population. Table 2-2 shows the percentage of Canada's 65+ population in 2010, projected to 2050, compared with other select countries. The figure for Canada was 14.1 percent in 2010 and will be 24.9 percent in 2050. This current percentage is lower than the proportions in Japan, Italy, and Germany, all with proportions above 20 percent. By 2050, according to these projections, over 30 percent of the population of Japan, the Republic of Korea, Italy, and Germany will be comprised of older adults, in other words, higher than that of Canada (United Nations, Statistics Bureau 2008).

Table 2-2   Percentage of Population Age 65+ in Selected Countries, 2010 and 2050

Country	2010	2050 (projected)
Japan	23.1	39.6
Korea, Rep. of	11.1	32.8
Italy	20.4	32.7
Germany	20.4	30.9
China	8.2	25.6
France	16.8	24.9
Canada	14.1	24.9
Sweden	18.2	24.6
UK	16.6	23.6
Russia	12.8	23.1
Brazil	7.0	22.5
US	13.1	21.2
India	4.9	13.5

Source: Statistics Bureau, MIC; Ministry of Health, Labour and Welfare; UN (Copyright © Statistics Bureau), 1996–2008. All rights reserved.

Dependency Ratios: Cause for Concern?

Another way to look at the population is to look at the proportion of older adults and/or children relative to those of working age. The *dependency ratio*, as it is called, is a popular means of summarizing demands on, and contributions to, society. This term is based on the assumption that neither older adults nor children contribute to the economic production of a society. This assumption, when applied to older adults, is largely erroneous. It fails to take into account those older adults who are in the labour force and more importantly the contributions of all older adults, as consumers and the large numbers who contribute in other ways, such as giving cash and other goods to their children and grandchildren, babysitting, etc. Similarly, it fails to consider children and teenagers who work for pay and those of working age who are not employed. Nevertheless, governments often use dependency ratios as a shorthand summary of current and future demands.

There are several types of dependency ratios. The *overall dependency ratio* includes both those 65+ and those under 15 as a ratio of persons of working age, 15 to 64. It was at an historic low in 2006 at 44 (in other words, for every 100 working age persons there were 44 persons who were above or below working age). This is less than it was in 2001, when the ratio was 62. It is projected to be only 61 in 2031 and 69 in 2056. However, the proportion of persons 65+ is increasing. In 1991, 11.5 percent of the total population was 65+; in 2000, this percentage grew to 12.5 percent; in 2006 it was 13 percent (Government of Alberta 2009; Statistics Canada 2008a). By 2036, projections place the proportion of those 65+ between 23 percent and 25 percent (Statistics Canada 2010e). Not surprisingly, following from these figures, the old age dependency ratio (those 65+ as a ratio of those of working age) does show a steady increase: 16.6 in 1991, 18.3 in 2000, and 20 in 2006. It is expected to reach 39 in 2036. In contrast, the youth dependency ratio is decreasing (45 percent in 1991; 39 percent in 2006; 34 percent in 2036).

Recent revisions to the estimates of the overall and old age dependency ratios now define the youth population as those between 0 and 19 (rather than 0 and 14 years of age) and the working age population as those between 20 and 64 (rather than between 15 and 64). This change increases the size of the youth population and shrinks the size of the working population. The result is an increase in the overall and old age dependency ratios. Using these definitions, Figure 2-1 shows that, between 1971 and 2006, the overall dependency ratio decreased from 89 to 60 and is projected to increase to 84 by 2056. The old age dependency ratio increased from 15 in 1971 to 21 in 2006, and is projected to be 50 by 2056. Given that many youth and young adults are staying in school longer than in the past, this is probably a more accurate reflection of current trends. However, with the disappearance of mandatory retirement, there could well be an increase in the normal retirement age and therefore in the size of the working age population. The consequence would be a decrease in the size of the dependent old age population. A further adjustment of the formulas used to compute dependency ratios would then likely reduce the size of the overall and old age dependency ratios compared to their more recent computations.

Interpreting Dependency Ratios

The extent to which these figures are a cause for concern depends on an individual's beliefs about the costs of children and older adults to society. Perhaps predictably, economists disagree. Magnus (2009) and Robson (2009), for example, argue that the cost of care for children is less than the cost of care for older adults, so that the decline in the proportion of young people will not offset the greater cost of caring for older adults. They argue that the potential cost of caring for older adults could be unaffordable. In a similar vein, Robson (2001) estimates that the implicit health care services

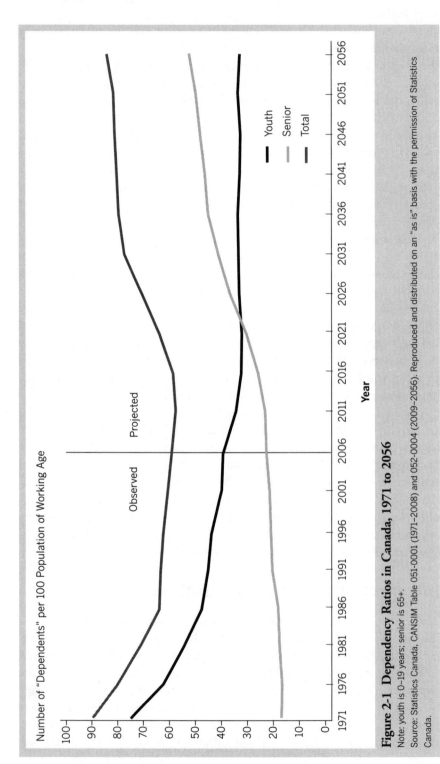

Number of "Dependents" per 100 Population of Working Age

Figure 2-1 Dependency Ratios in Canada, 1971 to 2056

Note: youth is 0–19 years; senior is 65+.

Source: Statistics Canada, CANSIM Table 051-0001 (1971–2008) and 052-0004 (2009–2056). Reproduced and distributed on an "as is" basis with the permission of Statistics Canada.

liability associated with the pressure of an aging population amounts to more than 50 percent of Canada's GDP.

Mendelson and Divinsky (2002) take a very different view. They state that, while those 75+ reveal disproportionate use of health care services, that age group will grow only from 5.8 percent of the population in 2001 to 6.7 percent in 2015. Even if we estimate that they consume 50 percent of all health care expenditures, their growth will likely add only 1.1 percent to health care expenditures as a percent of GDP. This number, while not insignificant, is well under expected economic growth. "In other words, everything else being equal, health care expenditures . . . due to the increased number of elderly . . . represents a real cost pressure, but it is hardly the Armageddon of health costs" (35).[1] Similarly, economists Denton and colleagues (1998) (also see Denton and Spencer 1999) argue that Canada can easily afford an aging population given at least moderate levels of economic growth.

Brown (2012) estimates that older adults cost public funds 2.5 times that of the young, per capita. Even using this weighting, however, Brown still concludes that both social security and health care are sustainable with an aging population, even without raising the age of normal retirement past 65, and even if GDP does not exhibit faster growth. Mérette (2002) further argues that a smaller workforce could result in increased wages relative to interest rates for younger cohorts, adding to an accumulation of human capital.

More is said about the health care system and associated costs in Chapters 4 and 5, but it is worth noting here that the Health Council of Canada (2009) agrees, adding that factors other than the aging population are the major causes of cost increases in health care services:

> Contrary to popular belief, aging and population growth are not the major causes of the rises in Canada's health care spending. The largest factor is our increase in use of services. On average we are all getting more care, undergoing more tests, and receiving more prescriptions. Are we healthier as a result? If we aren't, are we prepared to continue to pay more anyway? . . . The persistent belief that our aging population will overwhelm the health care system is a myth.

Research in Manitoba (CHSRF 2001) has established that most of the adults using more services are healthy adults, including seniors. In other words it is healthy, not sick, adults who are driving most of this increased usage (accounting for 57.5 percent of the increase in the late 1990s). The question that follows is whether this increased usage among those who are healthy is leading to improved health, perhaps in the future. This has not been established. As Brown notes (2011), the outcomes appear to be unchanged and there is no evidence of increased needs. Furthermore, the rising cost of high-end technological interventions (including pharmaceuticals) is a major factor in medical cost increases, much larger than the aging of the population (Di Matteo 2005). For example, Morgan and Cunningham (2011) find that per capita expenditures on acute hospital care and doctor visits increased only slightly more than inflation (17 percent) between 1996 and 2006, while spending on prescription drugs increased by 140 percent. In other words, increased medical intervention and changes in patterns of health care practices account substantially for rising costs, yet we lack evidence that it is appropriate and necessary, or that it increases the health and quality of life of older adults.

So the evidence suggests that factors other than the increasing numbers of older adults are much more significant in terms of rising health care costs. Nevertheless, while changing demographics need not cause alarm, the situation does require attention based on the best knowledge available.

The Health and Well-Being of Older Canadians

Older adults often have health care needs arising from declines in physical health. A starting point for considering aging in Canada is to determine those health care needs. However, first consider *health*. It is over six decades since the World Health Organization (WHO) proclaimed that health is more than the absence of disease; it includes physical but also psychological and social dimensions encompassing a more holistic resource for living than previously envisioned. Interestingly, of the many aspects of our health, it is our physical selves that are most likely to deteriorate as we age. This is most evident when examining the prevalence of chronic conditions.

Chronic conditions

Currently, chronic conditions are the major cause of death and disability in Canada and worldwide. WHO (2011) projects that chronic disease will account for 89 percent of all deaths by 2015. In Canada, prevalence rates vary depending on the conditions included, but Gilmour and Park (2006) report that 81 percent of those 65+ and living in the community have some chronic conditions. The figure is higher for older elderly people than younger elderly people: 80 percent among Canadian women age 65 to 74 and 86 percent among those 75+, with similar figures reported for men (Milan and Vézina 2011). As Table 2-3 and Figure 2-2 show, most people in Canada 65+ have at least one chronic condition. Additionally, 25 percent of this age group have four or more chronic conditions (Statistics Canada 2010b).

Table 2-3   Chronic Conditions among Canadians Age 45+, 2009

	Proportion Reporting Condition (%)	
Chronic Condition (based on self-reports from a checklist of diagnosed conditions)	Age 45–64	Age 65+
High blood pressure	24.0	52.9*
Arthritis	20.3	43.4*
Back problems	25.0	28.6*
Eye problems (cataracts or glaucoma)	4.6	27.9*
Heart disease	6.9	22.6*
Osteoporosis	6.1	18.1*
Diabetes	8.6	17.2*
Urinary incontinence	3.3	11.7*
Chronic obstructive pulmonary disease	4.0	8.8*
Bowel disorder	5.1	6.4*
Stroke	1.1	4.2*
Alzheimer's disease	0.1E	1.6*

Based on self-reports from a checklist of diagnosed conditions. Significantly different from estimate for 45 to 64 age group (p<0.05)
E use with caution (coefficient of variation 16.6% to 33.3%)
Sources: Statistics Canada, Canadian Community Health Survey – Healthy Aging 2009; Statistics Canada, Canadian Community Health Survey 2003. Reproduced and distributed on an "as is" basis with the permission of Statistics Canada.

Two common chronic conditions causing death are cardiovascular disease and cancer. Other chronic conditions include arthritis, diabetes, heart disease, high blood pressure, and mood disorders not including depression (CIHI 2009). The prevalence is higher among women than men, especially for arthritis/rheumatism, cataracts/glaucoma, and back problems, although men are more likely to have heart disease, diabetes, and cancer (DesMeules, Manuel, and Cho 2004; Gilmour and Park 2006). Living with chronic pain is also relatively common, with 27 percent of seniors reporting chronic pain. In addition, 16.7 percent of men 65+ and 23.9 percent of women 65+ suffer from pain that prevents activities; this is higher than any other age group (Statistics Canada 2008b; 2010d). In other words, women tend to live longer than men, but they live those longer lives with more illness. There is a saying in gerontology: men die quicker but women are sicker.

A major fear among middle-aged and older adults alike is the loss of mental capacities with age. A key concern in old age is dementia, a chronic condition of which Alzheimer's is the most common type. Dementia

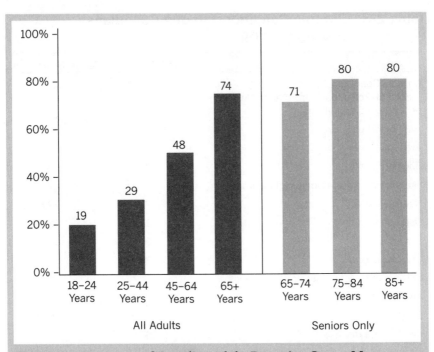

Figure 2-2   Percentage of Canadian Adults Reporting One or More Chronic Conditions

Note: The following chronic conditions are included: arthritis, asthma, cancer, chronic pain, depression, diabetes, emphysema or chronic obstructive pulmonary disease, heart disease, high blood pressure, a mood disorder other than depression and stroke. The analysis included "don't know" and "refusal" responses; the percentage of non-responses per chronic condition/survey question was less than 1 percent overall for all adults.
Sources: Based on Statistics Canada 2008b

increases in older age. The Canadian Study on Health and Aging (1994), Canada's first and only national study establishing the prevalence of dementia, documented between 7 percent and 8 percent of older adults with this disease, with women more likely to have dementia than men. This may change if men reach women's life expectancy. The prevalence of dementia increases dramatically within later life; from 8 percent among those 65+ to fully 35 percent among those 85+. Less severe symptoms of mild cognitive impairment are experienced by another 16 percent of older adults, also increasing with age (National Advisory Council on Aging 2004). Among those 85+, 65 percent have dementia or milder forms of cognitive impairment (Graham et al. 1997).

Another mental disorder of concern among gerontologists is depression. This is despite the fact that the risk of depression appears to lessen as we age. Among all Canadians age 12 and older, 11.4 percent suffer from depression. In 2002, only 1.9 percent of women and 2.1 percent of men age 65+ suffered from depression in the previous 12 months compared to 5.6 percent and 3.5 percent respectively for those between 45 and 65 (the next lowest age group). Those between 15 and 24 are the most likely to suffer depression (8.3 and 4.5 respectively). Until they reach 65, women are more likely to be depressed than men, but women over age 65 are less likely than are men (Canada, Government of Canada 2006). Østbye and colleagues (2005) report that the prevalence among older adults living in the community is between 1 and 5 percent but the Canadian Institute for Health Information (CIHI 2011b) recently reported high rates among those living in nursing homes. The rate in nursing homes is alarming if correct, with almost half (44 percent) having clinically significant symptoms.

Additionally, there is some concern about unreported depression and suspicions that "true" rates are higher. Indeed, the WHO ranks depression as first in middle-income and high-income countries in terms of the global burden of disease. For instance, suicide rates peaked among adults age 45 to 49 for both sexes, with male rates reaching 27 per 100,000 in 2007, and female rates approaching 9 per 100,000. But among males, rates rose again for seniors 75+, peaking at 24 per 100,000 for those between 85 and 89 (CIHI 2011c).

In terms of chronic conditions, it is unclear whether baby boomers will have the same, improved, or worse health in their older age compared with those now in older age. Wister (2005) reports that rates of cardiovascular disease, arthritis and rheumatism, hypertension, and bronchitis and emphysema have been declining from the 1970s to the late 1990s. However, rates for diabetes, asthma, migraine headaches, other respiratory diseases, and the total number of chronic conditions have increased in the same time period. Current concerns over increasing rates of obesity raise the possibility that the present generation of young adults might not live longer or even as long as their parents and that current trends toward the compression of morbidity might not continue much into the future. (*Compression of morbidity* is the later or delayed onset of illness until closer to death, thereby resulting in more years within old age in relatively good health and fewer years of ill health.) Russia's recent drop in life expectancy, down to 56 for men in the early 1990s following the collapse of the former Soviet Union (Ciment 1999; Magnus 2009) dramatically demonstrates the real consequences of poor health.

Whether health is better or worse in older age for generations to come depends, in part, on the overall health of the economy and the effectiveness of health promotion and disease prevention activities, a topic relevant to all aspects of health and discussed at the end of this chapter. First, however, we talk about several other aspects of health.

Functional disability

Suffering from a chronic condition does not necessarily translate into incapacity; that is, it does not necessarily limit daily functioning. Disability or activity restriction is where the "rubber hits the road." A diagnosis of a condition such as high blood pressure is manageable without dramatically changing what we do or how we live our lives, but a disease that restricts what we can do is a very different story. This can lead to dependency, one of the greatest fears of older adults (Gignac, Cott, and Badly 2000). *Dependency* is typically defined as the opposite of independence, the desired state of autonomy and control over one's own life. Disability is usually defined in terms of restrictions in ability to perform *activities of daily living* (ADL). *Basic ADL* include self-care tasks such as dressing, toileting, continence, feeding, and transferring from a chair to a bed. *Instrumental ADL* (IADL) include such tasks as using the telephone, shopping, preparing meals, housekeeping, laundry, using public transportation, taking medication, and handling finances (Heikkinen 2003). *Mobility disability* is particularly serious given that ambulation (the ability to walk around) is critical to so many other activities. However, there is wide recognition that disability refers to a relational perspective beyond simply diagnosing physical ability; it includes complex relationships between an individual's health condition and personal and external factors in the environment. If an individual is unable to go up and down stairs but lives in a one-storey house then, at least within the house, the individual is functionally able. The *disablement process* is a term that attempts to capture this dynamic interaction, interwoven as it is with cultural norms and socio-economic status, and encompassing attitudes, emotions, stigma, accessibility or lack thereof to various services, wheelchair accessible buildings, etc.

People adapt in different ways to disability and to different types of restrictions. Baltes and Baltes (1990) proposed three different processes.

- A process of *selection* occurs when we choose to avoid or cease certain activities (such as playing sports or walking up stairs), perhaps adjusting our goals and preferences in the process.
- *Optimization* occurs when we choose to enhance our reserves to be able to continue the activity. This would involve, for example, exercises to strengthen particular muscles or taking supplements or medication.

• *Compensation* refers to either psychological or behavioural responses that permit or improve functions (such as hand bars in the shower to enable continued showering and increased volume on the phone).

Assistance from others can also be considered a compensatory adaptation, although some researchers (such as Gignac, Cott, and Badly 2000) prefer to consider reliance on others as a distinct form of adaptation. In a study involving a group of primarily women above the age of 55 who suffered from osteoarthritis and/or osteoporosis, these authors found that, overall, older adults use a range of techniques to adapt, including optimization. They are proactive in anticipating problems and often act to avoid them when pro-active; they do not simply react after the fact. Furthermore, different adaptation strategies are implemented for different problems. For example, more discretionary activities tend to be dropped or limited (selection), while more necessary activities are maintained through compensation.

What do chronic conditions and disability mean for health care needs? As ever, the answer is complex. Taking all chronic conditions into account, 81 percent of adults 65+ suffer from at least one chronic condition (see Table 2-3 for selected chronic conditions), yet fully 80 percent of older adults are functionally able to live independently. Nevertheless, activity restriction does increase with age: 12 percent of those between 15 and 64 experience some restrictions on activity, with this number increasing to 43 percent for those 65+. It is even higher—56 percent—for those 75+ (Statistics Canada 2006; 2008b). Women experience more disability than men. While severe disability is related to higher rates of mortality among both men and women, women nevertheless survive longer, albeit with more disability (Chappell and Cooke 2010). Among those who are older, the likelihood of experiencing disability accelerates over age 70 and causes increased need for assistance over age 80. For this reason, the WHO argues that, in terms of disability, *old age* can be considered as beginning at 75. Because disability can vary considerably, researchers are interested in disability-free life expectancies (the number of years we can expect to live without disability) (Sanderson and Scherbov 2010) or in distinguishing the severity of disability. While recent reports of declining rates of severe disability in some countries have led to optimism for the future, the trend does not characterize all nations. In particular, it does not characterize Canada, where the trend is currently stable (OECD 2009b; Manton 2008). Indeed, a recent study finds that the overall rate of disability among older adults in Canada has decreased from 1996 to 2001, but the rate for moderate disability increased by 4 percent and severe disability increased by 2 percent (Keefe et al. 2012).

Self-perceptions of health

What about self-perceptions? Canadian seniors rate their physical health less well than any other adult age group: only 39.3 percent of men and 38.9 percent of women 65+ report their health as excellent or very good. This is a decline from 48.8 percent of men and 53.2 percent of women age 55 to 64. This likely reflects an accurate perception of physical health: it does in fact decline with age. Importantly, some have found that, when objective differences in health status are taken into account, older elderly consider their health more positively than do younger elderly persons (Hogan et al. 1999). Cott and Fox (2001) report similar findings among those who live in long-term care institutions.

A slight decline with age is evident when examining perceptions of mental health, although most rate it as at least "good" and the gap with younger age groups is barely if at all perceptible. Of those 15+ living in the community, 27.8 percent rate their mental health as excellent; 39.2 percent as very good; 26.1 percent as good; 6.9 percent as fair or poor. Among those 65+ the figures are as follows: 28.7 percent rate it as excellent, 37.3 percent as very good, 27.5 percent as good, and 6.5 percent as fair or poor (Penning and Chappell 2010). Put differently, 70.1 percent of elderly men and 69.4 percent of elderly women report their mental health as excellent or very good (the figures are 72.7 percent and 73.3 percent respectively for the next lowest age group, those 55 to 64) (Statistics Canada 2010c; 2010a). That is, almost three quarters of older Canadians assess their mental health in very positive terms.

Summary of physical health in old age

Thus, objective and some subjective measures show that health declines as we age and continues to decline during older age, although chronic conditions do not necessarily translate into functional limitations, and objective physical decline does not translate in a straightforward manner into perceptions of poor health. Moreover, these health difficulties do not necessarily mean diminished perception of mental health. Indeed, it would appear that, despite age-related declines in physical health, most older adults view themselves as psychologically healthy, and may even be healthier in this respect than younger individuals (both younger adults and youth). The reason for this is not known. We can speculate that in old age, many of the concerns of younger adulthood such as employment and childrearing are no longer as salient, and/or that older adults compare their situation with others who are worse off (passed away). Another possibility is that our experiences throughout our lives have led to psychological strength when faced with adversities.

Well-being

Another important area of health is well-being or mental health as opposed to mental illness. The Public Health Agency of Canada (PHAC) defines mental health as "the capacity of each and all of us to feel, think, and act in ways that enhance our ability to enjoy life and deal with the challenges we face. It is a positive sense of emotional and spiritual well-being that respects the importance of culture, equity, social justice, interconnections and personal dignity" (CIHI 2009, 3). That is, *well-being* is a holistic concept referring to how we feel, think, and act. It is often studied in terms of overall well-being, happiness, and/or life satisfaction, where these terms may be defined as an overall evaluation of one's life, as feeling and experience, as well as the degree to which one assesses overall quality of life favourably. Sometimes the terms are used interchangeably, sometimes not (Deaton 2008; Knight and Rosa 2011; Veenhoven 1991).

Over lifetimes, people do not seem to become less happy as they age despite deteriorating physical health. Statistics Canada (2006) reports that adults between 65 and 74 experience more life satisfaction than do adults between 25 and 64. Levels of happiness decrease after age 24, reaching a low among those between 35 and 44, and then increase until those 55 to 64 are as happy as those 18 to 24. Persons 65+ are much happier (Helliwell 2002). In 2008, a large majority of women 65+ said they were happy (79 percent) or somewhat happy (19 percent), barely more so than men (77 percent and 19 percent respectively) (Milan and Vézina 2011).

Regarding older adults who are institutionalized, Cott and Fox (2001) report varied responses by age group: middle-old persons are almost twice as likely to report being happy compared with the young-old, and close to four times more likely to say they are happy rather than unhappy. Old-old persons are more likely to say they are happy than are middle-old persons or young-old persons, and over five times more likely to say they are happy than unhappy. These figures are in sharp contrast to those cited earlier concerning depression within nursing homes in Canada; this discrepancy has not yet been investigated although it could reflect the years in which the studies were conducted. The recent study is more than 10 years after the Cott and Fox (2001) study, so the difference in findings could reflect a much older and frailer nursing home population than was evident in the late 1990s.

Recent research on life satisfaction is incorporating environmental sustainability into the concept. After finding that increased consumption of goods and services does not result in higher levels of well-being and that very large increases in consumption in the US since 1961 (but prior to the recent financial collapse) had not led to substantial improvements in life satisfaction, researchers became intrigued. Economic determinism dictates that we want to continue economic growth indefinitely on the grounds that increased consumption will lead to a higher quality of life and therefore greater happiness. Yet multinational studies have revealed a different picture, known as the *Easterlin Paradox*. As countries become richer (beyond a minimum level), their inhabitants do not become happier; among high-income countries there is either a negative relationship between economic growth and life satisfaction or a curvilinear relationship (Deaton 2008; Knight and Rosa 2011). Knight and Rosa's concept of environmental efficiency of well-being seeks to incorporate minimal environmental impact plus maximized human well-being. When applied to several countries they find that environmental efficiency producing well-being increases with affluence at low to moderate levels of economic development, but declines at high levels. There is no research yet applying this notion to aging, but the concept both illustrates the complexity of human happiness and promising directions for future research.

Frailty

Despite the good news when examining well-being among older adults, there are increasing health difficulties for many during old age—difficulties with which they must cope and for which they frequently require care. This is especially true for those who become frail. Even though frailty does not characterize everyone in old age, it does apply to a substantial proportion of seniors and increases with age. The term *frailty* refers to something broader than just disability or disease state alone, but it is difficult to distinguish from both. It also includes dependency. On the whole, frailty suggests a vulnerability resulting from the interaction of the simultaneous deterioration in several organ systems leading to adverse outcomes but without reference to a particular disease. Since the late 1990s, frailty has received focused attention in the research literature (Abellan van Kan et al. 2008). Hogan, MacKnight, and Bergman (2003) note an emerging consensus that frailty largely refers to a state of vulnerability to experiencing adverse outcomes, that is, multiple health failures. Rockwood and Mitnitski refer to it as "a nonspecific state of increasing risk, which reflects multisystem physiological change. The more individuals have wrong with them, the higher the likelihood that they will be frail" (Rockwood and Mitnitski 2007, 722). And, at some point, if too many deficits accumulate, people die, although women survive longer than men with more deficits.

The prevalence of frailty varies, depending on how it is measured, and there is no consensus on the best way to do that. As Song and colleagues (2010) note, more older people are classified as frail if using the Frailty Index (22.7 percent) than if using the Cardiovascular Health Survey definition (range 3.8 percent to 16.3 percent). However, there is consensus that frailty has catastrophic consequences for older adults and their families (Abellan van Kan et al. 2010).

The fact that some of us become frail and others do not has been recognized for some time. Interest in distinguishing among older adults who maintain their independence throughout most or all of their later years, and those who become dependent, is evident in the gerontological literature since the 1970s. This search for categorizing older adults on the basis of their overall health reflects a desire to not homogenize older adults on the basis of age; it refers to efforts to divide old age into those who are healthy or independent, in some sense not "old," and those who are unhealthy, dependent, "old." Such attempts, perhaps inadvertently, continue to devalue those in the "old" or dependent group.

Others refer to "usual aging," "successful aging," "productive aging," "active aging," or "robust aging" to name only some of the nomenclature evident in the literature (Rowe and Kahn 1998; Dillaway and Byrnes 2009; WHO 2002). The definitions sometimes vary and sometimes overlap, with some focusing primarily on physical health but others embracing quality of life. In the latter instance, an individual with poor physical health could nevertheless age well. What they share is an attempt to distinguish "good" aging from less desirable aging, with an inevitable, albeit subtle, denigration of those who do not age well, therefore reinforcing ageism (Chappell and Penning 2012).

Subpopulations

Care needs, furthermore, are not evenly distributed. They are higher among certain subpopulations. Poverty is a risk factor for many adverse health experiences (Huguet, Kaplan, and Feeny 2008; Kaplan et al. 2010; McIntosh et al. 2009), and even though the percentage of older adults living in poverty has been declining, poverty in old age has not disappeared, and many live just above low-income thresholds. The proportion of seniors with incomes below the low-income cut-off fell from 37 percent in the early 1970s to 5.9 percent in 2004 (Canada, National Seniors Council 2009). However, senior women's after-tax income from all sources, on average, was only 65 percent of senior men's in 2008 (CIHI 2011b). Relatively more women live in poverty than men, and unattached individuals are more likely to live in poverty than couples:

> In 2006, 15.5 percent of unattached seniors were living below the Statistics Canada low income cut off, a rate 11 times higher than that of senior couples (1.4 percent). Furthermore, unattached senior women

are at greater risk of experiencing low income. The low income rate for unattached senior women is reported as 16.1 percent, compared to unattached senior men at 14 percent. (Canada, National Seniors Council 2009)

That is, those who are poor, female, and living alone are more likely to require care and assistance in old age than are those who have more economic resources, males, and those living with others, especially those who are married. The following chapters elaborate on different types and sources of care.

Social isolation is another risk factor during old age, although it is not a problem for most. While most older adults in modern day Canadian society are retired and therefore outside of mainstream economic society, they are by and large socially embedded, especially within families. More than four decades ago, Eugene Litwak (1960) described the concept of a modified, extended family, emphasizing mutual close intergenerational ties among kin, strength of intergenerational relations, continuity of responsible filial behavior, and contact between the generations. Such relations are a more accurate description of most older adults' social interactions than is isolation.

In 2003, 98 percent of Canadian older adults living in the community said they had a family member or a friend they felt close to (Lindsey 2006; Gilmour and Park 2006). Most also have companionship and confidantes (Chappell, McDonald, and Stones 2008; Cranswick 2002). Interaction between older Canadians and their adult children is characterized by intimacy-at-a-distance, a term coined by Rosenmayr and Kockeis (1963) half a century ago. It describes older adults' general preference not to live with their children but to maintain close ties. When asked only about friends, between 12 and 14 percent of those 65 to 74 say there are none compared with 5 percent of those between 25 and 54. The figure is 18 percent for those 75+ (Lindsey 2006; Gilmour and Park 2006). In other words, most older adults are not socially isolated. But for those who are, it can be a risk factor for poor health and requiring care. This means not everyone requires assistance from the formal health care system; it means those who use the projections of all seniors to argue they will bankrupt the system are greatly exaggerating their case.

Summary of health and well-being

Well-being and life satisfaction provide a more positive picture of aging than an examination of chronic conditions and functional disability. Overall, older adults tend to cope with their lives, and do so with grace and dignity. A closer examination reveals that only a portion of seniors are in very poor health, requiring much assistance. However, for those who become frail, they are vulnerable and at risk. The distinctions many researchers draw between successful aging and its opposite is in part due to a recognition that there is considerable heterogeneity among older adults. Only some seniors become frail, and of those who do, many do so in later old age. Furthermore, with now virtually everyone expected to live to old age it is not only the "survivors" in exceptionally good health who live past age 70. In old-old age many people have prolonged lives while living with diseases and disabilities (Crimmins 2004). That is, we have not achieved a compression of morbidity. For these seniors, care is required, but to paint all those who are 65+ with this same brush is inaccurate. The most vulnerable are the old-elderly, the poor, and those who are socially isolated.

We know not only who the most vulnerable among us are, but we also know many of the risk factors for the chronic conditions that afflict us in old age. In addition, we also know that many of these risk factors are amenable to change. If we can decrease deteriorations in health, then the quality of life increases and the demands on the health care system can consequently decrease.

Health Promotion and Disease Prevention

Demands for care can be decreased if the need for care can be prevented. Health promotion provides such an opportunity. We know that Canadians want to experience healthy aging to the extent possible. Health Canada (2002) defines healthy aging as "a lifelong process of optimizing opportunities for improving and preserving health and physical, social and mental wellness, independence, quality of life and enhancing successful lifecourse transitions." Health promotion, or the process of enabling people to increase control over and improve their health, has been embraced by several national reports, including that of the National Forum on Health (1997) and the Romanow Commission (2002).

There is much evidence demonstrating that many chronic conditions can be prevented and that investing in policies that do so is cost-effective in human, social, and financial terms (Kannus et al. 2005; Katz and Shah 2010; WHO 2002; WHO 2003). Smoking, lack of physical exercise, and an inadequate diet are established risk factors for virtually all chronic illnesses. In terms of prevention, it is estimated that a dollar put toward enhancing physical exercise results in a savings of $3.20 in medical costs (WHO 2002); a dollar invested in health promotion has been estimated to yield a return on investment of six to eight dollars in health cost savings.

A 20 percent decrease in falls experienced by older adults would result in 7,500 fewer hospitalizations, 1,800 fewer permanently disabled older adults, and a cost savings of $138 million per year in health care costs (Public Health Agency of Canada 2009).

Prevention takes us beyond areas of strict physiology to include cognitive abilities, personal health behaviours, and psychological and social factors. And it takes us to the area of the distribution of a country's resources, to differences in socio-economic status, to the fact that the gap between the rich and poor is increasing in all parts of the world, and to the related fact that health diminishes with increased inequality (Lynch et al. 2000; Marmor 2009; Navarro 2007). In short, population health and prevention take us to the social determinants of health. Without reiterating the widespread literature on the social determinants of health, it can be noted that population health efforts direct attention to the very structure of society and the current socio-economic disparities that affect the lifelong experience of many individuals. Addressing these issues ultimately requires the involvement of all levels of government, civil society and local communities, businesses and international agencies. It involves daily living conditions, education, the built and natural environments, fair employment and decent work, and social protection.

The valuing of older adults within society is a key social determinant of health. Even though older adults represent a wealth of experience and a huge resource, ageism remains a barrier to their full participation in society. In addition, there remain ageist attitudes throughout society. *Ageism* refers to the treatment of older people as a social category. Such attitudes have been documented, for example, in media portrayals of seniors, among school-age children, among health care professionals, and among employers facing older job applicants (Achenbaum 1995; Van Dalen, Henkens, and Schippers 2009; Wood, Wilkinson, and Harcourt 2008). The pervasiveness of ageism has led Stones and Stones (1997) to refer to it as a "quiet epidemic" that contributes to indifference. Interestingly, ageism does not necessarily lead to interpersonal antagonism: we may treat our grandmothers well, but simultaneously refer to and treat other older adults with indifference and even contempt.

In virtually all walks of life, visible signs of aging are associated with devaluation and an assumption that declines in physical health reflect diminished internal capacity (Clarke and Griffin 2008). The labour force is one example of many. The end of mandatory retirement can be seen as a step in the right direction in that it allows individuals the choice to continue working. On the other hand, pension policies that begin full benefits at a later age mean that those without economic resources will be required to continue working. The first step toward a later age to begin full pension benefits is evident in the federal government's change to begin the Old Age Security (OAS) payment at age 67 instead of age 65. Discrimination against older workers continues, despite increasing recognition that the work force will shrink as the baby boom generation retires. Whether these attitudes will change as employers encounter future labour shortages is unknown.

A related area is human resources: working with older adults is a growth area. Yet it is difficult to attract individuals to work in jobs with older adults, especially caring for older adults. In fact, the low level of interest of individuals in occupations related to older age (Gonçalves 2009) is of such concern that several national organizations in Canada, including the Association of Geriatric Physicians and the Canadian Association on Gerontology, formed a group known as the Geriatric Education and Recruitment Initiative, whose task it is to change the negative image of older adults within society (Hogan 2007). Among those who are employed in such fields, there is evidence of discriminatory attitudes reflected in how they perform their work. For example, Kane and colleagues (2008) found that social work students perceive older adults as vulnerable, marginalized, only moderately resilient in overcoming depression or substance abuse, and unlikely to seek professional help.

The need to change attitudes toward older adults generally has been recognized by the Special Senate Committee on Aging (Carstairs and Keon 2009). This group recommended the federal government take a lead in an aggressive public relations campaign to portray seniors in a positive light.

In the absence of a role as contributing, valuable members of society, older adults are denied self-worth, with predictable consequences to health and well-being. Meaningful roles for participation do not have to include employment. Voluntary roles supporting community groups, neighbourhood helping, peer mentoring and visiting, family caregivers and intergenerational programs in outreach services (WHO, 2002) can provide such venues. WHO's Age-Friendly Cities (now Communities) (AFC) initiative incorporates these opportunities, and much more. AFC is an example of health promotion embracing multiple levels of change. In 2002, the WHO launched the Active Aging Policy Framework, defining *active aging* as, "the process of optimizing opportunities for health, participation and security in order to enhance quality of life as people age" (Kalache 2009).

For WHO, active caregiving requires a variety of supports including personal, physical environmental, economic, behavioural, and health and social services. WHO's Age-Friendly Cities Guide was launched in 2006, targeting eight domains for action: outdoor spaces and buildings, transportation, housing, social participation, respect and social inclusion, civic participation and deployment, communication and information, and community support and health services (Kalache 2009). Encouraging the restoration of function and the expansion of participation of older people in all aspects of society is the age-friendly goal. This includes the following: barrier-free workplaces; well-lit streets; exercise programs; life-long learning and literacy programs; hearing aids and instruction in sign language; barrier-free access to health centres; credit schemes and access to small business; and changed attitudes of health and social service providers toward older adults. Within Canada, the Special Senate Committee on Aging (Carstairs and Keon 2009) recommends that the federal government promote the Age-Friendly Cities Guide (and Age-Friendly Rural and Remote Communities Guide). Thus far, four provinces are championing age-friendly communities (BC, Manitoba, Nova Scotia, and Quebec) (Public Health Agency of Canada 2011; available online).

While the challenges loom large, the potential payoff of illness prevention is great. It represents the possibility of reducing the care needs of older adults. For example, Keefe, Légaré, and Carrière (2007a) estimate that an increase in the health of Canadians could reduce the rate of growth in the population in need of assistance from 2.5 to 1.9 percent. Yet, at the present time, less than 3 percent of public health care funding is directed toward health promotion and disease prevention (Public Health Agency of Canada 2010). Along with other industrialized nations, Canada is struggling with the implementation of health promotion/disease prevention programs that draw on our knowledge of the social determinants of health. Incorporating structural elements together with individual and organizational level interventions has not proven to be easy, often resorting to little more than the provision of information about healthy lifestyles, such as proper nutrition and/or the harmful effects of excessive alcohol consumption or smoking (Chappell 2009). Presumably one of the stumbling blocks to broader social policies relating to health promotion is that they fall outside of the health care system and therefore encounter jurisdictional challenges in a system where administrative silos abound (Government of Canada 2010). How to handle cross-cutting responsibilities within and across different levels of government remains a challenge. No doubt longer time spans required to see the results of health promotion programs is another stumbling block.

The promise of disease prevention and health promotion is great, in terms of both cost-savings and quality of life. It is time for more serious attention.

Chapter Summary

There is much we know about health as we age. Some aspects of our health decline, notably our physical health, and continue to do so within older age. The extent and type of decline varies considerably from individual to individual and, while not everyone is characterized by incapacitating ill health, many experience different forms of decline. Those most at-risk of serious problems can be identified; they do not encompass everyone, but for some, assistance is often necessary. And it is assistance with chronic conditions for which there is no cure, and functional disabilities that interfere with day-to-day living, that is needed. In the absence of a cure, the goal is to maximize older adults' independence and quality of life as much as possible. As we shall see, most older adults requiring care achieve these goals with the help of family and friends while remaining within the community.

Given the needs of an aging society, it is instructive to examine how we currently provide care to those in need in order to better understand how, as a society, we can prepare to meet the needs of the baby boom generation as they become older adults. The next chapter considers the most prevalent source of care to seniors: informal care, from family and friends, primarily family and primarily women (wives and daughters).

Chapter 3

Informal Care

Introduction

We have looked at the health of older Canadians and their subsequent care needs. Before turning to the formal health care system and its role in providing for an aging society, we first examine where most care comes from: what is known as the informal network, consisting of family and friends. We ask about the adequacy of these arrangements from the caregivers' and the care recipients' points of view and the likelihood of the adequacy of this type of care in the future. These issues necessarily concern social policy relating to the family and intergenerational relations.

First, it should be noted that families today do not abandon their elderly members, even though many women are in full-time employment while raising their own children, many adult children move to geographically distant locations away from their parents, and we live in an individually oriented society. Furthermore, despite a belief in the independence and separation of the generations, older adults continue to contribute much to families. In fact, research on the flow of assistance between the generations suggests it is bidirectional and reciprocal, with older adults giving more to their children than their children give to them, at least until very old age. The older parent generation tends to give in-kind assistance such as baby-sitting and assistance with finances when possible. Adult children tend to help their parents more when the health of the latter begins to fail and they need assistance. Familial proximity with frequent and affectionate interaction among family members and across generations is the norm; furthermore, these relations remain stable over several decades (Roberts and Bengtson 1996).

Much research has been conducted on intergenerational relations including older parents. Silverstein and Bengtson's (1997) solidarity (and conflict) model of generational relations has been popular in this research area. That model originally postulated six dimensions of solidarity:

- structure (such as geographic distance)
- association (such as social contact and shared activities)
- affect (such as feelings and affection)
- consensus (such as agreement)
- function (such as exchange of assistance)
- norms (such as a sense of mutual obligation)

A seventh was later added:

- intergenerational conflict

Feelings of solidarity are related to the individual's feelings of psychological well-being (Bengtson et al. 2000). Those with greater feelings of inter-generational solidarity and support are more likely to experience better mental and physical health (Ajrouch 2007). Lowenstein (2007) reveals that, in England, Norway, Germany, Spain, and Israel, parents age 75+ who have more solidarity with their children also experience a greater quality of life than do parents whose relationships with their children are more ambivalent. In addition, solidarity has a greater influence on quality of life than does ambivalence.

Families, though, have been changing. Life expectancy, as we saw above, has been increasing while fertility has been decreasing. This has resulted in *vertical extension* (more generations alive at one time), *horizontal shrinkage* (fewer members of each generation), and an increase in "beanpole families" (four or five generations alive at one time). We have also seen the emergence of many different forms of families, including reconstituted and blended families, one-parent families, and gay and lesbian families. As divorce has become more common, there is an increase in step-siblings, former step-siblings, half siblings, and step-children, as well as an increase in older adults living alone. Families—and specifically intergenerational relations within families—nevertheless continue to form the context within which people age; as the context evolves, so do the relationships within them. Despite demographic changes in the family, it remains the mainstay of support and assistance to older adults.

Social Support and Caregiving

Social support, or the diverse exchanges between individuals, includes but is not restricted to caregiving. *Caregiving* refers to the support provided to individuals when their health has deteriorated and they can no longer function independently (Chappell, McDonald, and Stones 2008). Caregiving can be instrumental (tangible) or emotional (intangible). There are various terms for caregiving, and the terms are often used interchangeably, without definition, and without definitional consensus. Caregiving, caring, assistance, interaction, support, informal caregiving, and family caregiving are some of the more common terms.

Regardless of the nomenclature, caregiving is the major form of care in old age, far exceeding that provided by the formal health care system. In 1990, Kane and colleagues examined research across industrialized countries and concluded that the informal network provided between 75 and 85 percent of the total personal care received by seniors, irrespective of whether the country provided comprehensive health insurance. Data from the 2007 General Social Survey suggest they provide 80 to 90 percent of care to those with a chronic health problem or disability (RAPP 2010). At any one time, most older adults receiving care do so for IADL, such as shopping and transportation, and not ADL—that is, not those required for survival, such as eating and toileting.

In some other cultures, particularly collectivist cultures, there is a tradition of reverence for seniors and explicit teaching of the notion of *filial piety*: care and respect for parents as they age. In Asia, for example, children (and notably first-born sons) historically were obligated to care for their aging parents. Daughters-in-law assisted in caring for their parents-in-law, not their own parents (at marriage they belonged to their husband's family, not their family of origin) (Chappell and Kusch 2007; Liu and Kendig 2000). In the mid twentieth century this notion of filial piety was officially criticized as feudal; this criticism took place during the rapid political, social, and cultural change under the leadership of Chairman Mao. In the late twentieth century the notion was again embraced but this time women were exhorted to support their own parents as a matter of gratitude rather than purely as an obligation (Chappell and Funk 2011a; Ikels 2004). There is debate over whether, to what extent, and in which ways this cultural norm of filial piety is changing in Asia, whether it remains strong, is becoming more reciprocal, affection-based, and voluntary, or co-exists together with a value of independent decision-making (Whyte 2004; Traphagen 2008). We do know that adult daughters now tend to care for their own parents rather than their parents-in-law and that spouses are starting to provide more care for one another (Chappell and Kusch 2007).

The cultural ideal of filial piety, explicitly taught from a young age to children in China, contrasts sharply with an ideology of individualism and personal autonomy espoused in the West. Here ageism competes with notions of reverence and respect for older adults. Adult children have a vague mental awareness of responsibility toward their aging parents rather than a normative consensus on family obligations. Donorfio (1996) argues this vague awareness often requires a triggering event in order to be activated. Beck and Beck-Gernsheim (2001) argue that in the West we tend to reject obligation, replacing it with affection as the main tenet of family relationships. Exchanges are conditional depending on personal circumstances and perceived parental deservedness. Nevertheless, in virtually all societies, most children care for their older parents when the need arises, irrespective of cultural norms and beliefs regarding filial responsibility (Montgomery, Borgatta, and Borgatta 2000).

To examine the relationship between attitudes toward providing care for older parents and the caregiving that is actually provided, Chappell and Funk (2011a; 2011b) recently studied the attitudes toward filial responsibility and actual caregiving behaviours among filial caregivers in Hong Kong, diasporic caregivers with Hong Kong origins and now living in Canada, and Caucasian Canadian caregivers. They report that, among the sample as a whole, attitudes do not predict assistance with basic ADL, IADL, companionship, or financial support. Stronger ideals of filial piety are associated with greater emotional support to the parent but are not the strongest of correlates. (The strongest correlate is being of Caucasian descent; that is, Caucasian children provide more emotional support to their older parents than do Chinese Canadians or Hong Kong Chinese.)

Looking at each cultural group separately adds clarity to these findings. Attitude toward filial responsibility—what a given individual believes he or she should do for his or her parents—is unrelated to the provision of any of the five caregiving behaviours studied (help with ADL, IADL, emotional support, companionship, financial assistance) among Caucasian Canadians. That is, stated belief about the kind of assistance he or she *should* provide does not correspond to what he or she actually does provide. However, among both Hong Kong Chinese and Canadian Chinese, the more they believe they should assist their parents, the more likely they are to provide emotional support, but these beliefs are again unrelated to the other four types of caregiving behaviour. Among Chinese Canadians only, the stronger the belief in assistance, the more likely is the provision of financial support. These beliefs, however, are unrelated to the actual assistance they provide with ADL, IADL, or companionship. Even among caregivers in the two Chinese groups, their beliefs are unrelated to most of the caregiving behaviours examined. Irrespective of what adult children say they believe, most provide care for their aging parents when the need arises, irrespective of cultural prescript. This is true across countries and is true in Canada.

Caregiving in the West

When health declines, unpaid support by family and friends, notably family, is the mainstay of care in old age. Even with women entering the paid labour force and changes in family forms, families still provide care. Lafrenière and colleagues (2003) and Cranswick (2003) report that in Canada, 70 percent of the hours provided for housework, shopping, meal preparation, and personal care—the four activities most related to long-term home support—are provided by members of the informal network. The studies also found that 39 percent of elderly women and 46 percent of elderly men receive all of their care from informal sources, representing no change from 1996.

We know much about the characteristics of these caregivers: most, but far from all, are women (in 2007, 56.5 percent were women), most are between 45 and 65, most care for a parent or parent-in-law. Caregiving involves a gendered division of labour: women provide the equivalent of 1.5 work days per week, whereas men provide on average one work day per week; women are more likely to provide homemaking and personal care assistance and emotional support, while men are more likely to provide instrumental assistance with things such as home repair, and women are more likely to organize the care (Cranswick and Dosman 2008; Cranswick 2003; RAPP 2010). See Table 3-1. It should be noted, however, that when there is no female available, sons do step in and provide the care. Fully 43.5 percent of caregivers are men. In addition, in 2007, about one-quarter of caregivers were seniors caring for seniors; 16 percent of these seniors were between 65 and 74; 8 percent were 75+ (Cranswick and Dosman 2008; RAPP 2010).

Caregivers themselves sometimes receive support from others, typically from other family members. See Figures 3-1 and 3-2. Most care for one person although many (40 percent) care for two or more persons at the same time. It is typically close kin who are the care recipients (parents, parents-in-law, spouses), although close to 25 percent care for friends or neighbours. More than two-thirds care for those with only a physical disability while 20 percent care for those with both physical and cognitive/mental disabilities. Over half care for older adults who are more than 75 years of age. Just under 85 percent care for those living in the community while more than 15 percent care for someone living in a residential care facility or supportive housing. Most live close by, but one in seven live a half-day or more drive away (RAPP 2010). It is important to note that these statistics are based on those 45 and over; including caregivers who are less than age 45 could significantly change these figures. Notably, care continues when the care recipient enters a long-term care institution, but the nature of care shifts to become indirect (such as overseeing care) or task

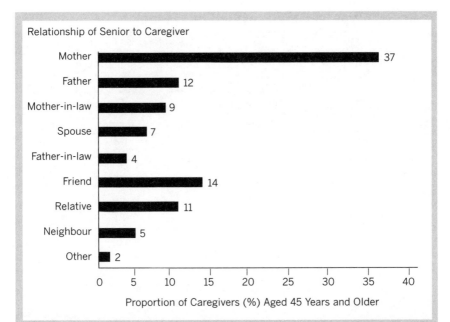

Figure 3-1 Who Receives the Care?

Notes: a) Close family members (mother, father, mother-in-law, spouse, father-in-law) made up 69% of those seniors who received care from caregivers 45 years or older. b) Due to rounding, totals might not add up to 100.

Source: Statistics Canada, General Social Survey, 2007

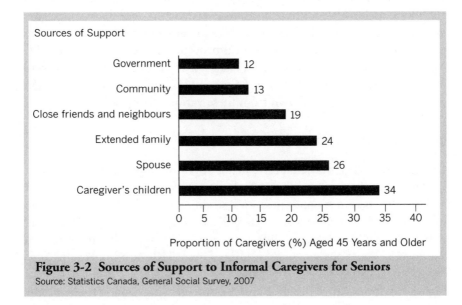

Figure 3-2 Sources of Support to Informal Caregivers for Seniors

Source: Statistics Canada, General Social Survey, 2007

Table 3-1 Type of Care Provided by Gender

Type of Care	Caregivers 45+			
	Proportion performing this task (%)		Among those performing this task, proportion who do so at least weekly (%)	
	Women[a]	Men	Women[a]	Men
Personal care	37	17*	74	75
Tasks outside the house	33	53*	59	52*
Tasks inside the house	57	32*	73	73
Transportation	80	82*	66	63*
Medical care	25	14*	81	77*
Care management	42	33*	64	62*

[a] Reference group.
* Statistically significant gender difference (when comparing 99 percent confidence intervals).
Source: Statistics Canada, General Social Survey, 2007

specific (such as reading to the family member); nevertheless, emotional support continues (Keefe and Fancey 2000).

Spouses are the first resort for care and are often themselves seniors. As noted above, a quarter of caregivers are seniors providing care to other seniors. This includes both spouses and older children who are themselves elderly (as well as friends and neighbours). Women, who have longer life expectancy and typically marry men older than themselves, tend to be there to provide care as their husbands' health declines; once a woman is widowed and her own health declines, a daughter often steps in to provide care for her mother. See the textbox "A Composite Caregiver" for a description of a composite caregiver drawn from these various characteristics.

Caregiver stress and burden

Caregiver stress and burden receive major attention in gerontology research.

The stresses of caregiving can include depression, guilt, worry, anxiety and loneliness, emotional stress and strain, lower physical functioning, lower social functioning and worse general health (Hirst 2005; Ho et al. 2009; Christakis and Allison 2006). Vitaliano, Zhang, and Scanlan (2003) conducted a meta-analysis of 23 studies of negative health impacts for family members caring for older persons and concluded that caregivers are at higher risk for negative physical health outcomes than non-caregivers. The

A Composite Caregiver

Ann is a 50-year-old female who cares for her mother, a 78-year-old widow (Shirley). Ann's mother lives in the family home alone, 35 minutes drive away. Ann organizes all of the care required and spends about a day and a half a week tending to her mother's emotional needs, doing her laundry and grocery shopping, and making some meals as well as scheduling a homemaker for two hours a week. She tries to stop by on her way home from work and at least once on weekends. She prepares sufficient food at one time that she can freeze and that Shirley can defrost quickly in the microwave. On days when Ann cannot visit, she is sure to phone her mother. If an emergency arises, Ann must leave work to tend to her mother's needs. Her mother is mentally alert but suffers from severe arthritis, high blood pressure, and diabetes, and is bordering on obesity. Her cancer is in remission. Ann's children are grown and no longer live in the area. Her husband occasionally helps with household repairs and yardwork at his mother-in-law's. Ann has two siblings, a sister who lives out of the country and a brother who lives in town. Her brother also helps out when the lawn needs cutting and repairs are required around the house. When her sister visits, she stays with their mother to provide Ann some respite from the daily assistance she provides. Ann and her husband seldom go away for more than a day or two, worried about leaving her mother for long.

list of risk factors for caregiver burden is long. Those who are at greater risk are those who are experiencing strain (Schulz and Beach 1999), experiencing difficulty (Navaie-Waliser et al. 2002), feeling overburdened (Sherwood et al. 2005), and providing more extensive assistance (Pinquart and Sörensen 2003). Those with low income (Robison et al. 2009), with lower formal educational levels (Navaie-Waliser et al. 2002), and females (Ho et al. 2009) are also at greater risk.

Younger caregivers are more stressed than those who are older (Health Canada 2002), a finding often attributed to the fact that older caregivers are more likely to be spouses who are more committed to caring for their often lifelong partners. However, living with the care recipient, not receiving formal services, and a poorer quality relationship between the caregiver and care receiver have also been related to greater stress and burden (Lyonette and Yardley 2003; Robinson et al. 2009). The health of the care recipient in terms of cognitive impairment and physical disabilities, the behavioural disturbances encountered, and the amount of caregiving provided (either number of tasks or hours of care) also tend to emerge as predictors of caregiver stress and burden (Andrieu et al. 2003; Chappell and Reid 2002). Findings, though, are not always consistent.

Much of the research on caregiver burden draws on Pearlin's (Pearlin et al. 1990) stress process model, either in its original conceptualization or a modified version. Designed specifically to understand and examine caregiver burden, this model consists of four domains:

- background and context
- stressors
- mediators of stress
- outcomes of stress

The context includes, for example, the caregiver's socio-economic characteristics, caregiving history, and family and network composition. Stressors can be either primary to the caregiving role (such as objective indicators of cognitive status, problematic behaviour, and ADL/IADL dependencies of the care recipient as well as subjective indicators such as the caregiver's perceived overload and relationship deprivation) or secondary to the caregiving role (such as job-related conflict, family conflict, economic difficulties, and restricted social activities). Outcomes can be secondary or primary (such as self-esteem, mastery, competence, burden, depression, anxiety, and physical health). Mediators such as coping strategies and social support can intervene at various points within this process.

Various modifications of this model have emerged in the quarter century since it was first published but no other conceptual model of caregiver burden has received such popularity. For example, burden is sometimes considered a more immediate outcome, with overall well-being as a more inclusive and less immediate outcome; sometimes family composition is considered as part of a social support mediator, and overall self-esteem might be an outcome.

The role of cultural beliefs in the experience of stress and burden is not known. It could be that a belief in filial responsibility normalizes the meaning of caregiving and helps adult children cope, and/or it gives greater value to the care work and lowers the burden (Houldin 2007; Marks et al. 2008). Supporting this view, Lai (2010) argues that Chinese Canadians who believe more in filial piety may experience reduced burden. Also consistent with this view are findings suggesting that when beliefs in such responsibility are low, and care is therefore not expected, there are barriers to satisfaction (Kirsi 2000). Similarly, Zhan (2006) argues that when expectations are not prescribed, caregivers derive less satisfaction from this role. However, Selig, Tomlinson, and Hickey (1991) note that high adherence to filial obligation can result in feelings of guilt and inadequacy and ultimately more burden. Lyonnete and Yardley's (2003) research reporting that strong beliefs in such responsibility are related to higher stress and subjective burden support this contrary view. It may be that, for some, prescriptions result in lower stress, but for others, it results in more stress.

And there is an argument that it may be culturally specific, as we discovered when comparing attitudes of filial responsibility to actual caregiving behaviours. As others have noted (Fine 2005), caregiving in the West may allow for greater choice, involving more affection, which could lead to filial responsibility being interpreted as negative. Lee and Sung (1998) find strong filial responsibility associated with lower burden among Korean caregivers, but not among American caregivers where high gratification from caregiving is associated with lower burden. However, contrary findings have been reported by others studying Asian caregivers (Tang et al. 2007; Zhan 2006).

Whether employment is an added burden for caregivers (and how much of a burden) is also controversial. It may provide necessary respite for the caregiver. Some studies find that combining employment and caregiving results in negative effects for caregivers (Covinsky et al. 2001; Kemp and Rosenthal 2001) while others find that it is positive or there is no difference in the burden experienced by caregivers who are employed and those who are not (Dautzenberg et al. 2000; Penning 1998) and still others report some positive together with some negative effects. For example, Edwards and colleagues (2002) studied employed and non-employed caregivers of cognitively impaired older adults and report no difference between the two groups for depression, role overload, worry, and strain; however, they did report that role conflict contributes to negative outcomes for many.

Most studies examine whether the caregiver is employed or not, but not how caregiving affects employment. Reid and colleagues (2010) examine several possible effects of caregiving on working outside the home and find that the status of employment (that is, working or not) is unrelated to caregiver burden, self-esteem, or well-being. Of note, when examining only those who are employed, the total number of work interruptions added to burden, but not well-being or self-esteem. This finding confirms earlier research (Chappell and Reid 2002) reporting that burden and well-being are two related but distinct concepts (elaborated below). Those who report that their performance at work is affected by caregiving are more likely to feel greater caregiver burden and lower levels of well-being and self-esteem. In other words, subjective assessments of the impacts of the caregiving role on their work is an important correlate of the impact of caregiving on their quality of life. This is not to say that work interferences are lacking, rather (as Table 3-2 shows), that it is the perceived impact on the caregiver's work that determines whether occupying the two roles leads to burden and lessened well-being.

Despite the focus on adverse caregiver outcomes, and the many, many studies reporting correlates of burden, studies asking caregivers whether they are coping reveal that the vast majority are. Health Canada (Canada,

Table 3-2   Interferences at Work as a Result of Caregiving

Interference Type	Proportion of Respondents Who Reported this Interference (%)
Decreased work hours and changed work shifts	29.40
Work performance affected	46.30
Arrive to work late	31.60
Missed work	41.90
Left work suddenly to take care recipients to doctor	36.00
Left work suddenly for other reason	38.20
Phone calls by or concerning care recipient	26.50

Source: Reid, Stajduhar, and Chappell 2010

Health Canada 2002) notes that 43 percent of caregivers report that they are coping with their care responsibilities very well and 49 percent say that they are coping generally well. This does not appear to be related to the frequency of caregiving tasks performed. Importantly, these findings do not suggest that they do not feel burden or stress within the role. Indeed, less than 5 percent of those who give care to older adults indicate that they are not doing well, but simultaneously, 70 percent report that providing care has been stressful. This is true even among those saying that they are coping very well. Close to 80 percent report experiencing emotional stress. Of these, 29 percent say it is significant; 54 percent report some difficulties with finances and 50 percent with their physical health (but less than 20 percent of these say it has been significant); and 70 percent say they need a break, either frequently or occasionally (Cranswick and Dosman 2008; Health Canada, 2002).

In addition to the above, there are the so-called hidden costs of caregiving (Fast et al. 1999) that have received less research attention. Hidden economic costs include employment-related costs such as lost income and benefits as well as reduced productivity. Additionally, there might be out-of-pocket expenditures for the older adult and any of a variety of forms of assistance such as paid help and home modifications. Unpaid labour would be another economic cost. Non-economic costs include social costs such as effects on relationships and activities as well as emotional costs (stress, morale, control/independence). There can also be physical costs for the caregiver in terms of a negative effect on their own health.

An important distinction between caregiver burden and caregiver well-being has emerged from this literature. While caregiver burden is related to overall well-being, it is a separate concept, so that caregivers can be burdened in that role while nevertheless experiencing good overall well-being (Chappell and Reid 2002). This stems from the fact that caregiving is not the only part of their lives, although it is more important and more all-encompassing for some than for others. Spitzer and colleagues (2003) observed that South Asian and Chinese immigrant caregivers strongly support familial caregiving, which may buffer their subjective burden but ultimately harm their well-being as a result of high cultural expectations within a context of diminished resources. Funk, Chappell, and Lui (2011) compared filial responsibility among Caucasian Canadians, Chinese Canadians, and Hong Kong Chinese, and found that attitudes of filial responsibility are unrelated to burden or overall well-being among any of the cultural groups. However, consider these findings:

- among Hong Kong Chinese, an attitude of filial responsibility is unrelated to self-rated health;
- among Caucasian Canadians, lower filial responsibility is related to better self-rated health; and
- among Canadian Chinese, an attitude of filial responsibility is related to higher self-rated health (perhaps promoting ethnic pride and affirmation when compared with other groups; see Pyke 2000).

In other words, these attitudes may be important only for specific domains of well-being (in this case the health domain) and not for overall assessments of our lives.

How do we make sense of these apparent inconsistencies and contradictions? Are caregivers burdened or not?

Understanding caregiver burden

First, not all caregivers are burdened and not all that are, are burdened to the point of burn out. Furthermore, while many caregivers experience burden, this does not mean that they want to relinquish the role; but neither does it mean that their current situation is ideal. Some caregivers are in difficult situations, burdened, stressed, and experiencing detrimental effects, and some of these caregivers nevertheless want to continue. Said another way, there is great diversity among caregivers, in their situations and in their reactions to those situations. There is also research that points to particular groups of caregivers who are more likely to be burdened and more likely to be experiencing heavy demands and having difficulty coping. This heterogeneity is good news: providing care to an older adult does not automatically mean that the provider necessarily requires assistance, from government or from elsewhere. It also means that existing knowledge can help us know who is most at risk and most likely requiring outside help. Those who are in disadvantaged positions in society are more likely to experience worse mental and physical illness, and therefore require more care. They place heavier demands on family and friend caregivers. In addition, it is these caregivers who most likely have the least resources to help them help their elderly family members. Disadvantages are embedded within the social structure of society and include such factors as gender, social class, and race and ethnicity. They represent unequal distributions of resources and opportunities.

Much has been written about gender inequality in Canada and elsewhere and does not need to be repeated here; suffice it to say that gendered differences in behavioural and role expectations are still apparent, evident in occupational differences, continuing wage gaps, and household divisions of labour. While the differential is disappearing in some areas, it is far from extinct. In terms of caregiving, as we have seen, women predominate as caregivers. We also know that women are more likely to experience strain than are male caregivers (Brazil et al. 2009), a finding often explained in terms of the lack of resources, poverty, vulnerability, and relatively powerless position of women that results in a lack of choice (Daly and Rake 2003; Robinson et al. 2009). This is the result of both social structure and ideology. Social structure—reflected in government, employment organizations, health insurance arrangements, and so on—limits the formal assistance that is available, that in turn necessitates informal assistance. This informal assistance comes primarily from women. Ideologically, paid work has been the primary forte of men, whereas caregiving has been part of women's nurturing role (Walker et al. 1998). Roles are reinforced and facilitated by the *mating gradient*, a term that refers to the fact that women tend to marry or cohabit at younger ages than men; over time, there is a widening of the initial differential between the wife's and the husband's economic resources. The result is that it then becomes good economic decision-making for the woman to undertake more care work so the man can concentrate on his greater earning power.

Social class differences in caregiving have also been investigated. Early research by Arber and Ginn (1993) suggested that middle-class non-manual workers in late mid-life tend to provide less hands-on care to older adults compared with manual workers. Among those providing care, manual workers are more likely to be co-resident with the care recipient while non-manual workers tend to provide extra-resident care. However, Arber and Ginn did not include the social class of the care recipient in their research. Glaser and Grundy (2002) sought to expand the inquiry, taking social class of both husband and wife (for a married couple) and of caregiver and care recipient into account. They conclude that:

Social class differences in the provision of co-resident care largely reflect the greater likelihood that those in manual class groups provide care for a spouse. This clearly reflects the higher prevalence of disability in manual groups [reflecting the relationship between lower social class and more disability]. There were almost no social class differences in the provision of co-resident care apparent among married respondents who had at least one living parent. (Glaser and Grundy 2002, 338)

Furthermore, among couples, the husband's social class is more important than that of the wife in terms of care provision for a spouse. However, among unmarried persons providing co-resident care for a parent, women from the non-manual group are more likely to be providing care than women from manual groups, reflecting the greater proportion of unmarried women among this group. The social class difference disappeared when controlling for marital status. These more recent findings support the earlier finding (Brody et al. 1995) that the unmarried, especially the never married, are more likely to provide parental care. Furthermore, Glaser and colleagues (2008) find that partnership dissolution does not necessarily have the expected detrimental effect on support in later life (but more is said about this later on). Rather, health needs and increasing age are the strong predictors of increased contact and increased informal and formal assistance, regardless of partnership dissolution.

In gerontology, ethnicity, minority status, and race typically refer to individuals living in a country where most of the population is from a different ethnicity, race, or cultural background (Chappell 2007); many are immigrants. In Western countries, including Canada, these individuals often share a history of disadvantages similar to class- and gender-based inequalities, notably socio-economic, health, physical environment, and formal social network disadvantages (Bajekal et al. 2004). By older age, the hardships of a lifetime accumulate (Nazroo et al. 2004). In these situations, exposure to stressful lives is attributed primarily to their typically low socio-economic status and subsequent prejudice and discrimination and, for immigrants in particular, disruption to their support systems and social networks as well as cultural adjustments in a new country (Driedger 2003). In other words, the poorer health of immigrants in old age is not considered a consequence of race or ethnicity per se.

Much gerontological literature assumes these subcultures also share a high value on family, including care for their older members; notable here is care by adult children of older parents. Some research supports this point of view, noting that familism accounts for a good quality of life in old age despite poor health and low incomes. Moriarty and Butt (2004) report minority groups consistently have high social support and, in Great Britain, it is associated with good quality of life. Ajrouch (2007) demonstrates that, among the poorly educated, good relationships with their adult children protect them from poorer health.

Other research, though, reveals that the structure of social support varies depending on the group. Nazroo and colleagues' research in Great Britain (2004) exemplifies some of the differences. The researchers find that South Asian people in Britain have intense routine support systems while black-Caribbean older adults and mixed white- and black-Caribbean older adults tend to live close to one child but the other children are geographically dispersed. Also in Britain, Butt and Moriaty (2004) find that Indian, Pakistani, and Bangladeshi people live in close proximity to each other with many members of their own families proximate. Chinese, black, and black-Caribbean people in Britain live farther away from one another and often kin live in another country. In Canada, historically, Chinese immigrants formed ethnic enclaves, but Li (1998) finds that currently immigrants from China are younger and better educated, have well-paying jobs waiting, and are settling outside of these Chinatowns, dispersing among those in the wider Canadian society. Interestingly, geographically mobile families, whether moving across or within countries, maintain their ties with older family members and put much effort into meeting their needs. While geographic distance poses its challenges, the connection is maintained, and concern flows in both directions (Antonucci, Jackson, and Biggs 2007).

What we do not know is whether the support to older adults in these groups is provided out of necessity (for example, they cannot afford nursing homes and other forms of paid assistance, or cannot access culturally appropriate services), if it is due to cultural preference, or if both factors are at work. We do know that many of these groups experience a "double whammy"—worse health in old age and fewer economic resources in both the parent and adult child generations that could be used either for assistance for the senior and/or for the caregiver. We know that the relative disadvantage experienced by specific social groups throughout their lives (including women relative to men, lower social classes relative to higher social classes, and specific ethnic and racial groups and immigrants) continues into old age. In particular, it results in worse health for members of these groups and in fewer economic resources for either the older adults or their adult children that can be used to ease the demands of care. Their jeopardy is greater and different, intersecting in ways we are only beginning to study. For example, being female and a member of an ethnic immigrant group and caring for one's parents is qualitatively different than being female and Caucasian and caring for one's parents or being male and a member of an ethnic immigrant group and caring for one's parents.

Other directions in caregiving research

Although much of the research has focused (and continues to focus) on caregiving-associated tasks, caregiver characteristics, characteristics of those they care for, and burdens and demands, there are nevertheless many other aspects of caregiving that have attracted research attention.

There is so much attention paid to the negative consequences of caregiving that it is easy to assume there are no satisfactions from this role. As noted above, the majority of caregivers are able to cope, and they do not feel overly burdened, or if they do, it is periodic, not constant (Chappell and Dujela 2008). Less studied than the stresses and burdens of caregiving are the satisfactions derived from this role, yet the vast majority of caregivers report deriving benefits. Positive aspects of caregiving include self-affirmation, self-confidence, and enjoyment, learning about oneself and about aging, a sense of satisfaction, a closer relationship with the care recipient, improved well-being, and greater tolerance of others (Braithwaite 1998; Tarlow et al. 2004). Adult children derive satisfaction from fulfilling their filial obligations and giving back, while spouses do so in fulfilling their marital vows (Pinquart and Sörenson 2003). What we do not know is whether and the extent to which the expressions of the positive aspects of caregiving reflect social desirability in caregivers' answers (they say what they think they are supposed to say) and/or caregivers attempt to cope with the difficulties by focusing on the positive (Funk and Stadjuhar 2009). More recently, it is being recognized that both negative and rewarding aspects of caregiving likely co-exist, sometimes simultaneously, for most caregivers (Andrén and Elmstähl, 2005).

The emphasis on the negative aspects of caregiving stems, in part, from the dominance of a practical or social-problems orientation in the field (Dannefer et al. 2008). This practical focus directs attention to the tasks of caregiving (such as assistance with ADL and IADL) with less attention on emotional aspects even though it is the emotional aspects that, conceptually at least, largely distinguish informal from formal caregiving, together with the absence of remuneration (Calasanti and Slevin 2001; Mac Rae 1998). However, we see ever more literature on emotional aspects (such as the famous "caring about" versus "caring for" distinction, with the former drawing attention to the emotional side of such work). There is also increasing recognition that the lines between informal and formal care are blurring as family caregivers undertake more skilled tasks (Ward-Griffin and Marshall 2003) and formal care providers describe emotional, even family-like, relationships with their clients (Chappell 2008; Lan 2002). Without good longitudinal data from the past we do not know whether this is a change in the relationships or primarily a growing awareness of the various aspects of both roles. The distinctions become even more complex when taking into consideration the fact that some older adults pay informal caregivers either directly or indirectly or receive formally organized unpaid volunteer support.

Another aspect that has not been studied extensively in its own right is the overall management of the older adults' care, although it has sometimes been captured in the caregiving literature. Referring to care management or managerial care as including care-related discussions with the older adult and/or other family members concerning finances and formal service arrangements, pertinent paperwork, and seeking out information, Rosenthal and colleagues (2007) find that caregivers often engage in this type of work. Most report providing care management together with direct care. Furthermore, both men and women report that it is the orchestration of care that extracts the greatest personal and job cost.

Another area that has received some attention is what additional roles caregivers fill and when. Much concern about those who give care to older adults has been encapsulated in phrases such as "the sandwich generation," "hidden victims," and "generation-in-the-middle" to depict the role overload encountered by middle-aged children caring for their parents while still raising children and sometimes also being employed. However, despite the popularity of this term in the media, being "sandwiched" is not typical of most caregivers. Penning (1998) and Williams (2005) have established that no more than one quarter of middle-aged caregivers are caring for children at home and for a parent simultaneously; that is, at least three quarters of caregivers are not sandwiched. Typically, care of a parent takes place after children have grown and left the home and, for women, prior to caring for an ailing husband. A more accurate term for this situation is *serial caregiving*. This is not to argue that serial caregiving is any less demanding or stressful than providing all or most of the care simultaneously. We do not know whether having more demands within a lesser period of time or the demands stretched over a longer period of time is more or less stressful or for whom.

There has also been interest in estimating the monetary value of caregiver contributions, either at minimum wage or in terms of replacement value. This research tends to focus on the tasks of caregiving, the care that would likely need to be provided from formal sources if not available from family and friends. That is, it does not assume that all support provided informally, especially emotional support, would be replaced by formal services (Harrow et al. 2004; Langa et al. 2002). A recent Canadian study (Hollander et al. 2009) documents the involvement of informal caregivers in meal preparation and cleanup, housecleaning, laundry and sewing, maintenance and outdoor work, shopping for groceries and other necessities, providing transportation, banking and paying bills, and personal care (assistance with bathing, toileting, care of toenails and fingernails, brushing teeth, shampooing and hairdressing). A conservative estimate is that informal caregivers age 45 and older provide approximately $25 billion of care yearly to older adults living in the community in Canada. The authors note that providing care is something that caregivers typically want to do, and prefer to do, rather than see formal care come into the home. The authors are not suggesting that all informal care be replaced with formal care, but rather that caregivers be supported in the care they willingly provide. (Table 3-3 provides an illustration of the types of hours caregivers devote to this role.)

There is also increasing recognition that those providing care and assistance to older adults may not define themselves as caregivers, nor see what they do as "work" (Henderson and Forbat 2002; O'Connor 2007). Furthermore, the point at which support evolves into caregiving per se is not well understood. The boundaries between caregiving and normal or everyday assistance is often confounded by gendered divisions of labour within households. For example, women typically prepare the meals and do the housework when men in the family are capable of (whether or not they have learned how to) undertaking the tasks themselves. Typically if assistance is provided within reciprocal exchanges or interdependencies,

Table 3-3 Average Annual Hours of Informal Caregiving in Victoria and Winnipeg

Care Level	Victoria, Community	Victoria, Facility	Winnipeg, Community	Winnipeg, Facility
Level A: Somewhat independent	222.93	143.98		
Level B: Slightly independent	475.67	181.37	643.65	175.82
Level C: Slightly dependent	580.45	223.87	826.84	241.45
Level D: Somewhat independent	1345.66	350.83	1131.23	268.74
Level E: Largely dependent			722.58	180.85

Source: Hollander et al. 2002

where the parties are able to do the activities, this would not be considered caregiving. O'Connor (2007) studied the process of self-identifying as a caregiver and reports that it occurs mainly through interactions with others. Often the individual will view what they are doing as an extension of their relationship with the person they are caring for and only come to consider themselves "caregivers" through the external influence of others. Viewing themselves as caregivers can be beneficial when it facilitates the effective use of support services and a sense of connectedness with others. It can have negative consequences though if the caregiver unintentionally marginalizes the care recipient. Relatedly, an understudied area is the negotiation of changing divisions of labour as older couples grow old together and one or both require assistance in areas in which they were previously independent.

Although there are many areas left to explore, we nevertheless know much about caregivers to older adults in Canada today. The caregivers are the baby boomers whose parents generally raised several children, who had a relatively structured life course in which the husband was the breadwinner and the wife raised the children and cared for the house. These older adults helped create universal medicare and lived the optimism of post– World War II, helped create pensions, and experienced retirement as a new life stage. In contrast, the aging baby boomers have fewer children and an increasingly less structured life course with more women working outside of the household, increasing prevalence of diverse family forms, increasing rates of divorce and remarriage, and increasing geographic mobility. Baby boomers are entering old age in a period during which medicare and the existing health care system are undergoing criticism, concerns have been raised about the sustainability of health care and pensions for their old age, and there are concerns about the availability of jobs for the baby boomers' children. How similar will caregiving be in the future?

Caregiving in the future

With longer life expectancies, the time spent caregiving is lengthening— soon we can expect to spend more time providing care to our parents than child rearing (CIHI 2011a). This greater longevity is bringing with it such issues as increasingly complex health problems as we live longer but with numerous chronic conditions (Crimmins 2004). It is not clear that caregivers can provide much or any more care than they currently do or that caregivers of the future will be able to provide the complex care required or be able to do so for extended periods of time. Current projections for the situation when the baby boomers are the care recipients, and their family and friends the caregivers, suggest reason for both optimism and pessimism.

Projecting the population age 75+ in Canada to 2030, Gaymu and colleagues (2007) estimate that widowhood will decrease considerably among women as the result of an increase in male life expectancy; this increase will exceed the increase for women, resulting in a smaller gap between the sexes. Women in the future, therefore, will be more likely to grow old with, rather than without, a partner, as is the case today. In addition, a greater proportion are likely to have at least one surviving child. Keefe and colleagues (2007b) project the proportion of seniors living alone will not increase from 2001 to 2031 and may decrease slightly from 2031 to 2051.

However, even though during the baby boomers' later years, the proportion who are still married and have living children is likely to increase, the sheer numbers of older adults will likely result in more individuals who are not in a marriage and who are without surviving children than was true in 2001 (the baseline used for the computations). Gaymu and colleagues (2007) estimate that those age 75+ will increase by over 146 percent in Canada by 2030, and that all categories of family composition will at least double (with partner and surviving children; with partner and no surviving children; with no partner and with surviving children; with no partner and no surviving children). Those age 75+ with a spouse and those with at least one surviving child will increase the most; that is, the size of the groups most likely to be in need will increase, but will do so at a slower rate than the other groups. These changes, however, are not dramatic until after 2020. At this time, the baby boom generation starts to turn age 75, after which time the pace of change will accelerate.

Keefe and colleagues (2007a) further note that, between 2001 and 2021, the proportion of women 85+ decreases from 22 percent to 16 percent as the parents of the baby boomers enter this age group. After this, between the years 2021 and 2051, as the baby boomers enter old-old age, those without surviving children increase to 20 percent in 2031 and to 28 percent in 2051. Projecting seniors in need of assistance (with shopping, personal care, housework, and meal preparation, i.e., everyday activities), they estimate that, assuming no change in disability rates or severities, those requiring assistance from 2001 to 2031 will be stable (from 15 percent to 18 percent). The same proportion, however, results in more than a doubling of the *numbers* of seniors in this situation due to the increasing size of that population. Both the proportion and size of the older adult population 65+ requiring assistance between 2026 and 2051 will steadily increase as the baby boomers enter old-old age.

These projections must be evaluated in light of several mitigating and unknown factors that will affect the family situation in the years to come. While living with at least one other person is a strong predictor of having informal support (Carrière et al. 2007), we do not know how well old-old couples, each with their own complex health problems, will be able to cope. As Pinquart and Sörensen (2003) report, older spouse caregivers with their own medical issues find the physical demands, financial strains and relationship strains more demanding than do other caregivers. At the present time, men caring for their wives are more likely to request formal care than are women caring for men; as well, they are more likely to institutionalize their wives (Martel and Légaré 2001; Delbès, Gaymu, and Springer 2006). In addition, yet unknown increases in marriage dissolution through separation or divorce could drastically effect those in old age; at present those living alone who require assistance are more likely to use more formal care than those similarly in need living with others, typically a spouse (Grundy 2006). And, having surviving children is not necessarily advantageous for older men who live alone; indeed, divorced men see their children less and receive less assistance from them than do divorced women (de Jong Gierveld, Van Tilbrg, and Lecchini 1997; Lin 2008) and the willingness of new partners to provide extensive care for those who remarry in later life is unknown.

Whether and how much adult children will shift in their willingness and the ways in which they provide care is open to change as are the relations between other family members. Guberman and colleagues (2011) suggest that, in Quebec at the present time, baby boomers who are the caregivers to older adults are maintaining multiple identities, setting limits to their caregiving, and expecting services through public support to assist in the care their parents require. The caregivers do this while adhering to norms of family responsibility. In addition, recent research reveals that adult stepchildren provide little or no emotional or instrumental care to remarried care recipients (Sherman and Boss 2007). It can be noted, though, that the baby boom generation has more siblings than older or younger cohorts even though baby boomers have fewer children than their parents' generation—a potential for informal care from siblings could see a change from past practices.

Expectations for old age are another consideration. Much has been said about the baby boom generation wanting and expecting old age to be different than it is for their parents. Both Phillipson (2007) and Gilleard and Higgs (2007) argue that baby boomers' lifetime experiences are distinctive, characterized by a mass consumer culture imbued with mass communications, the commodification of life, and an individualistic lifestyle. In middle age, they fuelled a new self-help orientation and a promise of a "new" old age, different from that of their parents. A recent Revera poll (News Canada 2012) finds that 85 percent of Canadian baby boomers want a better old age than their parents (News Canada 2012). According to Gilleard and Higgs (2007), the new consumer-based organization of life has replaced the old class-based distinctions within society. For baby boomers, status rises and falls based on consumer lifestyles that, in old age, are defined by the leisure we experience including our activities, exercise, travel, eating out, self-maintenance, and self-care. If these characterizations of baby boomers are correct, they portend a very different old age than older adults currently experience.

Caregiving in summary

What we know about caregivers today is that they carry out the vast majority of care for older adults who can no longer remain independent and care for themselves. They do so willingly and at times through great sacrifice to themselves. We also know that there is great diversity in terms of caregivers—who they are, the care they provide, and how well they are coping. For many, the experience is manageable. Not for all caregivers, but for some, the care they provide is complex, difficult, and burdensome. It is possible to identify those at greatest risk of adverse outcomes for their own health and well-being. However, we do not know the long-term toll caregiving may be taking on the physical and mental health of many; nor do we know the implications of the work for caregivers' own future need for care. Unless both the need for care decreases and utilization of health care services is restricted only to those services that are clearly beneficial, demands on both informal and formal care providers will increase.

There is wide consensus that older adults today and their caregivers require expanded policy and programming over and above what is available at the present time in Canada. Future projections add urgency to this matter. As the number of elderly people increases, especially into old-old age, the prevalence of chronic diseases will also increase, barring unexpected improvements in health. In all likelihood, informal caregivers have no capacity to expand their contributions. For them to continue, many require assistance; in other words, the assistance is not so that they can be replaced, but enabled to continue doing what they want to do—care for family and friends. The following section turns to a discussion of current and potential policy and programming for caregivers.

Social Policy and Caregiving
Caregiving policies and programs in Canada

The issue of who provides care for older adults is a question of the boundaries between the state and the family: that is, who should be providing what care and how much? No one is suggesting that families and friends should no longer provide care and assistance. As noted by Keefe and Rajnovich (2007), virtually all countries accept the notion that families have some responsibility to care for their members. And providing care is something that informal caregivers typically want and prefer to do rather than having formal care providers enter the home. This suggests that one of the first policy interventions required is to support caregivers in the care they willingly provide. However, at the present time, except for a few modest tax measures or programs (such as the compassionate care leave available through the employment insurance program), there is no national policy addressing family members (or others) caring for disabled older adults in Canada. Home care programs are under provincial jurisdiction.

In Canada at the present time, the Federal Family Caregiver Tax Credit is available. The federal government is proposing to increase and expand it (Government of Canada 2011). However, this is a tax *credit*, so that individuals must first have sufficient income to pay their additional expenses and claim the credit afterwards. This differs from a tax benefit that would assist those with fewer resources in the first place (BC Law Institute and the Canadian Centre for Elder Law 2010; Canadian Cancer Society 2011). Other suggestions to support caregivers that are advocated by a variety of individuals and groups but not currently in place in Canada include the following: greater financial support through tax initiatives, more adequate compassionate care leave provisions, flexible workplace arrangements, greater pension security, and other income support measures (BC Law Institute and the Canadian Centre for Elder Law 2010; Canadian Cancer Society 2011).

In addition to adequate labour policy (including labour standards and employment insurance), the Special Senate Committee on Aging (Carstairs and Keon 2009) also recommends providing direct payment to caregivers for reimbursement of expenses, and compensation and indirect financial support such as tax credits, pension credits, and dropouts from pensions. They urge a lead role for the federal government with all levels of government working together to ensure that caregiver needs are formally recognized and integrated into policy and the delivery of formal health care services. In 2008, the Canadian Caregiver Coalition also argued that the value of family caregiving be acknowledged in federal legislation, policy, and practice. They proposed a framework consisting of several essential elements to ensure the following:

- safeguard the health and well-being of family caregivers and increase flexible and available respite care;
- minimize excessive burden;
- enable access to user-friendly information and education;
- create work environments that are flexible and respect caregiving obligations; and
- invest in research and evidence-informed decision-making in this area.

Such a guiding framework can provide a yardstick or benchmark against which progress or the lack thereof can be assessed.

At the provincial level, services target older adults in need rather than caregivers. Typically, though, limited respite services are available. *Respite care* appears in three guises: sitter attendant services giving short breaks to the caregiver to run errands to go to a doctor's appointment and so on; adult daycare, where the older adult leaves the home for a few hours a week; and respite care beds within nursing homes for short stays. At the present time, there are no other programs that target caregivers, and in some jurisdictions (for example, BC), caregivers are eligible for respite services only when the older adult is already receiving formal care services. Those who are doing such a good job that the recipient does not need formal services are, by definition, not considered for support. And with those services that are provided, the fact that they are provided does not mean that they are necessarily funded sufficiently to meet the need.

Manitoba (Manitoba, Manitoba Finance 2008; Manitoba, Government of Manitoba 2012) recently passed provincial legislation in the hopes of increasing awareness and recognition of informal caregivers and their contributions. The Caregiver Recognition Act does the following:

- proclaims an annual Caregiver Recognition Day;
- provides general principles for how caregivers should be treated by the public, health staff, and in the workplace;
- recommends caregiver needs and supports be evaluated every two years; and
- creates a Caregiver Advisory Committee to advise the minister and to consult with the minister, caregivers, and relevant organizations.

The first Caregiver Recognition Day was April 3, 2012.

This is not to say that services delivered to older adults are unimportant in supporting the caregiver. Services provided to older adults can allow respite, much needed rejuvenation, and rest for the caregiver, and they can help prolong the caregiver's involvement by lifting some of the burden. This is an option that most caregivers state they prefer, but those services must take caregivers' needs into account (Chappell, Reid, and Dow 2001). Various authors point to the importance of long-term home care policies and programs to incorporate caregiver needs assessments and to provide services to support them in their role. For example, Chappell and Hollander's (2011) policy prescription for unpaid caregivers includes the following:

- assessing the needs of caregivers;
- providing information;

- adjusting labour and tax policies;
- providing support for respite; and
- conducting demonstration projects to inform policy on direct payment to caregivers.

Keefe and colleagues (2007a) categorize potential directions for supporting caregivers in terms of the following policy areas:

- home care policies—including assessment of caregivers, increasing services targeted to caregivers (such as respite services), and including non-family members as caregivers;
- workplace policies—broadening the eligibility criteria and length of leave allowed in the Canadian Compassionate Care Benefit, permitting family leave days in the federal labour code, and incentivizing private workplaces to include care of older adults in their policies on family leave; and
- income security policies—including financial support for caregivers (such as a non-taxable allowance), a refundable tax credit for caregivers, a drop-out clause for caring for an older adult, and credits for caregiving work in the Canada Pension Plan.

The experience in other countries is especially instructive for Canada. Several nations have implemented policies and programs for caregivers that hold lessons for Canada.

International experience

Many of the recommendations noted above for supporting caregivers have been implemented in European countries. Denmark, often considered a leader in this area, has financial provisions to facilitate care recipients remaining in their own homes for as long as possible. They also provide financial incentives for caregivers. Since the 1980s, Denmark has provided home help free of charge to seniors (those 65 and over) regardless of their economic situation. An assessment of the older person's functional capacity and needs determines eligibility for personal care and practical help through this program (Leeson 2004). Danish policies reject the notion that family members should necessarily be the care providers. Furthermore, if a medical assessment determines that hospital treatment can provide no further benefit to a dying relative, an informal caregiver is entitled to lost earnings. Since 2003, it has been the seniors themselves together with their family members who decide whether needed care should be provided by the local authority, a private person, or an authorized private service provider. The local authority pays for the private service provider if that is the chosen option.

Finland also has policies not found in Canada (Parkatti and Eskola 2004; Finland, Ministry of Social Affairs and Health 2006). Finland's Social Welfare Act provides allowances for the caregiver, whether a relative or some other person, and the family caregiver has the right to two days off per month. The municipality arranges for the care of the older adult during these days off and also insures the family caregiver against injury and issues pension benefits while the caregiver is in their employ.

Through the national Home and Community Care Program, established in 1984, Australia recognizes caregivers as both clients and as integral to care for seniors. Respite care options, general community support services, information and counselling, employment-related benefits, and cash benefits were introduced at the same time as the Home and Community Care Program. For example, compensation for extra costs of co-residence with the care recipient is set at 20 percent of the single-rate retirement pension and is not means tested or taxable. Those unable to work due to caregiving can apply for a means-tested caregiver payment that is equivalent to the retirement pension (Goodhead and McDonald 2007).

Chappell and Pridham (2010) recently reviewed the international literature on interventions designed to promote the health of family and friend caregivers for seniors. They conclude that successful interventions include the following:

- an assessment by trained assessors;
- an assessment of caregivers early and on an ongoing basis;
- sufficient resources to adequately address the needs identified;
- the active involvement of the caregiver in developing multidimensional and flexible programs tailored for them;
- caregivers seen as partners as well as clients who have needs and are treated accordingly;
- the facilitation of caregivers' self-identification and recognition of their own needs;
- options that are culturally sensitive; and
- implementation that is evaluated and outcomes monitored.

One of the areas of concern in the provision of services to older adults as well as to caregivers is the relationship between formal provision, especially government-funded services, and those provided informally. This raises the question: if additional services are made publicly available, will this result in less care by family and friends? British researcher Linda Pickard (2001) notes two basic approaches to government policy on caregivers. One is to support the continuation of family care through the provision of short-term breaks to caregivers with the aim of assisting them in the continuation of their caregiving roles. The other, the "carer blind" approach, uses an assessment of seniors' needs that does not take the existence or capabilities of caregivers into account in deciding service eligibility. In this approach, formal services could substitute for informal caregiving, arguably giving the care receiver greater autonomy and the caregiver greater freedom.

In Canada, only the first approach is evident. It is assumed that a large amount of family care is available, and family caregivers do not benefit from any direct public support. The health care system acts as a safety valve when family care is not available or not sufficient. As such, the lack of social policy that would share care between the family and the state results in a minimizing of the state's commitment to social care; rather, it opts to sustain the primacy of the family. When older Canadians do enter the health care system, policy is oriented toward the older adult, not the needs of the caregiver or the caregiving unit. This is not to say that caregivers are ignored in decisions about the provision of formal care, but that policy does not involve joint decision-making with one of the decision-makers being the family caregiver.

The question remains: do family members give less care when formal services are available? There is a growing body of research on this question, most of it international. Early Canadian research (Chappell and Blandford 1991), however, shows the relationship to be complementary, rather than one of substitution, and this has recently been confirmed (Dosman et al. 2005). In other words, formal care is called upon either when there is no informal care or when the demand is such that informal caregivers cannot cope on their own.

Studies examining the effect of informal care on the use of formal care usually find that informal care substitutes for formal services (Van Houtven and Norton 2008; Bolin, Lindgren, and Lundborg 2008). As one would expect, informal care is more likely to substitute for formal care that requires lower skill levels (grocery shopping, cleaning house, etc.) rather than, for example, physician services. Examining data from 11 European countries, Bonsang (2009) finds that the relationship varies depending on the type of services under consideration. Informal care substitutes for paid domestic help, but is a complement to high-skilled home care (in this instance nursing and personal care). For older adults with significant disability, the substitution effect vanishes, raising questions about the ability of informal caregivers to increase care provision in the future.

At issue here is the nature of the relationship between social policy and intergenerational relations. Walker (2002) notes that, while usually care provided by children to their older parents is accompanied with a feeling of obligation for past help from their parents, a minority do not experience these feelings yet assist their parents and attribute this to external pressures to do so.

Daatland and Lowenstein (2005) also looked at the relationship of social policy and informal care by families to consider the hypotheses of *crowding out* versus *crowding in* care, as outlined below. The researchers studied the division of responsibility for caring for older adults between the family, the welfare state, and others. More specifically, the researchers asked whether greater provision of care by the state leads to less care from families and/ or to a financial bankrupting of the state. They sought answers from five countries with differing state policies (Norway, England, Germany, Spain, and Israel). Germany and Spain are examples of countries with familialist welfare states; that is, they tend to favour family responsibility rather than state responsibility. Both countries have legal obligations for adult children toward their older parents and low levels of social care services. (However, this does not mean that they have low levels of medical services.) England and Norway have more individualist social policies (with no legal obligation for adult children to care for older parents) and high levels of social care services. Both England and Norway also have high employment of

Hypotheses of Relations between the Provision of Social Care Services and Family Help to Older Adults

Crowding out: the hypothesis that providing high social care service levels will result in low levels of family help.
Two variants:
- *substitution*—services push families out due to lack of need, demoralizing the family (referred to as a moral risk argument)
- *compensation*—a decline in family care leads to the need for services to be provided

Crowding in: the hypothesis that the provision of social care services complements or stimulates family efforts, leading to no decline in care from families or to more care than provided before.
Two variants:
- *complement*—services are added to the assistance already being provided by the family
- *stimulate*—family help increases due to a sharing of the burdens

Source: Daatland and Lowenstein 2005

women and higher fertility rates. Israel is a mixed welfare state, with legal family obligations but also high social care service levels.

For all five countries in the study, spouses, daughters (most frequently), and sons are the most important sources of family assisatance—confirming past research for Western countries, including Canada. *Affectional solidarity* (emotional closeness) is equally strong in all countries. Furthermore, emotional support flows both ways between the generations, instrumental assistance is more likely to flow upward from children to parents and financial support is most likely to flow down from parents to adult children (when the economy allows for it). Their findings in regard to the provision of social care services show that family help is not crowded out by the availability of these services. Instead, the services increase the total level of care to older adults—in other words, care is now provided by both formal services and family members. Finally, the availability of services allows the older adults to establish more independent relationships with their family members.

Jönsson (2003) also studied European countries and the changing intergenerational relations and expectations given differing socio-political contexts.

- She categorized the southern European countries of Greece, Italy, and Spain as having strong family responsibilities due to their underdevelopment of social services to support older adults (and children). These are countries where care of older adults is left to the family. These countries also have low rates of female employment.
- France and Germany were classified as having "regulated shared responsibilities." Here the state specifies legal obligations of families while also providing support for the care of older adults (and children).
- The UK and Ireland have "unregulated sharing of responsibilities" where state responsibility is not clearly defined. Neither the state nor adult children are legally required to care for older adults in need.
- The Scandinavian countries are characterized by state responsibility for care for older adults (and children).

Despite varying involvement of the state in the provision of services to older adults in these countries, Jönsson (2003) reports that across all countries, there is widespread support among its citizens for state responsibility for older adults through support services that facilitate older adults remaining in their own homes. At the same time, family solidarity and intergenerational support is evident in all countries, regardless of state involvement. In countries where state support is weaker, the demand for the state provision of services is stronger; in countries where it exists, it is more or less taken for granted but public support is strong. In all countries, care for elderly persons remains women's work but with an increasing differentiation among women. Among families with few economic resources, family members provide care to older adults. However, well-educated women with high economic resources in countries with poor public provision of services tend to hire less well educated and low-paid women (either from their own country or from elsewhere) to provide care for their elderly members.

To summarize, research does not support the position that providing formal services results in a lessened role for informal caregivers. Indeed, the bulk of the evidence suggests families continue helping one another irrespective of state policy but, when formal services are available, it results overall in more care for the older adult. Formal services, therefore, become important and necessary when the informal care system cannot cope with all of the care required by the senior. As noted above, this does not apply to all older adults but only a proportion. However, as the baby boom generation reaches older old age, the numbers of those requiring more care than the informal network can manage, and those without family to provide the care, will increase. That is, Canada should be attending to care for older adults now, and part of that effort should be directed to care for caregivers.

The Need for Care for Caregivers

Policies that support the needs of caregivers are important for several reasons: the formal care system could never replace all of the support provided informally; caregivers express a desire to continue in this role; and many caregivers make great sacrifices in order to provide the care that they do. Without assistance, caregivers' health can deteriorate and result in greater demands on the formal health care system. Such policies are particularly important for women, who constitute the majority of caregivers. However, policies may inadvertently encourage women to leave the labour force, thus pushing them back into the private sphere and reinforcing the gendered division of labour that so many have sought for so long to change. On the other hand, if women are reducing employment or quitting paid work to provide care anyway, support may provide real assistance and recognition of the value of their contributions. If we believe individuals should have choices, support for caregivers must be sufficient so the individual has alternatives, in terms of both whether to be a caregiver and also the extent of caregiving provided. Keefe and Rajnovich (2007) summarize the issue:

> The debate should focus less on whether family or state should be responsible for providing care, and focus more on how caregivers can

be supported if they choose to be a caregiver, while ensuring that the choice does not carry [negative] short- and long-term consequences. Policy must be based on the needs of persons of all ages in the society, not just those in need of care. It must also consider the interconnections among individuals and families and how social policy affects these relationships. (87)

It might also be noted that support for the caregiver can and often does take the form of arrangements outside of the formal health care system, including voluntary organizations, churches, and other not-for-profit and neighbourhood organizations as well as informal groupings of friends and neighbours. The health care system at present is not organized to act as a coordinator or broker for bringing any such resources together. There is no place in society mandated with this task. Some targeted experiments, however, suggest that such coordination is achievable. For example, the McConnell Foundation of Montreal gave funds to various groups within the formal care system with a mandate to *not* do business as usual. They were tasked with providing respite to caregivers in need on an innovative basis: caregivers themselves defined what would give them a break. Drawing on the concept of "respite is an outcome not a service" (Chappell et al. 2001), the program devised solutions for each client that responded to individual needs while taking into account the caregivers' context of family, friends, neighbours, volunteers, local not-for-profit and charitable organizations, and health care and social services by coordinating and drawing on any number of these sectors.

An examination of three such rural projects (Chappell, Gibbens, and Schroeder 2008) concluded there were six foundational principles for facilitating such respite:

- embracing caregivers as partners;
- raising awareness of caregiving issues among caregivers themselves, their family and friends, and the general public;
- networking and engaging stakeholders (not only the formal care system);
- creating advisory structures inclusive of the key stakeholders;
- caregiver leadership; and
- building community capacity that encourages creativity and individualizing support.

At present, not only do various units within the formal health care system work largely in isolated silos, lacking communication with one another, but they also function independently from organizations within the third sector. There is no coordination/collaboration function either within or external to the health care system that brings different systems together in the interests of meeting the needs of dependent older adults.

Looking Forward

It is wrong to assume that families can continue providing more care without adverse consequences for themselves and the older adults they care for. There is good reason to support these caregivers in the role in which they are willingly engaging. At least some of that support, we suggest, must come from the formal health care system.

In the next chapters, we consider a brief history of how the formal health care system came to be the way it is, the research on the cost-effectiveness of continuing care, and a model of integrated care that has the potential to provide services appropriate to an aging society while being cost-effective. The focus of the discussion is not on medical care *per se* but on continuing care services typically including community-based home care and supportive services. These are the services most required by older adults to help them deal with their chronic conditions and functional difficulties, that is, to remain living independently in the community where they prefer to live. The discussion, like the majority of research on older adults and their informal caregivers, targets care within the community rather than in long-term care institutions because that is where most older adults reside and where they want to stay. It is, that is, the site of the vast majority of care.

Chapter 4

The Evolution of Continuing Care for Older Adults

Introduction

Formal care services for older adults and persons with disabilities—often known as *continuing care*—have developed over time and have important historical roots in the evolution of health and social services in Canada. This chapter begins with an overview of continuing care and concludes with a discussion of health and social policy in Canada. While there is considerable commonality, continuing care has evolved differently in each of the provinces and territories. The result is variation in service provision, policies, and terminology. The evolution of organizational models and terminology is ongoing.

Defining continuing care

It is important to note that continuing care is not a type of service, such as hospital care or physician services, but a complex "system" of service delivery. This system has a number of components and is integrated conceptually as well as in practice through a "continuum of care." The efficiency and effectiveness of the system depends not only on each component, but also on the structure of the service delivery system itself (Federal/Provincial/Territorial Subcommittee on Continuing Care 1992).

Tables 4-1 and 4-2 summarize the core components of continuing care, and Table 4-3 provides a summary of other service components that are often included in a comprehensive continuing care system.

Table 4-1 Core Components of the Continuing Care Service Delivery System: Home- and Community-Based Services

Home and Community-Based Care

Assessment and Case Management Services constitute a process of determining care needs, admitting clients into service, and providing for the ongoing monitoring of care requirements, including the revision of care plans as necessary.

Meal Programs Meals-on-Wheels is a voluntary community program that provides and delivers a hot nutritious meal to the client's home. The goal of Meals-on-Wheels is to supplement a client's diet by delivering an attractive nourishing meal to help maintain or improve health. Other programs that connect people to meals such as Wheels to Meals may also be provided.

Home Support Services are provided to clients who require non-professional (lay) personal assistance with care needs or with essential housekeeping tasks. Personal assistance needs may include help with dressing, bathing, grooming, and transferring, whereas housekeeping tasks might include activities such as cleaning and meal preparation.

Home Nursing Care provides comprehensive nursing care to people in their homes. A home nursing care program coordinates a continuum of services designed to allow clients of all ages to remain in their homes during an acute or chronic illness. This community-based program provides one-to-one nursing care in the client's own environment. Home nursing care encourages clients to be responsible for, and to actively participate in, their own care. Goals for nursing care can be curative, rehabilitative, or palliative.

Community Physiotherapy and Occupational Therapy Services provide direct treatment and consultative and preventative services to clients in their homes, arrange for the necessary equipment to cope with physical disability, and train family members to assist clients. Community physiotherapy and occupational therapy programs also typically provide consultative, follow-up, maintenance, and educational services to patients, families, physicians, public health staff, hospitals, and nursing homes.

Adult Day Care Services provide personal assistance, supervision, and an organized program of health, social, and recreational activities in a protective group setting. The program is designed to maintain persons with physical and/or mental disabilities or restore them to their personal optimum capacity for self-care. Adult day care centres may be established within a residential care facility or may be located in a freestanding building.

Group Homes are independent private residences that enable persons with physical or mental disabilities to increase their independence through a pooling of group resources. They must be able to participate in a co-operative living situation with other disabled individuals. This type of care is particularly suitable for disabled young adults who are working, enrolled in an educational program, or attending a sheltered workshop.

Source: Adapted from Federal/Provincial/Territorial Subcommittee on Continuing Care 1992, 25–27

Table 4-2   Core Components of the Continuing Care Service Delivery System: Residential Services

Residential Care

Long-Term Care Residential Facilities provide care for clients who can no longer safely live at home. Residential care services provide a protective, supportive environment and assistance with activities of daily living for clients who cannot remain at home due to their need for medication supervision, 24-hour surveillance, assisted meal service, professional nursing care and/or supervision.

Chronic Care Units/Hospitals provide care to persons who, because of chronic illness and marked functional disability, require long-term hospitalization but do not require all of the resources of an acute, rehabilitation, or psychiatric hospital. Twenty-four hour coverage by professional nursing staff and on-call physicians is provided, as well as care by professional staff from a variety of other health and social specialties. Only people who have been properly assessed and who are under a physician's care are admitted to chronic care facilities. Care may be provided in designated chronic care units, in acute care hospitals, or in stand alone chronic care hospitals.

Assessment and Treatment Centres and Day Hospitals provide short-term diagnostic and treatment services in a special unit within an acute care hospital. These centres provide intensive assessment services to ensure that elderly persons with complex physical and psychiatric disorders are correctly assessed and treated. The objective of the centres is to assist the client to achieve and maintain an optimal level of functioning and independence. Centres may have beds for inpatient assessment and treatment, a day hospital service, and/or an outreach capability that permits staff to assist clients in care facilities or in their homes.

Source: Adapted from Federal/Provincial/Territorial Subcommittee on Continuing Care 1992, 25–27

Table 4-3   Examples of Additional Services Sometimes Included in the Continuing Care System

Other Examples of Additional Services Sometimes Included

Medical Equipment and Supplies may be provided as required to maintain a person's health (e.g., medical gases, assisted breathing apparatus) and to improve the opportunities for self-care and a better quality of life (e.g., wheelchairs, walkers, electronic aids). Equipment may be loaned, purchased, or donated.

Transportation Services may be provided to disabled persons to allow them to go shopping, keep appointments, and attend social functions. Many vehicles are adapted for wheelchairs and other devices.

Support Groups may be initiated by many sources such as community and institutional services, friends and families of clients, and clients having similar disabilities. The groups provide psychological support and foster mutual aid.

Crisis Support may be available in the community to give emergency assistance when existing arrangements break down (e.g., illness of the spouse caring for a disabled person), which could include emergency admission to institutional care.

Table 4-3 (Continued)

Life and Social Skills for Independent Living may provide retraining and support for independent living and for social and personal development. This service might be provided in group settings or on an individual basis.

Respite Services may be provided to primary caregivers to give them temporary relief by providing a substitute for the caregiver in the home or by providing alternate accommodation to the client.

Palliative Care may be provided to dying persons in their homes or in residential settings.

Volunteers may provide programs of volunteer help that are utilized in most aspects of long-term care.

Congregate Living Facilities (sheltered housing/assisted living) are apartment complexes that offer amenities such as emergency response, social support, and shared meals.

Family Care Homes are single-family residences that accommodate a maximum of two long-term care clients who require residential care. This is a type of adult foster care.

Special Extended Care Units for the behaviourally disordered are hospital units that provide a special program for residents who, because of serious disruptive (chronic, occasional, or episodic) behaviours, cannot be managed in the usual extended care or continuing care facility.

Discharge Planning Units (also called **step down care**) are units in acute care hospitals that receive elderly persons who have been transferred from regular hospital beds and whose discharge can be facilitated by providing a program of health services to aid recovery.

Quick Response Teams are located in hospital emergency departments. They review cases of elderly persons who are deemed to be eligible for admission to hospital by physicians to determine whether or not such persons can be returned to their homes, that is, can be diverted.

Sources: Adapted from Federal/Provincial/Territorial Subcommittee on Institutional Program Guidelines 1988, 31–33; Hollander and Pallan 1995; Hollander and Prince 2007

What formal care exists now in Canada and how it is described is complex and potentially confusing. This complexity stems from its history. Prior to the late 1970s, the components of what is now continuing care were generally housed in three separate areas: acute care, public health, and social services. This system of delivering services relied on coordination mechanisms between these three separate and distinct organizational entities that were typically housed in different divisions and/or different ministries of government. The new system that emerged in the mid-1970s and the 1980s integrated a range of different services within one service delivery system, in one branch or division. This allowed for system-wide planning, policy-making, administration, and care provision. Figure 4-1 lists services such as assessment and treatment centres, day hospitals, and chronic care hospitals that originate with the acute care tradition. Long-term care facilities originated from charitable hospitals, poorhouses, and other social welfare oriented institutions. They are now often combined administratively with other institutional services such as hospitals in jurisdictions where there is a split between residential and community-based services. Like long-term care facilities, home support services were originally in the social services sector. The home nursing care and rehabilitation components of continuing care were originally rooted in public health, and are now often referred to as home care services.

Figure 4-2 presents a classic example of a continuing care service delivery system, the system in place in BC in the early 1990s. Similar models were also in place in the early 1990s in other western provinces. More recently, the concept of continuing care has been expanded from caring primarily for elderly persons and persons with disabilities to a broader concept of an integrated system of care for persons with ongoing care needs that could also include chronic mental health clients and children with special needs.

Continuing care is generally used to describe a system of service delivery that includes all of the services provided by residential long-term care, home support, and home care; that is how it is used in this book. In a few instances, the term has been used to refer to community-based long-term care services and home care services excluding residential long-term care services. On the other hand, the term has also been used in some jurisdictions to refer to only long-term facility care. Whatever the definition, the original meaning of the term reflects within it two complementary concepts: care may "continue" over a long period of time and the program of care "continues" across service components; in other words, there is a continuum of care.

Yet another distinction we sometimes see is the use of *long-term care* to describe a range of institutional services primarily for the care of elderly persons, and *home care* to describe home-based services provided primarily by nurses and other professionals such as physiotherapists. In other in-stances, long-term care refers to home and community-based care provided over longer periods of time (over three months or over six months, depending on the jurisdiction). The specific services included, and under what umbrella, vary by jurisdiction. For example, responsibility for adult day care centres and group homes may be in home care in one jurisdiction and in long-term institutional care in another; elsewhere they may be split

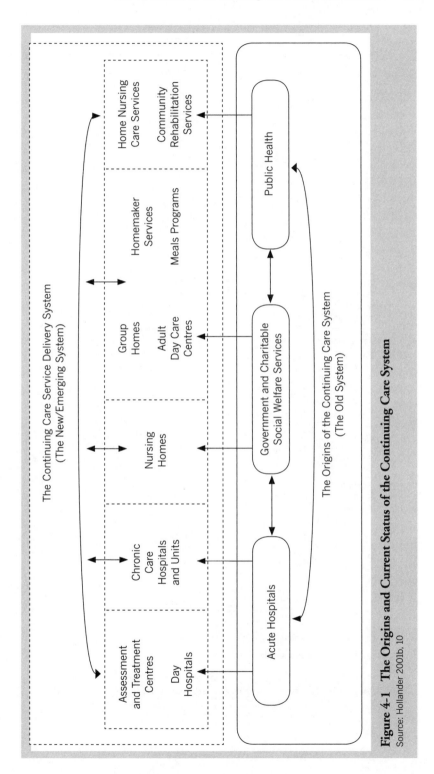

Figure 4-1 The Origins and Current Status of the Continuing Care System
Source: Hollander 2001b, 10

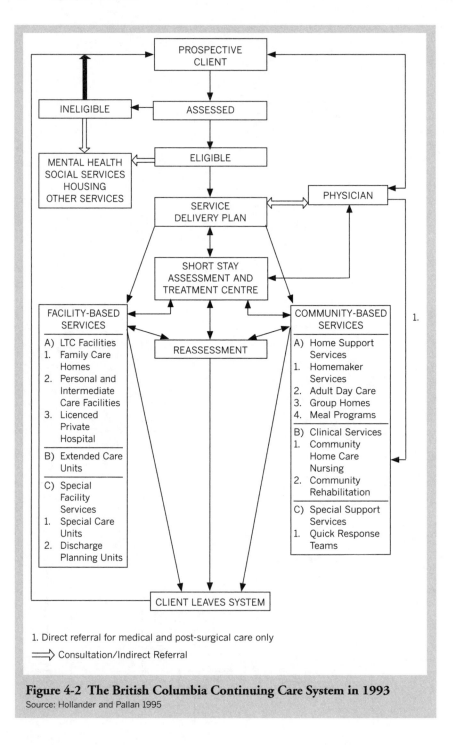

Figure 4-2 The British Columbia Continuing Care System in 1993
Source: Hollander and Pallan 1995

across jurisdictions, such as when facility-based adult day care centres are in institutional care, while stand-alone centres are in home care.

The term *long-term care* also has a second, very different meaning. It has come to refer to both residential and community-based services and to have a meaning similar to the term *continuing care*. This usage was reflected in the establishment in 1986 of the Federal/Provincial/Territorial Subcommittee on Long Term Care that combined the former Federal/Provincial/Territorial Subcommittee on Home Care and an interprovincial committee on long-term care. When the new subcommittee was established in 1986, it defined *long-term care* as follows:

> Long term care represents a range of services that address the health, social and personal care needs of individuals who, for one reason or another, have never developed or have lost some capacity for self-care. Services may be continuous or intermittent, but it is generally presumed that they will be delivered for the "long term" that is, indefinitely to individuals who have demonstrated need, usually by some index of functional incapacity. (Federal/Provincial/Territorial Subcommittee on Institutional Program Guidelines 1988, 2)

This definition includes residential long-term care services, as well as community- and home-based long-term care services—in other words, home support and professional home care services. Home and community-based long-term care services generally provided by persons other than professionals such as nurses or rehabilitation therapists (e.g., homemakers) are often referred to as *home support services*. The term may also include *personal care services* that provide more advanced, non-professional care, including care for activities of daily living. Sometimes personal care is seen as a separate service in its own right. Home support services are usually included in the term *home care*. Adult day care, group home services, and homemaker services are community-based home support services.

The term *home care* refers to non-physician medical services at home such as home nursing and home physiotherapy; as well, it usually, but not always, incorporates home support services. A working group established to review the major issues in home care recognized the conceptual confusion around the term: "there is no precise and universally accepted definition. Home care therefore has different meanings in different places" (Federal/Provincial/Territorial Subcommittee on Long Term Care 1990, 1). The report goes on to note that there are three distinct models of home care (known as "functions of home care"): the acute care substitution model, the long-term residential care substitution model, and the maintenance and preventive model.

To add to the confusion surrounding terminology in this area, organizational arrangements in the continuing care sector have been, and continue to be, in a state of flux. Most provinces and regional health authorities are reviewing the organization of these services, and changes continue to be made. For purposes of this discussion *home care* and *home/community care* refer to all home- and community-based home support and home care services.

The Historical Evolution of Continuing Care

Given that a significant portion of the services within continuing care emerged from the social welfare sector, its development is embedded in the evolution of both health and social services in Canada. In social policy, there is a robust body of literature (Armitage 1996; Graham et al. 2012) related to social policy and income redistribution, employment support programs and so on, but there is relatively little literature on actual service delivery mechanisms such as group homes or homemaker services. Similarly, in the health sector, much of what has been written focuses on the key milestones such as the development and financing of hospitals and medical services, population health, and federal/provincial relations and funding (Taylor 1987; Taylor 1978; Thompson 2010).

Continuing care comes from both the health and social welfare traditions. The social welfare traditions are often overlooked because continuing care is now seen primarily as located within the health system. However, many of the current debates about home support services, user fees for facilities, etc. fall more appropriately into the domain of social policy. A brief overview of the key issues is useful here.

Titmuss (1976), in his classic work *Essays on the Welfare State*, notes three types of welfare:

- *Social welfare* is part of a system of redistributing societal resources through income support (for example, the Old Age Pensions and the Guaranteed Income Supplement) or the provision of services in kind (for example, hospital care, home care, support for unpaid caregivers).
- *Fiscal welfare* refers to providing benefits to individuals, families, or groups through the tax system (such as the current federal and provincial tax deductions for family caregivers and tax breaks for seniors and persons with disabilities).
- *Occupational welfare* relates to benefits provided by employers (for example, company pensions and sickness benefits). This is more pronounced in countries where health benefits are provided through employers. The interest here is in social welfare.

Graham and colleagues (2012), building on the work of Titmuss, outline three conceptual and philosophical approaches to social welfare. These
models are at the heart of the debate about the role of the state versus the
role of the individual in terms of who is responsible for what and who pays
for what. These three approaches can be summarized as follows:

- *The Residual Welfare Model of Social Policy* argues that the private market
  and families are responsible for people's social needs. The government
  should only intervene when these systems break down.
- *The Industrial Achievement–Performance Model of Social Policy* argues
  that social needs should be met on the basis of merit related to work
  performance and productivity.
- *The Institutional Redistributive Model of Social Policy* argues that there is
  a role for the state to provide social and health services based on need.
  (Graham et al. 2012)

Within Titmuss's formulation of social welfare there are three major categories of activity. The first category relates to the *protection of the public*
by government such as the feeding of "vagrants, offenders, the diseased
and the insane." This is an example of Graham's residual welfare model,
where government has to act because individuals and families cannot adequately deal with issues of relevance to the larger society. The other two
categories of social welfare, which are particularly relevant to continuing
care, were initially in the sector of the private charities who provided
two things:

- *care* to those who could not help themselves, such as the sick, the or-
  phaned, and older adults; and
- *support* for the poor and destitute.

In other words, originally services were provided as a response to need for
those who could not care for themselves and as a means of protecting the
public from such persons. In this case, communities—rather than government—were responsible for care and support, and they were a type of societal insurance against risk. This was a type of societal response based on
the residual welfare model.

In the current era, continuing care and support are provided primarily
as a care-related response to need; that is, they fall under the redistributive model as government funds care- and support-related services. Thus,
while continuing care is considered a health care service, and is funded
by Ministries of Health, most of the policy issues around eligibility, user
fees, etc. reflect an ongoing tension between Graham's residual welfare and

redistributive models. As will be seen below, this tension is an ongoing feature of policy debates about continuing care.

Continuing care emerged as a new sector within the health care industry in the 1970s and 1980s. This chapter focuses on four periods in order to establish the historical context out of which continuing care emerged. First is the emergence of social security (the colonial period to the end of World War II); second, the consolidation of social security (1945 to the early 1970s); third, retrenchment in health and social services (early 1970s to early 1990s); and finally, reform and restructuring (early 1990s to the present). The development of health and social policy in Canada has been well documented (Graham et al. 2012; Thompson 2010; Armitage 1996; Crichton 1993; Meilicke and Storch 1980; Taylor 1987). The policy evolution, as noted in the subsequent sections, is primarily based on these sources. The following provides brief summary overviews of major policy milestones, trends, and developments that relate to the care of seniors. It focuses primarily on recent developments.

The emergence of social security in Canada (1700s–1945)

Health services in the colonial period were related primarily to the protection of the public and the housing of the indigent (people who are needy or poor). Meilicke and Storch (1980) note that buildings to provide for those termed "insane" were built as early as 1714, and provisions were instituted in 1844 for the care of individuals with leprosy. Local boards of health were established as early as 1832 to deal with outbreaks of disease and were often disbanded when the epidemic subsided. In the later years of the nineteenth century, the Red Cross, the Victorian Order of Nurses, and provincial Boards of Health were established.

In the early part of the next century, the medical care and hospital sectors emerged. The Canadian Mental Health Association and the National Institute for the Blind were established; Saskatchewan implemented municipal doctor and union hospital plans; the federal Department of Health was established; and municipal hospital plans were implemented. Hospitals were originally developed to house the indigent and were often attached to churches and run by religious or charitable organizations. Long-term care facilities and group homes were originally for people who where destitute and disabled. Until the early 1900s, health services could best be described as constituting a subset of social welfare services. There was a gradual evolution of hospital and physician services during the 1920s and 1930s.

Social services in the pre-Confederation era—in other words, services for people who were poor, sick, mentally ill, and delinquent—were primarily left to the family, religious organizations, and voluntary lay groups.

During this period, three major elements shaped the provision of health and social services: frontier life, the role of the church, and the example of the Elizabethan Poor Laws in England.

The period preceding 1867 included the consolidation of poor relief as a municipal responsibility in Canada West (Ontario). Towns and villages were given powers to pass bylaws regarding almshouses, houses of refuge, and workhouses. The period after Confederation (1867 to 1900) included the incorporation of most of the existing provinces into Canada and the opening up of the west by the railway. During this period, the workforce was shifting from family farms to urban and industrial centres. New voluntary agencies developed and there was a shift from institutional (care in facilities) to outdoor (care in the community) assistance. There were a number of initiatives undertaken in the early 1900s to protect workers, children, war veterans, and older Canadians, by addressing income security through the Old Age Pensions Act of 1927, which laid the groundwork for future federal-provincial cost sharing agreements and which were significant for health care later on.

During the Great Depression of the 1930s, ad hoc measures to provide assistance proved to be inadequate resulting in serious protests and mounting social tensions. The Unemployment Insurance Act of 1940 came into effect. The federal government also appointed the Royal Commission on Dominion-Provincial Relations (the Rowell-Sirois Commission) in 1937 (Smiley 1963) to examine the financial and economic basis of Confederation. The report, released in 1940, concluded that, with a few important exceptions, provincial autonomy should be maintained and strengthened, the federal government should be responsible for unemployment insurance, and old age pensions and a system of unconditional equalization grants to the provinces should be established so that social welfare programs could be provided across Canada in accordance with national standards.

The Beveridge Report in Britain, released in 1942, was a visionary plan for postwar reconstruction. Shortly after its release, a similar plan was devised for Canada. The Marsh Report (1943) argued for a social security system buttressed by a comprehensive employment policy. This report is now regarded as a landmark document that provided the conceptual framework for the development of social security in Canada. The Heagerty Report on health insurance and public health was also released in 1943, and called for a joint federal-provincial program of health insurance with a full range of benefits such as medical, dental, pharmaceutical, hospital, and nursing services. A Dominion-Provincial Conference on Reconstruction was convened in 1945 to synthesize the various reports and to map out a plan of action for the postwar era. The social security proposals included the following: making old age pensions universal; expanding the coverage of unemployment insurance to persons not previously covered; and establishing comprehensive health insurance. However, these policies (called the Green Book proposals) were not implemented due to disagreements between the federal and provincial governments about the mechanisms for allocating tax revenues.

In terms of *continuing care,* long-term care facilities, and group homes emerged from the early institutions for the destitute and disabled, influenced by the Elizabethan Poor Laws. Home care nursing and homemaker services emerged in the late 1800s and early 1900s with the work of the Victorian Order of Nurses and the establishment of homemaker services (Crichton et al. 1994). Individuals and families paid directly for these services until the 1950s. At that time, some provincial governments started to pay for them or to fund municipalities that, in turn, paid for such services.

The consolidation of social security (1945–early 1970s)

During this period, there was pressure on the federal government both for and against national action. In 1948, Prime Minister Mackenzie King announced the national health services grants program to provide funds for a variety of medical and public health purposes, including hospital construction and research. This initiative greatly increased the number of hospital beds and contributed to the concept of the scientific medical model of health care by its allocation of funds for scientific research (Taylor 1987). However, after 1948, the federal government took the position that it would only involve itself in the issue of health insurance if called on to do so by a majority of the provinces.

By the early 1950s, the Canada Sickness Survey and the Canadian Tax Foundation had pointed to Canada's high level of illness and existing disparities in health care, and four provinces had developed varied health insurance programs. These provinces demanded that the federal government honour its 1945 offer of cost sharing for health care.

Countervailing pressures included the Canadian Medical Association's (CMA) official reversal, in 1955, of its 1943 approval of government-administered programs. The Canadian Hospital Association (CHA, now the Canadian Healthcare Association) and the life insurance industry concurred with the recommendations of the CMA. However, public opinion, increasing press coverage, a commitment to health insurance in the 1953 election, and provincial pressure ensured that the issue was addressed at the 1955 federal-provincial meeting to negotiate tax arrangements. At this conference, several provincial premiers called for, or proposed, national health insurance schemes.

The Hospital Insurance and Diagnostic Services Act was passed in 1957. The law called for a detailed set of standards and required that services be delivered on equal terms and conditions across the country. This effectively prevented any province from accepting the private insurance model because a program calling for a means test would not be equal for everyone. The result was the establishment of an expensive hospital-based system of health care, with a medical and technological focus. Other services such as long-term care, tuberculosis, and mental health facilities were not covered, leading to an inequitable distribution of health services among the provinces. The decision to first develop a hospital-based infrastructure set the tone for Canadian health care as other alternatives were effectively ruled out once this decision was made (Taylor 1987).

An important factor in the establishment of the medical system in Canada was the medicare program in Saskatchewan (brought in under the leadership of Tommy Douglas, leader of the Co-operative Commonwealth Federation, or CCF, which later became the New Democratic Party, or NDP). This provincial example demonstrated the feasibility and effectiveness of such a program. A second factor was the 1964 report of the Royal Commission on Health Services (the Hall Commission) calling for a universal, portable, accessible, comprehensive, and government-administered medical care program. The Medical Care Act was passed in 1966,[1] completing the program of basic health coverage for Canadians. The law allowed for the maintenance of the fee-for-service, private enterprise model of physician services, and to a great extent, precluded the adoption of alternative forms of medical care. Furthermore, this action completed and consolidated the Canadian health care infrastructure based on "the acute care hospital and the individual patient–single doctor relationship" (Aucoin 1974, 57).

During the era from 1946 to the early 1970s, there was also a consolidation and expansion of social services policies and programs. In 1951 a constitutional amendment was passed that enabled the federal government to make laws to operate a federally administered old age pension program. This was followed in 1952 by the implementation of the Old Age Security (OAS) program that provided a universal pension to those 70 years of age or older, and the Old Age Assistance program that provided a means-tested pension for those between 65 and 70 years of age. The Disabled Persons Act of 1954 provided disability pensions to totally and permanently disabled persons. During the 1960s much of the Canadian social security system was consolidated. The National Welfare Grants program was introduced in 1962 to strengthen social services through training and innovative projects. The Canada Pension Plan (CPP) was implemented in 1966 to supplement old age pensions and provide coverage for widows and people with disabilities. The Quebec Pension Plan provided similar coverage for residents of that province. In the same year, the Old Age Security Act was amended to provide a Guaranteed Income Supplement

(GIS) to pensioners with low incomes. OAS benefits were phased in over a five-year period for those aged 65 to 70, so that benefits would eventually be paid out to people at age 65.

The year 1966 also saw the introduction of a major new initiative, the Canada Assistance Plan (CAP). This plan provided "a comprehensive program for federal sharing of provincial expenditures for public assistance and for welfare services on a conditional cost-sharing basis similar to that in health" (Meilicke and Storch 1980, 10). The main purposes of this program were to help people achieve, or retain, independence and to improve the standards of public welfare. CAP consolidated numerous federal-provincial programs based on need, or on means, into a single program to meet needs regardless of the cause (for example, what was perceived to be defects of character, laziness) of those needs. CAP benefits extended beyond the basic requirements for food and shelter to other benefits such as counselling, homemaker and day care services, and the care of persons in long-term care institutions. CAP represented the high point in Canada of the adoption of the redistributive model of social policy.

With regard to continuing care, there were some early home care programs initiated at this time. However, most continuing care services were still under the social welfare umbrella. The emergence of the Canada Assistance Plan was a major milestone for continuing care as it brought services such as long-term care facilities, group homes, and homemaker services under a federal-provincial cost sharing agreement. However, it left decisions to the provinces about which programs to include and whether they would be means-tested. As such, these services differed from physician and acute-care hospital services that were to be universal, based on need, and portable from province to province.

By 1971, Canada had built a medical care system anchored in the institutional model of the hospital and the professional privilege of physicians. The speciality of geriatrics was also emerging in the early 1970s. In 1965, the Canadian Medical Association journal called for greater emphasis on aging in the curricula of medical schools and in 1971, the University of Manitoba approved the establishment of a teaching unit in geriatrics. After 1971, departments of geriatrics were established in all medical schools. The Canadian Society of Geriatric Medicine was founded in 1981 (Hogan et al. 1997, 1136).

Fiscal retrenchment (early 1970s–early 1990s)

From the 1970s onward, the federal government was concerned with cost sharing arrangements and with continually escalating health care costs. The cost sharing arrangement required the federal government to match provincial contributions (that is, pay 50 percent of the total cost) for all hospital and medical services delivered by the provinces) and was open-ended. The initial arrangements provided an implicit incentive for provinces to increase expenditures as they were dealing in "50 cent dollars," reducing incentives to economize. In addition, increases in expenditures were not resulting in commensurate improvements in health indicators such as life expectancy (Alexander 1995; Taylor 1987; Van Loon 1978).

During this period, thinking about institution-based health care was also shifting. While fiscal considerations were no doubt paramount, the move to community-based services (Hastings 1972) and the "health field concept" enunciated by then federal Health Minister Marc Lalonde in his 1974 report *A New Perspective on the Health of Canadians* reflected a move to greater innovation and flexibility in the provision of health services. These reports, and the desire of the federal government to avoid direct public criticism for not funding health care, led to consideration of the block funding approach. Block funding would allow provinces greater flexibility as the federal contribution would no longer be restricted only to hospital and medical services but could be used to develop new health programs, such as residential long-term care and home care services. For the federal government, it would contain costs. A series of ceilings was placed on the growth of the federal contribution to the provinces. The principle of equalization was to be maintained (Van Loon 1978).

Block funding came into being in 1977 through the Federal-Provincial Fiscal Arrangements and Established Programs Financing Act (known as EPF). The new arrangement provided greater predictability of expenditure to the federal government and an incentive for provinces to restrain increases in health expenditures. The federal contribution was separated from program costs. The block grant formula included a transfer of tax points to the provinces and a cash grant equivalent to the remainder of its contribution for the 1975–76 fiscal year (the base year for purposes of calculation). The cash grant would escalate annually in relation to increases in per capita GNP. An additional per capita grant was also provided under EPF to provinces to assist them in developing alternative health services (called extended health care services) such as nursing homes and home care services (Alexander 1995). However, these alternative services were not insured services (in contrast to hospital and physician services), and the provinces still had to pay for escalating physician and hospital costs.

After wage and price controls introduced by the Trudeau Government in late 1975 and early 1976 came to an end in 1978, those in the health care sector tried to "catch up." There was an increase in extra-billing by physicians and a greater militancy among nurses and other unionized groups in the health care industry. These cost pressures led to charges that the federal government was not fulfilling its fiscal obligations to the medicare system and that provincial governments were diverting federal health contributions under block funding for non-health purposes. Justice Hall, the former Chair of the Royal Commission on Health Services, was asked again to review the state of Canada's medicare system in order to address two major questions: "Were the provinces, as charged, diverting federal health funds to non-health purposes? Were extra billing by doctors and hospital user fees violating the principle of reasonable access and thus eroding Medicare?" (Taylor 1987, 428). (*Extra billing* is billing by physicians above the rates set out in provincial fee schedules.) Justice Hall concluded that federal health funds were not being diverted to other uses by the provinces and that extra billing by physicians and hospital user fees would eventually erode and destroy the medicare program. Similar conclusions were reached by other reports (MacEachen 1981; Canadian Medical Association 1983).

In response to concerns, the federal government released in 1982 a White Paper on a Canada Health Act. The purpose was to ensure the integrity of medicare and the legislation recommended would consolidate the Hospital Insurance and Diagnostic Services Act of 1957 and the Medical Care Act of 1966, and would ban both extra-billing by physicians and hospital user fees. Despite controversy and rising tensions between the provincial governments and the federal government, the act was passed in 1984.

The Canada Health Act outlined the five major principles of the Canadian health care system: accessibility, comprehensiveness, portability, universality, and public administration. In addition, the act provided penalties for extra billing by physicians and for user fees for hospital care. However, in keeping with earlier traditions, the five principles of the Canadian health care system and the restrictions on extra billing and user fees only applied to the insured health services of hospitals and physician services. They did not apply to the extended health care services (EHCS) of the Canada Health Act, under which most continuing care services such as long-term residential care and home care services fall. This is why, for example, it is possible to charge user fees in long-term care facilities and why most continuing care services are not portable across provinces. The components of the continuing care system that come from the social services sector, such as home support services, continued to be covered by provisions of the Canada Assistance Plan (CAP).

When the CAP was enacted in 1966, most of the services that now come under the umbrella of continuing care were, in fact, in the social welfare/services sector. This included long-term care facilities, homemakers, and group homes. Only professional services, such as community nursing, were in the jurisdiction of the Ministries of Health. Chronic care hospitals were also in the health sector, where they could take advantage of the cost sharing provisions in place for hospital services, prior to the block funding arrangement of the EPF. With the advent of long-term care programs across Canada in the late 1970s many of the services tradition-ally in the social service sector were transferred to Ministries of Health. In 1996, CAP and EPF were amalgamated into the Canada Health and Social Transfer (CHST).

This period (mid-1970s to mid-1980s) was important for the evolution of continuing care. The establishment of the extended health care services (EHCS) in the block funding arrangement of the EPF provided the oppor-tunity for provinces to enhance their long-term care systems as it brought new money into this sector. Because federal funds in EPF were no longer tied exclusively to hospitals and medical care, they could be used for other health-related services. This allowed provinces to enhance their health care systems with a range of community- and home-based services. This change served as an impetus for the development of a full range of long-term care services, including those that had previously been in the social welfare sec-tor (Shapiro 1993; Crichton 1997). It allowed provincial governments to move more aggressively to provide comprehensive services for seniors and people with disabilities and allowed for greater flexibility at the provincial level. It may also have been a factor in moving some services previously housed in the social services ministries, such as long-term care facilities, into Ministries of Health. This, in turn, enabled provincial governments to more easily move into a phase of consolidating services from the acute, public health, and social services sectors into more integrated systems of care for elderly and disabled persons. In other words, the relevance of the EPF (Van Loon 1978) for the development of the continuing care sector was significant.

The period from 1977 to the early 1980s was a time of system build-ing. The period from the early 1980s to the early 1990s was when sys-tems were consolidated and various jurisdictions learned from each other. For example, by the early to mid-1990s, all services came under one ad-ministrative entity headed by an Executive Director or Assistant Deputy Minister in BC, Alberta, Saskatchewan, Manitoba, Ontario, Quebec, and Prince Edward Island (Hollander 1994). The Canadian Council for Health Services Accreditation was working on the development of standards for accrediting long-term care facilities in the late 1980s. A Federal/Provincial/Territorial Working Group on Home Care and an interprovincial com-mittee on long-term care were combined into one subcommittee for con-tinuing care in 1986. At a social policy level, the fact that continuing care services are not insured health services means that discussions are ongoing and that policy continues to shift with regards to matters such as user fees and the portability of services. These would not be issues if continuing care

The Influence of the EPF
in British Columbia

The EPF was a key factor in adopting the new Long Term Care Program in BC. As noted by Cutt (1989) and Prince (1996), BC had been able to have relatively balanced budgets throughout the 1970s with surpluses from some years used to offset deficits in other years. There were, in fact, significant surpluses for the period 1978–1981, and there was a modest surplus in 1977. In addition, the Social Credit party under Premier William Bennett had a focus on providing services for elderly persons during the mid to late 1970s.

There were at least four major catalysts for the emergence of the Long Term Care Program in BC: the change to EPF funding; surplus revenues; a will to do something for seniors by the politicians of the day; and a champion for developing a Long Term Care Program at the Assistant Deputy Minister level in the Ministry of Health. The program was planned in 1977 and became operational on January 1, 1978; the BC program was instituted one year after EPF.

The BC Long Term Care Program integrated health and social services components into the Ministry of Health. System building continued in 1980, when home care nursing and rehabilitation services were added to form the Home Care/Long Term Care Program, and it was completed in 1983, when the name of the program was changed to Continuing Care. The system allowed for a more rational approach to substituting community- and home-based services for residential care. The fact that all key services were under one administrative umbrella and covered by one funding envelope may have contributed to the ability of continuing care to weather the fiscal shocks of the recession of the early 1980s: in this case, there were no separated divisions or branches competing with each other for resources, taking independent fiscal measures without considering the implications for other parts of the system.

were an insured service. There are also major regional policy differences. Western provinces have had fairly modest fees for facility care that, at most, reflect the room and board portions of care, while until fairly recently income and means testing existed in some of the Atlantic provinces for up to the total cost of care.

Reform and retrenchment (early 1990s–present)

By the early 1990s, health services were under intense scrutiny. In almost every province in the late 1980s and early 1990s, Royal Commission and other inquiries produced reports on the health system.[2] Mhatre and Deber (1992) reviewed available reports and discovered remarkable similarities in their vision of a new health care system. That vision included the following: population health/health promotion; a broader definition of health that goes beyond only biomedical aspects to include social and psychological health; collaboration across sectors; a focus on community-based care; greater participation by patients in personal health care decision-making; decentralization to regional health authorities (typically excluding physician services and drug plans); alternative methods of payment for physicians; and increased funding for health services research.

Thus, the new vision embraced a health care system that would be more appropriate for an aging society with an emphasis on community-based care. However, shortly after this flurry of reports, the cash portion of the federal transfer payment was reduced, resulting in fiscal pressures at the provincial level. The consequence of this reduction was two major pressures for change in the health care system: changes in structure and changes in financing. The movement toward reform in these two areas opened the door for other types of change. However, much of what has happened to date is a restructuring of services, rather than a fundamental shift in philosophy or approach to care.

An important initiative from 1997 to 2001 was the $150 million Health Transition Fund (HTF) (Lewis 2002), which funded a wide range of demonstration and evaluation projects in health care in a collaborative effort between federal, provincial, and territorial governments. The projects were designed to foster and test innovations in health care services in four major areas: home care, pharmacare, primary care, and integrated care. Other major initiatives since 2000 include the Romanow Commission on health care, the Kirby Committee, and federal-provincial Health Accords. The Romanow Commission report (2002) proposed major changes for the Canadian health care system. Key recommendations are noted in Table 4-4.

There have been two federal-provincial Health Accords since the release of these reports. The first was in 2003 (Canada, Health Canada 2006a), and the second was in 2004. The 2004 Health Accord replaced the 2003 Accord, and continues today (Canada, Health Canada 2006b). The 2004 Health Accord was established for 10 years. The federal, provincial, and territorial governments agreed to focus on the following areas:

- wait times and access;
- strategic health human resources action plans;
- home care;
- primary care reform;
- access to care in the north;
- a national pharmaceutical strategy;
- prevention, promotion, and public health;
- health innovation;

- accountability and reporting to citizens; and
- dispute avoidance and resolution.

An important structural change in the financing of health care occurred in 2004 when the Canada Health and Social Transfer (CHST) was split into two separate transfer payments: the Health Transfer and the Canada Social Transfer (Canada, Department of Finance 2009). The Canada Health Transfer is a conditional, block transfer consisting of a combination of cash transfers and tax point transfers for the purpose of maintaining national criteria as set out in the Canada Health Act. The 2004 Health Accord establishes annual cash transfer levels to the fiscal year 2013–14. In fiscal year 2008–9 the estimated cash transfer payment was $22.6 billion and the tax points transfer was $13.9 billion (Canada, Department of Finance

Table 4-4 Key Recommendations of the Romanow Report, 2002

- Establish a new Canadian Health Covenant as a tangible statement of Canadians' values and a guiding force for our publicly funded health care system.
- Create a Health Council of Canada to facilitate collaborative leadership in health.
- Modernize the Canada Health Act by expanding coverage and renewing its principles.
- Enable the establishment of personal electronic health records for each Canadian building on the work currently underway in provinces and territories.
- Provide better health information to Canadians, health care providers, researchers and policymakers—information they can use to guide their decisions.
- Address the need to change the scopes and patterns of practice of health care providers to reflect changes in how health care services are delivered, particularly through new approaches to primary health care.
- Take steps to ensure that rural and remote communities have an appropriate mix of skilled health care providers to meet their health care needs.
- Establish strategies for addressing the supply, distribution, education, training, and changing skills and patterns of practice for Canada's health workforce.
- Implement primary health care.
- Better manage wait lists.
- Establish a new Rural and Remote Access Fund to support new approaches for delivering health care services and improve the health of people in rural and remote communities.
- Better integrate prescription drugs into Canada's health care system.
- Consolidate Aboriginal health funding from all sources and use the funds to support the creation of Aboriginal Health Partnerships to manage and organize health services for Aboriginal peoples and promote Aboriginal health.
- Ensure ongoing input from Aboriginal peoples into the new direction and design of health care services in their communities.
- Take clear and immediate steps to protect Canada's health care system from possible challenges under international law and trade agreements and build alliances within the international community.

Source: Based on Romanow 2002

2008). In late 2011, the federal Minister of Finance guaranteed to continue transfers at an increase of 6 percent per year to the fiscal year 2016–2017. According to this guarantee, the transfer amount will increase a minimum of 3 percent starting in fiscal year 2017–18 and last until the fiscal year of 2023–24, at which time it will be revisited (Canada, Department of Finance 2011). The year 2004 was also when the Health Council of Canada and the Compassionate Care Benefit were established.

Since 2004, there have been no major federal structural changes to health care arrangements with one exception: the Mental Health Commission of Canada was established in 2007. However, some individual provinces have started introducing new initiatives for seniors. For example, Manitoba in 2008, and Nova Scotia in 2009, instituted financial benefits for caregivers (Nova Scotia, Department of Health and Wellness, Continuing Care Branch 2010). Manitoba instituted a new caregiver tax credit of $1,020 (Manitoba, Manitoba Finance 2008). This case is an example of fiscal welfare in which benefits are provided through the tax system. More recently, Manitoba has passed the Caregiver Recognition Act and BC recently announced the creation of a Seniors' Advocate Office.

For the social welfare and social services sector, the changes initiated in the 1990s had momentous consequences: there was considerable retrenchment of payments and services and a completion of the flight from universality. In the area of seniors, the universal nature of Old Age Security was eliminated when claw backs were implemented through the tax system. In 1991, a limit or "cap" was placed on the Canada Assistance Plan, restricting transfers to BC, Alberta, and Ontario to a 5 percent annual rate of growth. The CHST was perhaps the most monumental fiscal change of the 1990s. It combined CAP and EPF funding into a block grant for social, health, and educational services and significantly reduced the total amount of money transferred to the provinces. The combined budget for CAP and EPF was $29.9 billion in the 1995–96 fiscal year of which $18.5 billion was a cash transfer. Under the CHST, this amount was reduced to $26.9 billion for the 1996–97 fiscal year, of which $14.7 billion was a cash transfer, and to $25.8 billion for the 1997–98 fiscal year, of which $12.5 billion was to be a cash transfer. The original intent was to reduce transfers to $11.1 billion; however, the federal government announced a policy decision during the 1997 federal general election to not reduce the cash portion below $12.5 billion. The government also announced a major increase in funding to the health sector in the 1999 budget (Government of Newfoundland 2000).

There was considerable controversy about the CHST. While it maintained the five principles of medicare as national standards, the CAP provisions of *need* as the sole basis for income support, an appeal system, data reporting and sharing requirements, and the non-profit provision of social services, were not included in the CHST. Only one of the five principles of CAP remained enshrined: the provision prohibiting provinces from imposing residency requirements on those receiving social welfare benefits. The retreat from standards that were part of CAP and the potential for provinces to deny benefits to the needy are of considerable concern to those working in social services. The Caledon Institute of Social Policy notes, "collapsing the Canada Assistance Plan into a larger transfer that includes health and post-secondary education will see social services suffer dramatically. By withdrawing CAP, there is no guarantee that provinces will invest in welfare and social services" (Torjman 1995, 4). This change constituted a major erosion of the redistributive model of social policy, where benefits are provided on the basis of need. As noted above, the CHST was split into separate health and social transfers in 2004.

In the late 1990s, the major social and health policy initiative was the 1999 Social Union Framework Agreement (SUFA) in which the federal, provincial, and territorial governments (except Quebec) agreed to a new mechanism to establish national programs without having to change the constitution. This agreement ensured mobility across provinces and territories for social benefits and established mechanisms for greater public accountability. Under SUFA, new cross-Canada social programs with federal financial support could be established with the joint approval of the federal government and the majority of provincial governments. The agreement also contained a provision whereby the federal government could introduce Canada-wide funding initiatives to individuals or organizations (Canada, Government of Canada 1999). The SUFA never got traction (perhaps because of that latter provision). As it stands now, the Social Union Framework Agreement has little support across federal, provincial, and territorial governments. However, its importance lies in its potential as a vehicle for bringing about a national continuing care program. This option would avoid concerns that any re-opening of the Canada Health Act would raise—specifically that re-opening that law would put physician and hospital funding at risk of change but would not guarantee that continuing care would be included. SUFA is already designed to be a vehicle for major new initiatives in health and social services and thus could accommodate a sector that incorporates both.

For continuing care, there was a significant downturn in the mid 1990s. The structure of the federal, provincial, and territorial advisory committees was reformed, and subcommittees and working groups were disbanded, in 1992. This included the subcommittee on continuing care. With regionalization came new priorities, exacerbated by the fiscal restraint of the time. The result was that continuing care departments disappeared and continuing care was no longer seen as a major component of the Canadian health care system. The elimination of senior continuing care positions in provincial organizational structures reduced the level of institutional memory and expertise in continuing care at this level. This was a by-product of three forces: regionalization, fiscal restraints, and the focus on primary/community care models of service delivery.

However, just at the time continuing care organizational structures were disintegrating, a new round of studies emerged on the cost-effectiveness of integrated continuing care systems (Hollander and Chappell 2002a). For example, one of the major projects funded by the HTF was the National Evaluation of the Cost-Effectiveness of Home Care, a national program of research with 15 substudies. Key findings were as follows:

- Home care costs significantly less than residential care for people with similar care needs (40 percent to 70 percent depending on level of need).
- Stable home care clients cost much less (50 percent) than residential care clients.
- The cost is in the transitions in that home care clients who changed their type and/or level of care cost close to those in facilities.
- Home care is not cost-effective for clients who die, as they usually have repeated visits to hospitals, increasing their costs.
- The costs of home care itself are often less than half of the overall health care costs—the additional costs coming from hospital care, primary care, and the use of drugs. In fact, hospital costs accounted for 30 to 60 percent of health care costs for home care clients.
- Home support services seem to be able to substitute for hospital care. During the restraint of the 1990s hospital costs in BC decreased while home support increased. In addition, home nursing and home support can be used to care for clients re-directed, in the emergency department, from hospital admission to a return to home with additional supports, by Quick Response Teams (home care nurses embedded in ERs redirect people to their homes who would normally be admitted to a hospital). (Hollander and Chappell 2002a)

A related study showed that it is more cost-effective to provide tertiary preventative care; that results in lower hospital costs and long-term care facility costs (Hollander 2001a). The major policy recommendations from the National Evaluation of the Cost-Effectiveness of Home Care are presented in Table 4-5.

Table 4-5 Key Policy Recommendations from the National Evaluation Synthesis Report

- Develop effective and integrated systems of continuing care service delivery for seniors and persons with disabilities. In order to make cost-effective trade-offs achieve seamless care and also to achieve cost avoidance, these systems should have the following characteristics: single entry; coordinated, system-level assessment and service authorization; ongoing system-level case management; a single, system-level administrative and funding structure; a consistent system-level approach to client classification.
- Enhance information systems and analysis.
- Enhance public policy and legislation regarding home care including: universal coverage; portability across jurisdictions; subsidizing drug costs in the community; and assisting unpaid family caregivers.
- Develop innovative pilot projects and test out new models of care delivery and their cost-effectiveness.
- Develop approaches to allocate new money to home care rather than facility care, as appropriate.
- Reduce the divide between health services and supportive services. Much of the care needed by home-based seniors is home support, not medical or nursing care. Recognize home support as a key component of home care, different from, but equal to, professional home care services.
- Develop a capacity for policy-relevant rapid response research (R^3) to assist with ongoing evidence-based policy and program decision-making.

Source: Hollander and Chappell 2002a

The Romanow Commission also made several specific recommendations regarding home care, including the following:

- Use the proposed new Home Care Transfer to establish a national platform for home care services.
- Revise the Canada Health Act to include coverage for home care services in priority areas.
- Improve the quality of care and support available to people with mental illnesses by including home mental health case management and intervention services as part of the Canada Health Act.
- Expand the Canada Health Act to include coverage for post-acute home care including medication management and rehabilitation services.
- Provide Canada Health Act coverage for palliative home care services to support people in their last six months of life.
- Introduce a new program to provide ongoing support for informal caregivers. (Romanow 2002)

The recommendations were part of the basis for the health accords described earlier. The Accords, like the Romanow report, focused on: short-term, acute replacement home care; home care for persons with mental illnesses; and home care for palliative care clients. What is most noteworthy in these recommendations is what is missing. There are no recommendations on long-term home care or home support services, of critical importance in addressing the chronic conditions that many older adults face. While there is some discussion of the broader concept of continuing care, of which home care is a part, the recommendations focus on home care per se, and on incorporating it into the Canada Health Act. The Kirby Committee's recommendations on home care were similar to those espoused by the Romanow Commission, arguing for expanded coverage for post-acute home care and palliative home care (Kirby 2002).

Governments did not recognize continuing care as a major component of the health care system in the subsequent health accords. In addition, the 2004 Health Accord further splintered home care by focusing on short-term (primarily professional) and specialty home care. Long-term home care and home support were not addressed. The 2004 accord made a commitment to provide first dollar coverage for short-term case management and short-term acute home care, and discharge-related intravenous medications for a two-week period; short-term acute community mental health home care; and crisis response services for a two-week period. It also covers end-of-life home care, case management, and palliative-specific pharmaceuticals (Canada, Health Canada 2006b).

Current Concerns

With the financial crisis of 2008, increasing alarm has been expressed about the sustainability of our health care system despite the fact that health care spending as a percentage of GDP barely grew over the 1992 to 2007 period, i.e., it increased from 10.0 percent in 1992 to 10.5 percent in 2007 (CIHI 2011b). However, the economic crisis resulted in an increase from 10.5 percent of GDP in 2007 to an estimated 11.9 percent in 2009 (CIHI 2011b) due to a decrease in GDP. This change may be temporary or continuous, depending on the level of economic growth going forward. If economic growth rates increase to earlier levels it is likely that there will be a commensurate decline in the percentage of GDP accounted for by health care.

In the absence of structural changes, and with concerns stemming from the economic crisis of 2008, key thinkers, researchers, and policy analysts have recently started to provide a range of analyses about the future sustainability of our health care system. David Dodge, former Deputy Minister of Finance and former Governor of the Bank of Canada, and Richard Dion, a former economist with the Bank of Canada, prepared a commentary in 2011 (Dodge and Dion 2011a; 2011b). They presented a fairly gloomy outlook regarding sustainability. These authors argue that the "spending disease" requires the following remedies: a sharp reduction in public services other than health care provided by governments, especially provincial governments; increased taxes to finance the public share of health care spending; increased spending by individuals on health care services that are currently insured by provinces, through some form of co-payment or through delisting of services that are currently publicly financed; and a major degradation of publicly insured health care standards—longer queues, services of poorer quality—and the development of a privately funded system to provide better-quality care for those willing to pay for it.

Another document questioning the sustainability of the Canadian health care system (Morneau 2011) also suggests that it is on an unsustainable track. The alternative solutions put forward in the document include the following: institute and/or increase user fees; develop health credits that could be used to pay for care with people being reimbursed, in whole or in part, for unused credits; gain greater efficiencies through evidence-based medicine; reduce costs by outsourcing the production of medical equipment to low-cost countries such as India or China; and/or focus on wellness and prevention.

Donald Drummond, the former senior vice-president and chief economist of the TD Bank documents the financial challenges faced by our health care system and notes that quick action is required if we are to sustain it (Drummond and Burleton 2010). The solutions suggested include changes to the funding of doctors and hospitals, scaling back benefits, and increasing taxes. Other options included in the Drummond report were expanding information technology, focusing on quality care and promoting healthier lifestyles.

In contrast, other writers argue that our health care system is sustainable and they offer other solutions. Hébert and colleagues (2011) argue that, with ongoing economic growth and stable tax revenues, our system is sustainable; what we should be concerned about is the quality of the care provided. In a 2002 paper, Ruggeri (2002) questions whether we have a crisis in health care. Another example is from a 2007 Canadian Health Services Research Foundation (CHSRF) "Mythbusters" series in which they summarize existing knowledge that debunks prevalent myths concerning health care. For example, they debunk the common perception that the Canadian health care system is unsustainable, noting that the percentage of GDP spent on health care has remained fairly consistent over time (CHSRF 2007). The Canadian Life and Health Insurance Association (CLHIA 2012) has also produced a progressive monograph on how to make our health care system more sustainable that includes a recommendation to restructure long-term care and to recognize the continuum of care.

A different solution to sustainability is presented by Snowdon and colleagues (2010). They argue that innovation leads to productivity and skilled leaders, so change agents are required to drive innovation. The authors contend that Canada needs to establish conditions that foster innovation to maintain the sustainability of our health care system and they present three solutions. The first is to grow the leadership capacity for innovation across Canada in order to develop a culture of innovation; the authors also argue in favour of starting with small projects to "learn early and fail cheap"; and finally, they recommend creating a culture focused on the adoption and commercialization of ideas and innovations, not just the creation of new knowledge. Canada has, in fact, recently developed a senior level Health Care Innovation Group (2012) headed by the premiers of Saskatchewan and PEI, under the auspices of the Council of the Federation (the provincial and territorial premiers). However, the focus of this group is on innovations to clinical practice guidelines, team-based health care models (mainly primary care), and human resource management. Thus, at least at present, there does not appear to be a focus on continuing care or the kinds of aspects related to developing a broad range of innovations and fostering skilled leaders as called for by Snowdon.

The Conference Board of Canada has recently established the Canadian Alliance for Sustainable Health Care. Whether or not the group will focus on continuing care and its potential contribution to sustainability remains to be seen.

Another approach is to examine how to enhance value for money—in other words, how to "get more bang for the buck." Over the past decade, the primary focus of health discourse has been on requesting more money for health care. While more money may, in fact, be needed, the goal should be to make our health care system as efficient and effective as possible first. In a recent set of papers by McGrail and colleagues (2009) entitled "Getting What We Pay For? The Value-for-Money Challenge," the authors note that value-for-money systems are akin to high performing health systems where the focus is on the system of care, including structure, delivery, and financing. They map out persistent cost differences across geographic areas, the potential of electronic health records, and the importance of identifying relevant and useable outcome measures.

There are also a number of major reports related to continuing care and the care of elderly persons. These include the Special Senate Committee on Aging chaired by Senators Carstairs and Keon (2009), a lead paper in *HealthcarePapers* by Chappell and Hollander (2011), the proceedings from five regional and one national workshop hosted by the Canadian Health Services Research Foundation (2011), a report by the Canadian Institute for Health Information (2011a), and one by the Health Council of Canada

(2012). Their messages are similar, although each emphasizes different aspects. Table 4-6 presents the main recommendations from the Special Senate Committee on Aging (Carstairs and Keon 2009). As a result of these reports, there is now an established consensus among policy experts and major national bodies about the "best" directions for the care of Canada's elderly population.

Table 4-6 Key Recommendations from the Special Senate Committee on Aging

- Address ageism and age discrimination.
- Develop comprehensive, integrated models of continuing care service delivery.
- Ensure comparable services for seniors across Canada.
- Promote active aging and the development of age-friendly cities and rural communities.
- Eliminate/reduce poverty and income security.
- Support unpaid caregivers.
- Support the volunteer sector.
- Address health and social core human resource issues and shortfalls.
- Develop a focus on new technologies and research.
- Lead by example by improving health services for seniors in the areas of federal responsibility, for example, veterans and First Nations and Inuit.

Source: Based on Carstairs and Keon 2009

There are many suggestions for improving our health care system and making it more sustainable. However, it is worth noting that there is a glaring omission in all of these discussions: how to implement integrated systems of continuing care that have the potential for significantly increasing value-for-money and for making our health care system more sustainable. These matters are discussed in more detail in Chapters 5 to 7. Finally, there is, or at least appears to be, a lack of political will to decide on an optimal plan of action and to implement major change. As noted by Martin (2009), "it may be . . . that it is not the goal itself but, rather, simply the courage to act to achieve this goal that is elusive" (48).

Discussion

The material presented in this chapter leads to several observations. The first is that, in the modern era, social policy and economic policy are interrelated. The major Canadian social security reforms reached their zenith in the 1960s, a period of relative economic prosperity. Provincial initiatives, minority federal governments, and pressure by the Co-operative Commonwealth Federation/New Democratic Party combined with a sound economic backdrop to bring about medicare. However, no sooner was this accomplished than the forces for fiscal austerity came back into play. Crichton (1993) notes that, concerned with the potential costs of medicare, the federal government decided against extending matching grants beyond those to hospitals and physicians. Consequently, programs were not created that would designate dental care and prescription medications as insured services. This decision to exclude certain services is still with us today, and the debate about the inclusion of these services under the Canada Health Act continues. In addition, this decision had a major impact on continuing care services over time: these services were included as Extended Health Care Services in EPF and the Canada Health Act, but they were not insured services.

A second observation has to do with structural arrangements. In the 1970s and 1980s, continuing care was an emerging hybrid of health and social services struggling to find a place. Crichton (1993) captured the reality for much of continuing care services in this period:

> Within provincial health departments, it was difficult to change the proportional amounts allocated to institutional services versus community care. The hospitals were well organized to resist reduction of their budgets and community care was divided between a number of small government departments and numerous voluntary organizations who were grateful for any subsidy they could get. (306)

This also meant that, unlike hospitals and doctors, and even public health, continuing care had no major institutional champions at the provincial and territorial decision-making tables.

In 1992, the Federal/Provincial/Territorial advisory committee structure was changed, eliminating all other levels of committees and leaving only three advisory committees in the area of health: the Advisory Committee on Health Services (the former Advisory Committee on Institutional and Medical Services), the Advisory Committee on Population Health (the former Advisory Committee on Community Health), and the Advisory Committee on Health Human Resources. With the dissolution of the sub-committee on continuing care, there was no longer a major institutional forum for continuing care. It did not appear to be a priority of the advisory committee on health services. Thus, there was little progress made in continuing care until late 1997, when a Working Group on Continuing Care was established under the Advisory Committee on Health Services. However, this working group lasted only a few years.

A third observation relates to overall philosophy—including the concept of universality and the models for social policy, which were discussed earlier in this chapter. Universality for income support programs died in the late

1980s and early 1990s. There has been a reversion to the residual model of welfare (Wilensky and Lebeaux 1965, 135) in the social sector. The tension noted above in regard to the relationship between economic and social policy is also linked to the overall philosophical debate between the residual welfare model and the institutional or redistributive welfare model. These opposing philosophical positions were mirrored in the debates on medicare in the House of Commons as far back as 1966. Opposition to the residual welfare model has been countered by statements that health care is a right, not a privilege, and should not be tied to income. Another common statement is that medicare is part of our national character.

Those who have opposed the practice, if not the principles, of the Canadian health care system have consistently made their arguments primarily on a financial basis: for example, perhaps we are no longer able to afford medicare, a viewpoint reflected in the Dodge and Dion report (2011a). Another argument borders on ageism: the growing elderly population will bankrupt our health care system. Opponents of these arguments respond that our system is sustainable and health care is a right available to all Canadians.

These two viewpoints confuse fundamental principles and values with operational and economic issues. If health care is a right of citizenship, then it follows that the state has an obligation to provide adequate, appropriate, and sustainable funding for our health care system, to a reasonable standard. It also follows that taxpayers have an obligation to help fund services, and that health administrators, researchers, and policy analysts have an obligation to make the health care system as efficient and effective as possible. In other words, the adequacy of funding is not a valid issue. Citizens either have a right to health care or they do not. If they do, governments must provide adequate services. This view of health care as a right does not mean that every individual should be provided with what he or she wants immediately upon demand. It does, however, mean that people should have access to a reasonable standard of care based on their needs. If citizens do not have a right to health care, then the societal contract that addresses this needs to be renegotiated with the public in a clear and transparent manner.

Arguments about costs are a red herring. They attempt to frame the debate in terms of the existing status quo where existing budget allocations are an inviolable constraint. Existing tax structures were developed by people and can be changed by people. In other words, arguing that there is too little money to cover a right is based on a false logic. There are a range of clear options: seek greater efficiencies; develop growth-oriented policies that increase the tax base; or ask citizens to pay more through the tax system. Paying more through user fees does not meet government's obligation to ensure its citizens' right to health care. Rather, it simply shifts costs from the government to individuals and thereby fails to represent an appropriate response to meeting the rights of its citizens.

The arguments above about costs typically refer to the insured services of hospitals and medical care that constitute our medicare system. Technically, government could only provide hospital and medical services and meet its obligations to ensure the right of citizens to medicare. However, the federal government and most provincial governments subscribe to broader definitions of health. Thus, governments have taken on the responsibility of providing a wider range of health (not just strictly medical) services and continue to do so.

Continuing care was essentially established as a major component of the Canadian health care system in the late 1970s to the early 1990s. While some services did have some user fees, continuing care was basically designed as a redistributive service, in which service provision was based on need. However, need was eliminated as the primary basis for assistance when the CHST was established. This started the slide from a national policy based on the redistributive model to a focus on the residual welfare model. Several things happened. In the mid-1990s, governments started to disenfranchise from home care people who had lower, but legitimate, care needs. Thus, people who were previously eligible for home support services in the early 1990s were shifted from a redistributive model to a residual welfare model. Responsibility for care was transferred from the state to individuals with care and support needs, their families, and local communities.

The mid-1990s also marked increases in user fees for facility care, and these fees have continued to escalate. The poor who cannot afford to pay are covered, but for the more affluent the focus has shifted from "need" (the Redistributive Model) to ability to pay (the Residual Welfare Model). While provincial governments have continued to provide home support services, the 2004 Health Accord does not address people with ongoing care needs. It only deals with short-term and specialty home care. Thus the federal policy focus on short-term hospital replacement home care shifts the policy focus away from those with ongoing or longer-term home care needs. Recently, there has been little or no policy focus on long-term home care, even though the history of social services in home/community care incorporated payments for home care and home support in federal/ provincial transfers, and despite the continued provision of longer term home/community support services by provincial governments.

It appears that we have witnessed a hidden policy shift from continuing care services based on the needs of a broad population to home and community care services provided only to a limited number of individuals. This is supported with national figures revealing a shift to medical services and away from social services, and a shift to restricting services to those requiring high-level intensive care, within home care (CIHI 2007; Penning et al. 2009). Those who would have been covered in the early 1990s but are not covered now have been shifted from the Redistributive Model to the Residual Welfare Model. It is important to note that this has happened without public debate and without clear policy choices in the electoral process. Thousands of seniors have been disenfranchised without the public knowing about it. This trend has led to visible problems in the provision of care for older adults. This has prompted documents such as those by the Special Senate Committee on Aging, the Health Council of Canada, the CHSRF, and academics, identifying problems and proposing solutions. Their efforts are essentially attempts to reassert the Redistributive Model.

Canada must make policy choices but these choices should be made in a clear and transparent manner. The fundamental philosophical and policy choice is whether or not we choose to have a Redistributive Model or a Residual Welfare Model for continuing care services. We can opt for a variant of a universal Redistributive Model, with moderate and affordable user fees, for all people in need, or we can choose to formally and transparently go back to a Residual Welfare Model where individuals, families, and communities are responsible for the provision of continuing care services. Intermediate choices based on the Industrial Achievement Model of meeting needs for those who are "socially worthy," such as seniors with high care needs and veterans can also be considered but are unlikely to gain acceptance.

Our argument in this book is that people have made choices to arrive at the current reality or status quo. In turn, people can make choices to change the status quo and develop a new reality, but we believe that these should be made in a transparent manner. For example, since the mid-1990s, seniors and people with ongoing care needs have received less-than-optimal care without government formally asking Canadians what they feel is appropriate and reasonable, or presenting the continuing care framework per se to the public for discussion. The public should be presented with unambiguous choices. The public should understand the potential increases in value for money if continuing care and the health care system were managed more effectively. They should also be given cost estimates about the actual impact of tax increases, or special levies for the care of older adults and, if the government role continues to decline, when and how insurance instruments can be structured so people can purchase affordable continuing care insurance.

Chapter 5

The Economic Evaluation of Continuing Care

Introduction

This chapter reviews the current state of the literature on costs and outcomes, across several sites of care, for those receiving continuing care services. (The continuing care sector generally refers to people in care as "clients," while the hospital/medical literature generally refers to them as patients; this chapter will follow the terminology used by the authors of the respective papers.)

There are three main functions of home and community care. The first is to prevent or delay further deterioration and to maintain the client at his/her optimal level of care for as long as possible. The second function is to act as a substitute for residential long-term care, for those with higher level care needs and, in the absence of home care, those who would likely be admitted to a long-term care facility. Home/community care, then, acts as a substitute for residential long-term care for people who are deemed to be eligible for placement in a long-term care facility.

The third function is to substitute for hospital care where people are discharged early from hospitals at the end of the acute care phase of their illness. Instead of spending the convalescent part of their illness in the hospital, they convalesce at home with the assistance of professional health care providers such as nurses and/or physiotherapists, and home support workers, as required. Home care is also used to prevent new admissions and re-admissions to hospital and, thus, can be an indirect substitute for acute care. While the focus of home care is often on substitution, home care is also a valuable service in its own right that can complement other components of the health care system.

An Overview of Economic Analysis

Economic analysis deals with two aspects. The first is the inputs and outputs, or costs and consequences, of activities; the second is the issue of choices among alternatives. This kind of analysis can be defined as "the comparative analysis of alternative courses of action in terms of both their costs and consequences" (Drummond, Stoddart, and Torrance 1987; see also Canadian Agency for Drugs and Technologies 2006) as noted below.

Full economic evaluation has four main approaches:

- Cost-effectiveness analysis measures the costs and consequences of programs in comparable units. In cost-effectiveness analysis, no attempt is made to place a monetary value on the quality of outcomes. The result, therefore, is a determination of the relative cost per unit; an example of this would be cost per year of life gained. Totally different interventions for different groups of people can be compared to determine which has the most impact; for example, which intervention will maximize the number of life years saved at a given cost.
- Cost-minimization analysis compares the costs of alternative services where the consequences of services received are deemed to be equivalent (for example, in a search for the lowest cost alternative). Because the benefits are assumed to be equivalent, no separate valuation of outcomes is required; rather, only a valuation of the comparative costs of two or more programs takes place. Cost-minimization analysis can be considered a variant of cost-effectiveness analysis and is relevant for evaluations of continuing care services where outcomes can be assumed to be similar across sites of care.
- Cost-utility analysis measures the costs and consequences of programs in time units adjusted by health utility weights. For example, costs are related to one or more effects that are not necessarily common to each alternative, by a standardized utility measure such as Quality Adjusted Life Years (QALYs). This is an advance over cost-effectiveness analysis in that one can incorporate the QALYs saved into the analysis. QALY scores can be determined in a number of ways. One may wish to adopt values already published in the literature, conduct studies of persons with a given condition to obtain their utility scores for that condition, or ask experts such as physicians to assign values to different conditions. Another option would be to ask informed members of the general public to assign values.
- Cost-benefit analysis values both the costs and consequences of programs in monetary terms. For example, costs are related to one or more effects that are not necessarily common to each alternative, by the

standardized measure of money. It is usually difficult in a health-related cost-benefit study to value the outputs of health care interventions in strictly monetary terms. It is possible to ascribe costs to a life saved, but determining the cost of a human life is controversial, and analysts who have attempted to do so typically estimate a wide range of costs. Another possibility is to assign dollar values to foregone income or the willingness to pay for avoiding some condition. Currently, there appears to be little substantive consensus on the valuation of the benefits of health interventions in monetary terms.

Methodologically, many of the more advanced techniques of economic analysis have similar characteristics to experimental research, clinical trials, and outcome evaluations. All of these approaches have certain common elements. Some type of program or experimental condition (e.g., a new drug) is introduced, it is applied to some set of subjects, and the outcome is analyzed. There is a temporal dimension to this approach such that the intervention is typically introduced at one point in time and the consequences of that action are studied over time. Programs receiving the experimental condition are usually compared to control groups or to other alternative programs.

Perhaps the most essential feature of an economic analysis is the perspective inherent in the question posed. Perspective has significant implications for analysis. Ideally, the widest range of costs and benefits should be considered in conducting an economic analysis—that is, the perspective of society as a whole. However, this is often not the case. Rather, writers often consider costs and benefits from a more restrictive perspective—such as the government, the agency, or the client. Even within a government or funder perspective, it is possible to only consider a given agency or type of service, rather than the whole system of care. Erroneous conclusions may be the result of failing to adopt a comprehensive perspective.

For example, consider the following: (1) clients who pay a user fee for home support services but who pay no fee for home nursing care services; (2) a government that wishes to reduce costs; and (3) a home care agency that wants to maximize profits. Government may ask for an economic analysis of a new program where certain functions typically provided by nurses are transferred to home support workers through an agreement to transfer a function. An economic analysis of this situation may find, for example, that 20 percent of the volume of work can be transferred and that home support workers are paid half as much as home care nurses. The result would mean that government can save 10 percent of the costs of its home nursing care program by instituting the transfer of function program. However, the client sees it differently. Clients who are affected may pay more for the home support service (for which they may pay a user fee) than they would if nurses, for which no user fee is required, continue to provide the service. The position of the agency in this scenario is determined by its comparative profit margins for nurses versus home support workers. That is, depending on the relative ratios of user fees and staff-specific profit margins, the result of adopting a program change could be any of the following: a shift in cost from government to clients and/ or agencies; an overall saving to government, but less than projected from the government perspective alone; or an increase in overall governmental costs, particularly if home support workers take longer to provide the service than nurses, or to the client if there are high user fees.

In the same scenario, there is also a fourth group that could be affected: informal caregivers such as family members. Home support workers may provide care to the client but may not teach family members how to care for the client in a correct and efficient manner. To the extent that nurses do so, there could be a different impact on the amount of time and resources family members would have to devote to caring for the client. Time may constitute real direct costs to family members if they take non-paid leave from work. Thus, the decision to transfer nursing functions to home support workers may have economic impacts not only on the government, the agency, and the client, but also on the client's family.

Another issue is the determination of the range of costs and benefits included in a given study. An important issue is how costs for non-market goods, such as the time of family members, should be assigned. There are four possible approaches, of which the first two are the most common:

- Market valuations—taking actual valuations where these exist (for example, for most resource items) or imputing valuations by reference to the market price of similar commodities (for example, the value of housewives' time could be imputed by reference to the wages paid to domestic staff).
- Client's willingness-to-pay estimates—assessed directly by asking them or indirectly by observing their behaviour (for example, asking people what they would pay for a quicker form of travel, or observing the trade-offs they make between expenditures and travel-time savings).
- Policy-makers views—either explicitly stated or implicit in their actions (for example, the decisions made about building safety regulations could be used to impute policy-makers' valuations of human life).
- Practitioners' views or professional opinions—such as those on the appropriateness of different forms of care for given categories of patients (for example, court awards might be used to impute the value of the unpleasantness of a disfiguring injury). (Adapted from Drummond, Stoddart, and Torrance 1987, 149–50)

Furthermore, in economic analysis, future costs and benefits are discounted back to present values. Thus, the further out in time a cost or benefit occurs, the lower its present value is because it is discounted at a given annual rate—for example, 5 percent. Discounting occurs because it is believed that people have a "time preference"—for example, there is the belief that goods received now have a higher value than goods received in the future. If an inflation factor is added to time preference discounting, one is said to be using an inflation-adjusted discount rate.

To look at the cost-effectiveness of home and community care, the following examines it in terms of its three main functions. While there are different types of economic evaluations, we shall use "cost-effectiveness" as a general term for simplicity and because most studies in continuing care use a cost-effectiveness approach (including cost minimization).

The Cost-Effectiveness of the Maintenance and Preventive Function of Home Care

The literature evaluating the cost-effectiveness of the maintenance and preventive function of home care per se is relatively limited. Studies typically focus on certain types of preventive programs rather than on the broader preventive functions of home care. That said, there are three levels of prevention:

- *Primary prevention* focuses on general preventive activities for a population and includes programs such as lifestyle counselling and immunization. Specific activities include the promotion of regular aerobic exercise, tobacco reduction, and safe driving initiatives.
- *Secondary prevention* focuses on the identification of individuals at risk through preventive activities related to early detection of subclinical disease by screening or case-finding to prevent disability. Examples of such activities include screening questionnaires for problem drinking, hearing impairment and diminished visual activity, and regular mammography and clinical examinations for breast cancer.
- *Tertiary prevention* focuses on minimizing disability and handicap for people who already have established diseases or functional disabilities. (Adapted from Patterson and Chambers 1995)

Some early Canadian studies suggested that home care is not cost-effective. In the mid-1990s, Patterson and Chambers (1995) concluded that, while there is some evidence for the effectiveness of primary and secondary prevention, the evidence on tertiary prevention seems to indicate that it is not cost-effective for improving the functional status of older people. Patterson and Chambers note that prevention initiatives result in greater utilization of community services such as physiotherapy, domestic help, and chiropody, and that there are more referrals for specialist opinions. In a study designed to evaluate whether preventive home care is cost-effective, Contandriopoulos and colleagues (1986) examined two different Quebec cohorts, one before a home care service was introduced and one after it was introduced. In both the global and specific impact analyses, the presence of home aid services did not significantly reduce the use of hospital inpatient services, emergency and outpatient hospital services, physician services, or home care services.

A retrospective, observational cohort study using administrative data was conducted in Saskatchewan (Saskatchewan 2000). The seniors were studied for eight years, revealing that 50 percent of those receiving preventive home care were more likely to lose their independence or die than those not receiving this service. In addition, costs for clients receiving preventive home care were three times as high as for clients not receiving this service. This study has been questioned in terms of the comparability between clients receiving home care and those not receiving home care, with concern that individuals receiving home care had higher care needs and greater functional deficits than those not receiving home care, but the data did not allow this to be taken into account. In addition, the study did not have information on the availability of informal supports, another important factor that can impact service utilization and health outcomes.

In contrast, more recent evidence indicates that tertiary prevention in home care may be cost-effective. Hollander (2001a) studied a natural experiment in BC in 1994 and 1995 in which comparisons were made between some health regions that cut clients from care who were at the lowest level of care need and were only receiving housecleaning services (one component of home support services), and other regions that did not make such cuts. The overall costs to the health care system for the people who were cut from service in two health regions compared to people who were not cut from service in two similar regions where there were no (or limited) cuts indicated support for the preventive function of home care. In the year before the cuts, the average annual cost per client for those who were cut from service was $5,052 and the cost per client for the comparison group was $4,535. In the third year following these cuts the comparative costs were $11,903 and $7,808, respectively (see Table 5-1). The conclusion is that costs increased over time for each group, but the increases were more pronounced for those who had had their service cut.

Most of the differences in costs were accounted for by the increased use of acute care and long-term residential care services (see Table 5-2).

Table 5-1 Per Person Annual Average Costs of Care for Health Regions with and without Cuts

		Period		
		Year Prior to Cuts	**First Year after Cuts**	**Second Year after Cuts**	**Third Year after Cuts**
All costs $	Health regions with cuts	5,052	6,683	9,654	11,903
	Health regions with no cuts	4,535	5,963	6,771	7,808

Source: Hollander 2001a, 21

Table 5-2 Per Person Average Costs for Health Regions with and without Cuts

Types of Cuts		Costs in Year before Cuts ($)	Costs over 3 Years after Cuts ($)	Percentage Change in Costs over Three Years (%)
All	Cuts	5,051.84	28,240.36	559.01
	No cuts	4,535.02	20,542.52	452.98
Medical Services Plan (MSP)	Cuts	1,142.90	3,957.07	346.23
	No cuts	1,085.33	3,566.47	328.61
Pharmacy	Cuts	705.2	2,153.85	305.42
	No cuts	577.26	1,681.41	291.27
Acute hospital (including day surgery)	Cuts	1,256.42	9,616.51	765.39
	No cuts	1,019.58	7,068.98	693.32
Other hospitals (excluding extended [chronic] care)	Cuts	46.4	554.65	1,195.48
	No cuts	97.69	495.93	507.67
Professional home care	Cuts	112.85	786.36	696.79
	No cuts	66.25	426.31	643.53
Homemaker	Cuts	1,666.68	5,384.39	323.06
	No cuts	1,603.58	4,601.66	286.96
Adult day care	Cuts	103.96	297.76	286.42
	No cuts	81.86	418.95	511.77
Long-term care facility	Cuts	17.42	5,489.77	n/a
	No cuts	3.46	2,282.79	n/a

Source: Hollander 2001a, 22

Thus, the findings seem to indicate that even basic home support services can have a significant impact on the cost-effectiveness of our health care system. Anecdotal accounts indicate that the findings are consistent with the following scenario: Those clients who were receiving cleaning services had been assessed by a health professional as being frail and therefore in need of government-funded services to enable them to remain independent; in other words, a limiting condition meant that clients needed cleaning to maintain a normal, sanitary home environment. We can hypothesize that, if these clients were unable to pay for cleaning, or did not have family members who could assist and attempted to clean and vacuum by themselves, this could have led to an accident requiring hospitalization, or a more rapid deterioration in function, thus leading to institutionalization.

Darby (1992) found that a quick response team in an Ontario hospital was able to prevent 206 admissions out of 237 referrals of frail elderly adults from the emergency department to the hospital over a 12-month period. While Darby does not provide a cost comparison, he does indicate that, by being able to send people home with enhanced services, the quick response team freed up the equivalent of 8 to 10 beds for a one-year period.

Most of the international studies on preventative home care refer to specific initiatives focused on preventing admissions or readmissions to hospitals. In Great Britain, Townsend and colleagues (1998) implemented a randomized controlled trial (RCT) to analyze the impact of a community support program using care attendants compared to standard care. After 18 months, they found that hospital readmission rates were significantly higher for the control group with standard care, resulting in 30.6 hospital days for the control group compared to 17.1 days for the treatment group. If the results are extrapolated to all patients 75+ who live alone, an average-sized health district could save some 23 hospital beds using this approach, at a net annual savings of £220,000.

In the US, Rich and colleagues (1995) conducted a study on the effects of a nurse-oriented, post-discharge multidisciplinary intervention to prevent readmission to hospital by elderly patients with congestive heart failure. In this RCT, the treatment group had 56.2 percent fewer readmissions for heart failure and 28.5 percent fewer admissions for other causes within 90 days of hospital discharge, compared to people receiving conventional care. For the treatment group, the overall cost of care was $460 less per patient than for the control group. In a study of a seniors' health promotion program, Nuñez, Armbruster, Phillips, and Gale (2003) found that, in a community-based, nurse-managed health promotion and chronic disease management program for older adults living in the community, such adults had better health and social functioning, not to mention fewer doctor visits and hospital days per year, than a national comparison group.

In Australia, Lim, Lambert, and Gray (2003) found that patients receiving post-acute care coordination used fewer hospital days during six months after discharge than patients receiving the usual care, resulting in an average net savings of $1,545 per person for the treatment group. Stewart and colleagues (1999) also found in a randomized study of patients who had experienced some form of congestive heart failure that a multidisciplinary home-based intervention, consisting of a home visit by a cardiac nurse, resulted in fewer unplanned readmissions and associated days in hospital compared to usual care. The overall hospital costs for the treatment group was $490,300 (in Australian dollars) compared to $922,600 for the control group. Graves and colleagues (2009) studied "a comprehensive nursing and physiotherapy assessment and an individually tailored program of exercise strategies and nurse home visits with telephone follow-up, commencing in hospital and continuing after discharge for 24 weeks" designed to reduce emergency readmissions to hospital. The mean net benefit per individual in the intervention group for the 24-week period was $7,907 (Australian dollars).

In Scandinavia, Melin and Bygren (1992) evaluated the impacts of a primary home care intervention program for people discharged from a short stay in hospital. Clients were randomly assigned to an intervention group and a control group. The intervention group received services from a physician-led primary home care and home assistance team providing 24-hour services. The control group received standard care. The clients were frail elderly individuals with higher level care needs. At a six-month follow-up, the intervention group members showed significant improvements in the instrumental activities of daily living (IADL) and outdoor walking. They also used less long-term hospital services than the control group. (The authors, however, do not provide a comparative cost analysis for the two groups.) Robertson and Kayhko (2001) also found that supportive home follow-up reduced in-patient hospitalizations by more than half for first-time post-myocardial infarction patients.

In Israel, Peleg and colleagues (2008) studied a multidimensional intervention program designed to reduce the number of hospitalizations of elderly patients in a primary care clinic. The intervention included the re-engineering of existing work processes with a focus on case management, communications with outside agencies, and care quality. Compared to the period prior to the introduction of the intervention, the adjusted hospitalization costs (per 1,000 patients) dropped from $32,574 to $18,624, a reduction of 43.8 percent. The number of hospitalizations, hospital days, and average length of stay all decreased.

While it is generally thought that there is little economic evidence to support preventive activities, these studies suggest that prevention, particularly tertiary prevention, can reduce readmission to hospital, improve IADL function, and help clients to maintain their independence and continue to live at home. In the process, there is the potential for considerable cost avoidance.

Home Care as a Substitute for Residential Care

A considerable amount of research has been conducted on the cost-effectiveness of home care in the US, and much of that evidence suggests that home care is *not* a cost-effective alternative to care in long-term care facilities. Two series of federally funded American studies including 14 community care demonstration projects were funded in the late 1970s and early 1980s. An additional 10 projects were funded from 1982 to 1985 as part of the National Long Term Care Demonstration, generally referred to as "channelling" (Mathematica Policy Research 1986, May). These studies all used a rigorous methodology that included random assignment to experimental and control groups. They tested two types of case management: the first was a basic case management model, introducing case management into the existing service delivery system, and the second was a financial control model introducing case management plus additional resources. These additional resources could be used at the discretion of case managers to purchase additional, new services or enhancements to existing services.

Generally, in these studies, researchers found that the experimental group had greater satisfaction and quality of life and somewhat reduced costs (Mathematica Policy Research 1986, April). However, when the costs of the enhanced home care program were added into the equation, the overall costs were generally greater for the experimental group than for the control group, as the intervention did not sufficiently decrease the rate of admission to long-term care facilities. As such, it constituted an add-on cost (Haskins 1985; Mathematica Policy Research, 1986, May).

Illustrative of the general approach used in the studies is the analysis of the Georgia Alternative Health Services Project by Skellie and colleagues (1984). The experimental group received a comprehensive range of community-based services including alternative living services, adult day rehabilitation, and home delivered services. They also received screening and case management services. The control group was eligible to receive existing community services. After the first two years, 22 percent of the control group and 21 percent of the experimental group were admitted to a long-term care facility. In other words, there was no significant difference between the groups. While the costs for the experimental group were higher than the control group, the authors did note that the cost for the experimental group was, nevertheless, considerably lower than the cost for residential care per se. The authors suggested that savings should be possible where home care could be more directly substituted for residential care.

Many of the clients in the channelling studies had relatively low levels of care needs and, therefore, there was a low probability that such clients would be admitted to long-term care facilities during the study period. Put differently, there was little opportunity for a cost-effective substitution of home care for residential care. Weissert, an influential American writer on the cost-effectiveness of home care services during this period, argued that it is difficult to make home- and community-based services cost-effective. His classic work (Weissert 1985) entitled "Seven Reasons Why It Is So Difficult to Make Community-Based Long Term Care Cost-Effective" summarized the findings of a number of studies on this topic:

- Community care is an add-on to other services and is not a substitute for residential care.
- Only short nursing home stays can be avoided by community-based care as some studies note that as many as 25 percent of residents return to their own homes within three months of admission.
- Community care has not reduced the rates of institutionalization.
- Patients at high risk are hard to find because they are relatively low in number.
- Screening and assessment costs are high.
- Because most community services are small, unit costs are relatively high, due to overhead costs, particularly when all service slots are not filled.
- There is limited effectiveness in improving health status.

Weissert and colleagues (1988) expanded the analysis in a review of the 27 most rigorous and generalizable studies on the relative costs of community- and home-based services versus residential long-term care services that were published since 1960. They concluded that home- and community-based long-term care services usually raise overall health care service use and costs for the following reasons: targeting patients at high risk of institutionalization has been uneven and is best accomplished when accompanied by a mandatory nursing home preadmission-screening program; too little money has been saved on institutional care to offset costs of new home and community care services; hospital use may actually have been increased by home and community care; and health status effects are primarily limited to patient and caregiver satisfaction and the reduction of unmet needs.

There is also some evidence from Taiwan that home care is not a cost-effective alternative to residential care. Two studies (Chiu, Shyu, and Liu 2001; Chiu and Shyu 2001) indicate that residential services are considerably more cost-effective than home care. However, a significant portion of the cost is attributed to the labour provided by informal caregivers at replacement wages. If informal labour costs are eliminated, then home care (including out-of-pocket expenses of informal caregivers and clients) is less costly than residential care.

Given these findings, it is not surprising that researchers concluded that home care was not a cost-effective alternative to residential care. This research—especially that from the US—is important. In the late 1980s and early 1990s, when Canada was beginning health care reform, many turned to the US to understand whether or not there was a role for home care services; at the time there was little Canadian research available. As a result of the findings at the time, home care was not seriously considered in Canada. However, the research described above generally does not directly compare the costs of community- and home-based services to those of long-term residential care. Rather, the studies tend to compare costs associated with the introduction of a new home care service to existing community services. In other words, they compared the costs associated with introducing a new and expanded home care service with enhanced case management (and the costs associated with additional services) with what had already been in place, existing community services. And, as noted above, many of the studies included older adults whose level of need did not warrant long-term residential care.

In contrast to the above, other studies have shown that when the costs of community-based services are compared directly with the costs of long-term care services, home care has the potential to be a cost-effective substitute for facility care. For example, among the set of channelling demonstration projects, a study in South Carolina (Mathematica Policy Research 1986, May; Haskins 1985; Capitman 1986) included only subjects who were eligible for, and in need of, residential services. In this instance, home care was a cost-effective alternative to residential care. This model had single entry, assessment, and case management functions within a state-administered system of care. The evaluation of On Lok (Haskins 1985; Mathematical Policy Research 1986), a system for high care needs patients, also reported the cost-effectiveness of home care, although the number of cases was small and the authors advised considerable caution in the interpretation and extrapolation of their findings. Both of these studies included clients with high care needs.

Since the early 1990s, there has been a growing body of literature that contradicts the conclusions of the channelling studies. Greene and colleagues (1993) note that an element that is key to cost-effectiveness is risk targeting. The authors reanalyzed the data from the channelling studies and found that there was some potential for net cost reductions among 41 percent of those in the control group by adding home care services to existing services. These are, however, potential rather than actual gains as the findings are based on statistical modelling of existing data.

Weissert and colleagues (1997) showed that home care can be cost-effective when home- and community-based services are designed to substitute for facility care. Examining the Arizona Long Term Care System, the first *capitated* (population-based funding) long-term care Medicaid program in the US, and conducting a simulation study, the authors report the estimated costs of an integrated care program with case management and home care as less costly than a regular American care delivery system. They noted the cost reductions were due to reductions in admission rates to facility care. The suggested reasons for these cost savings include the use of a capitation payment methods that encouraged program contractors to place clients in lower-cost home- and community-based services rather than risk losing money by using more facility days than their monthly capitated rate allowed.

Other international studies also demonstrate the cost-effectiveness of home care. A Belgian study of people with dementia (Scuvee-Moreau, Kurz, Dresse, and the National Dementia Economic Study Group 2002) found that the average monthly cost in Belgian francs was 445.50 for dementia patients treated at home and 2,301.70 for dementia patients in institutions. The comparable costs for persons with severe dementia were 556.88 and 2,465.28 francs, respectively.

Stuart and Weinrich (2001) compared the cost trends in Denmark and the US. For many years, Denmark has had an integrated system of care delivery for elderly persons and persons with disabilities that prioritizes home care, and includes a home support component. Since this integrated system was implemented in Denmark in the mid-1980s, Danish long-term care expenditures leveled off; in contrast, American expenditures continued to increase over the same time period. More specifically, for the period 1985 to 1997, per capita expenditures on continuing care services per person 65+ increased by 8 percent in Denmark and by 67 percent in the US. For those clients age 80 and over, costs decreased by 12 percent in Denmark but increased 68 percent in the US. It appears that the savings in Denmark were the result of reducing the number of nursing home beds. Over the same period in the US, however, there was a 12 percent increase in nursing home beds. In a related study comparing France and the US, Stuart and

Weinrich (2004) note that the French health care system is considerably less costly than that in the US. The authors attribute this difference in costs to a range of factors, including lower physician salaries, lower administrative costs, and the preventive care and disease management systems that exist in France for persons requiring chronic (long-term) care.

Canadian studies conducted during the 1990s and later also point to the cost-effectiveness of home care. Hollander (2001b) examined BC data and found that home care, on average, was significantly less costly than care in a long-term care facility for all levels of care needs. For example, for those with moderate care needs in the mid-to-late 1990s, average annual costs to government for continuing care, drugs, hospital care, and physician care was $9,624 per person in home care and $25,742 per person in an institution. For people at the highest, or chronic, level of care (extended care) the corresponding costs were $34,859 in home care and $44,233 in an institution. A related study conducted in Victoria and Winnipeg (Chappell et al. 2004; Hollander and Chappell. 2002b) found similar cost differences when looking at clients with 120 hours or less aide time per month in the community versus in facilities (see Table 5-3). This same study also incorporated into the analysis a broader societal perspective by considering out-of-pocket expenses and the care time of informal caregivers (see Table 5-4).

In a Veterans Affairs Canada study, Pedlar and Walker (2004) report on an Overseas Service Veterans (OSV) at Home Pilot Project for veterans who were previously only eligible for residential care. The veterans were offered the alternative of remaining at home with home support services. The veterans preferred this option, which resulted in significant reductions in waiting lists for facility care. The study led to two additional studies, one on this particular veterans group and one on the general veterans population receiving care. Both studies showed that home care was a cost-effective alternative to residential care when analyzed from the perspectives of costs to government and costs within a broader societal context (Hollander et al. 2009).

Some Canadian studies have focused on the cost-effectiveness of home care for individuals with cognitive impairments. Using data from the Canadian Study of Health and Aging (CSHA), Østbye and Crosse (1994) calculated the net economic costs incurred specifically as a result of dementia. This study considered both direct costs (such as home support, physiotherapy, respite care, day centre care) and indirect costs (such as time spent by informal caregivers in assisting clients with activities of daily living). The annual direct costs of caring for someone without dementia in the community was estimated at $1,790. In contrast, the annual direct costs of caring for someone with mild dementia in the community were $4,506 and for someone with severe dementia, $8,109. Using the broader societal perspective, it was estimated that the annual societal cost of providing

Table 5-3 Cost to Government of All Health Services for Continuing Care Clients (for Clients with 120 Hours per Month or Less of Care Aide Time)

Care Level		Victoria Sample		Winnipeg Sample	
		Community	Facility	Community	Facility
Level A: Somewhat independent	Mean annual cost	$12,249.20	$24,092.59		
	Standard deviation	$8,025.57	$7,622.32		
	Number	37	12		
Level B: Slightly independent	Mean annual cost	$17,188.25	$29,141.49	$17,989.32	$33,655.59
	Standard deviation	$6,996.46	$11,898.78	$10,217.75	$18,076.34
	Number	23	42	14	11
Level C: Slightly dependent	Mean annual cost	$14,544.56	$36,014.93	$16,559.31	$32,151.75
	Standard deviation	$10,941.38	$17,894.51	$6,418.52	$13,523.96
	Number	12	50	10	37
Level D: Somewhat dependent	Mean annual cost	$16,870.76	$44,309.55	$15,528.02	$28,595.75
	Standard deviation	$13,465.77	$16,940.92	$7,731.96	$13,897.39
	Number	8	26	13	52
Level E: Largely dependent	Mean annual cost			$23,815.54	$33,422.73
	Standard deviation			$4,254.38	$16,864.30
	Number			4*	29

*Due to there being fewer than five cases for some categories, the reported statistical analysis for Winnipeg was based on Levels B to D only.

Note: All clients studied are those who have fewer than 120 hours of care aide per month. "Mean deviation" refers to the extent to which the costs vary for the group as a whole. Due to there being fewer than five cases for some categories, the reported statistical analysis for Winnipeg was based on Levels B to D only.

Source: Chappell et al. 2004

Table 5-4 Annual Cost of Continuing Care Services, Physician and Hospital Costs, Out-of-Pocket Expenses, and Informal Caregiver Time Valued at Replacement Wages (for Clients with 120 Hours per Month or Less of Care Aide Time)

Care Level		Victoria Sample		Winnipeg Sample	
		Community	Facility	Community	Facility
Level A: Somewhat independent	Mean	$19,758.59	$39,255.44		
	Standard deviation	$11,590.57	$7,594.13		
	Number	37	12		
Level B: Slightly independent	Mean	$30,975.22	$45,964.23	$27,313.02	$47,618.22
	Standard deviation	$16,943.63	$12,566.70	$21,219.16	$19.486.61
	Number	23	42	14	11
Level C: Slightly dependent	Mean	$31,847.92	$53,847.62	$29,094.46	$49,207.31
	Standard deviation	$13,764.31	$17,417.82	$8,851.74	$13,805.44
	Number	12	50	10	37
Level D: Somewhat dependent	Mean	$58,619.30	$66,310.18	$32,274.54	$45,636.77
	Standard deviation	$35,473.65	$21,491.15	$9,200.12	$15,735.47
	Number	8	26	13	5
Level E: Largely dependent	Mean			$35,133.75	$50,560.38
	Standard deviation			$6,302.44	$17,196.53
	Number			4*	29

Note: all clients studied are those who have fewer than 120 hours of care aide per month. Costs have been adjusted to incorporate physician and hospital costs, out-of-pocket expenses, and informal caregiver time valued at with a replacement wage.
* Due to there being fewer than five cases for some categories, the reported statistical analysis for Winnipeg was based on Levels B to D only.
Source: Chappell, Havens, Hollander, Miller, and McWilliam 2004

dementia-specific care for those in the community was $10,100 ($4,970 for direct costs and $5,130 for indirect costs). The annual societal cost of providing dementia-specific care to individuals in a facility was $19,100.

Finally, Hébert et al. (2001) report mixed results in a comparison of the costs by level of care for home care services, long-term care facilities, and "intermediate care" residences (similar to supportive housing). This comparison found that, clearly and consistently, home care was the most cost-effective type of care for government, while long-term facility care was the most expensive. Intermediate care residential settings were positioned between the other two. When a broader societal perspective was used, intermediate care residential settings were still less costly than long-term care facilities. However, home care costs were higher for clients with moderate and high care needs than costs in the other two settings. This is primarily due to the costs attributed to informal caregivers. The extent to which these costs were strictly limited to activities and/or out-of-pocket expenses due solely to the health condition of the client is unclear. A similar study (Chappell et al. 2004), using strict criteria to ensure that non-government costs were directly attributable to the health condition of the client, did not find the same kind of cost escalation as the level of care increased. In fact, this study reported that, even using a broader societal perspective, home care costs were lower than residential care costs at each level of care.

It should be noted that the savings from substituting home care services for residential services are not only theoretical. Actual savings were achieved in BC during the 1980s and 1990s by holding down future construction of long-term care facilities and making investments in home care (Hollander 2001b). The utilization rate of home and community care services in the fiscal year 1984–85 amounted to 92 person years per 1,000 persons age 65+ and 71.7 person years, for residential care, for a total utilization rate of 163.7. The overall utilization rate was also 163.7 for the 1994–95 fiscal year, but residential services (long-term care and chronic, or extended care, services) were reduced to 50.7 and home care increased to 113 (see Figure 5-1). Thus over a 10-year period, due to a pro-active policy of substituting home care services for residential services, the utilization of some 21 person years per 1,000 population 65 and over was shifted from residential care to home care. This transfer from residential care to home care resulted in an estimated annual costs avoidance of some $150M in 1995 (Chappell and Hollander 2011).

Although early research on home care was concentrated in the US and revealed that home care was not cost-effective, subsequent research points to flaws in this work, which led to erroneous conclusions. The very different system (or lack thereof) in the US, combined with methodological design inadequacies meant that the results did not translate to the Canadian context. Later research, including Canadian research, has demonstrated that, for older adults with higher care needs, home care has the potential to cost less when substituted for long-term residential care. Although these later findings came too late for the early days of health reform in the 1990s, they are timely and relevant for ongoing reform within the current context.

The Cost-Effectiveness of Home Care Compared to Acute Care Hospitals

Current Canadian policy related to short-term home care appears to be based primarily on the assumption that home care can act as a substitute for

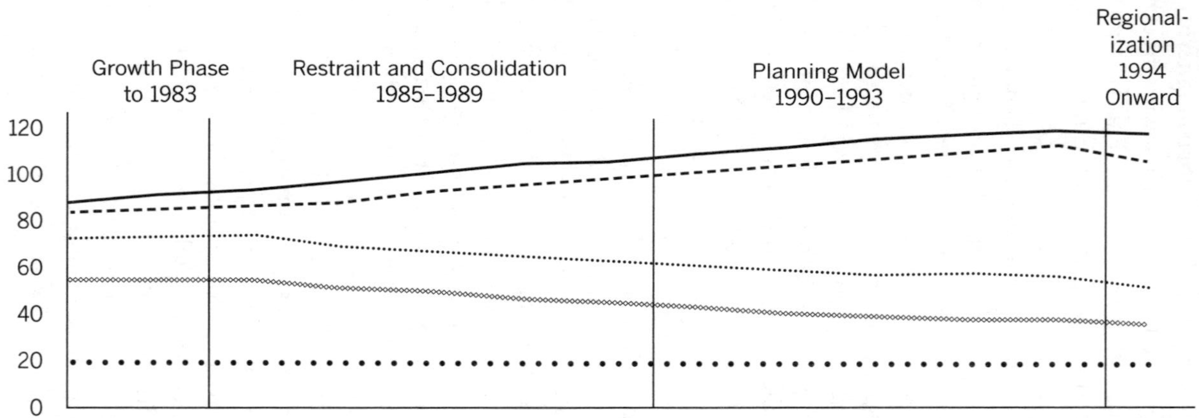

	1983	1984	1985	1986	1987	1988	1989	1990	1991	1992	1993	1994	1995
Community	87.2	89.5	92.0	96.5	98.7	100.7	102.4	105.8	110.8	113.8	114.8	116.2	113.0
Homemakers	80.9	83.1	84.9	88.7	90.9	93.3	95.1	98.4	103.0	105.5	106.5	107.6	101.2
Residential	71.5	71.6	71.7	69.7	67.2	65.1	63.0	60.4	58.2	56.5	55.2	53.5	50.7
LTC Facilities	52.5	52.7	52.0	50.1	48.1	46.1	44.0	42.1	40.3	38.6	37.8	36.7	34.4
EC Hospital	18.9	19.1	19.7	19.6	19.1	19.1	19.0	18.3	17.9	17.9	17.4	16.9	16.3

Growth Phase to 1983   Restraint and Consolidation 1985–1989   Planning Model 1990–1993   Regionalization 1994 Onward

Utilization per 1,000 population aged 65+ by fiscal year and type of care
Fiscal year 1983 is for the period April 1, 1982 to March 31, 1983

Figure 5-1 Substituting Home Care for Residential Care over Time
Source: Adapted from Hollander and Chappell 2007

hospital services through early discharge combined with follow-up during home care. However, there are in fact three aspects to the relationship between acute care and home care. The first is the direct substitution of home care for hospital care by allowing hospital patients to be discharged earlier and cared for in the community by home care. The second is the substitution of community-based care for acute care. The third is a preventive function relating to the reduction of hospital admissions, or readmissions, by using targeted home care services. This preventive function was previously discussed in the section on the cost-effectiveness of preventive home care.

The cost-effectiveness of early discharge from hospital has been studied in several countries. In a British study, Hollingworth and colleagues (1993) studied early discharge of hip-fracture patients to *hospital at home* (that is, care in a home setting in which there are some hospital-related services as well as home care) compared to regular hospital care. The authors found that the patients in the experimental group spent 9.2 fewer days in hospital, resulting in a comparative cost reduction of £722 per patient. Roberts' (2001) RCT of early discharge plus home and community care in Edinburgh reported that, while outcomes were similar, the costs were lower for the home/community option than for people who stayed in hospital (£877 versus £1,753). Similar results were reported in an Irish study (Murphy, Byrne, and Costello 2002), an inner-city London study (Beech et al. 1999), and an Australian study (Caplan et al. 1998; Nicholson et al. 2001).

In a review of studies on the cost-effectiveness of early discharge and home/community rehabilitation for clients who had suffered strokes, Anderson and colleagues (2002) concluded that the overall costs for the early intervention group were 15 percent lower than for the standard care group. This was confirmed in a British Cochrane Collaboration paper (Anderson et al. 2002) looking at early discharge plus home rehabilitation for stroke patients. The authors found that the group that had been discharged early but given support had hospital stays reduced by some nine days compared to patients who remained in the hospital. In a Swedish study, Holmqvist and colleagues (1998) conducted a RCT to evaluate early discharge plus rehabilitation at home for stroke victims. In this instance, there were no differences in outcomes, but over a three-month period there was a 52 percent reduction in hospitalization for the home rehabilitation group. In similar vein, Teng and colleagues' (2003) RCT found that, for patients requiring ventilation, the initial costs were similar for the early discharge stroke group and the hospital group; however, the standard care (hospital care) group had considerably more readmissions, resulting in comparative costs of $7,784 versus $11,065 for the early supported discharge group compared to the standard care group.

It should be noted that there are studies that report different findings. Consider a Canadian study of joint-replacement patients in which patients referred to the home care group stayed longer in hospital than other patients, had overall higher costs, and higher readmission rates (Coyte, Young, and Croxford 2000). In this case, early discharge did not seem to work as intended. However, sufficient studies now indicate that cost savings are possible. Importantly, though, there may be less potential for cost-effective substitutions of home care for early discharge today than in the past because hospital stays have become increasingly short. This is illustrated by a study of the cost-effectiveness of early discharge for pre-term infants. At the outset of the study, it was estimated that one half day in hospital could be avoided by the early discharge of mother and infant pairs. By the time the study was completed, the time in hospital was almost the same for the early discharge group and the control group (Stevens et al. 2001). In other words, the potential efficiencies had simply been absorbed by the hospital. Increased pressure to reduce hospital stays resulted in less opportunity for cost-effective substitution because the time spent in hospital in the convalescent period had already been reduced.

There are also a number of studies of specific types of home care programs that could act as a substitute for hospital care. Studies in the 1980s and 1990s showed evidence of cost-effectiveness for wound care (O'Brien et al. 1999; Morrell et al. 1998), home parenteral (intravenous) nutrition (Detsky et al. 1986; Cade and Puntis 1998; Richards and Irving 1996), home intravenous therapy (Coyte, Dobrow, and Broadfield 2001; Harjai et al. 1997), home chemotherapy (Lowenthal et al. 1996; Rischin et al. 2000), and home ventilation (Guber et al. 2002; Larson, Odegard, and Brown 1992; Rizzi et al. 2009; Tuggey, Plant, and Elliott 2003). Research in these areas seems to have dropped off in recent years.

Finally, there is also some evidence that integrated home care programs can substitute home/community care for acute care. For example, two Italian studies of the impact of an integrated home care program (including social and health services) on hospital use (Landi et al. 1999; Landi et al. 2001) are relevant here. Both studies indicated a significant reduction in hospitalizations, hospital days, and costs in a comparison of the same patients before and after the implementation of the integrated home care program. Similar findings were obtained by Leung and colleagues (2004) in a Hong Kong RCT of the impacts of case management for community-dwelling individuals. They found that, after the introduction of case management, hospital admissions were reduced by 36.8 percent and bed days were decreased by 53.1 percent, compared to the control group. A review of international models of systems of care delivery for older adults (Johri, Beland, and Bergman 2003) found that home care, as part of an integrated system of care delivery, tended to result in overall system efficiencies due to reductions in the number of hospital admissions and hospital days and admissions to long-term care facilities.

In sum, these findings indicate that the issue of home care and its relationship to hospital care is much broader and more complex than is currently understood. At a policy level, we currently see a focus on short-term home care to replace acute care. This is certainly an important area. However, the research indicates that it may also be useful to focus on approaches to prevent admissions and readmissions to hospitals. Long-term and supportive home care could usefully be considered as a substitute for acute care.

The Cost-Effectiveness of Other Continuing Care Services

In addition to home care, other components of the continuing care system can also be cost-effective. An example is respite care for family caregivers, discussed in Chapter 3.

Assisted living is an emerging component of the care continuum for seniors. While to some, assisted living may seem to be a new concept, in fact, there are various forms that have a long history. What is new is a shift by policy-makers to focus more on this sector and to begin promoting and integrating assisted living arrangements more formally into the care continuum. There is no current, widely accepted definition of assisted living. Rather, it is an umbrella term that currently incorporates a number of new, and previously existing, housing arrangements such as group homes, congregate living, room and board (to the extent that some additional supportive services are included), group living situations, and supportive housing. The generally recognized components of this model of care are captured in the Assisted Living Federation of America's definition of assisted living as "a special combination of housing, personalized supportive services, and health care designed to respond to the individual needs of those who require help with activities of daily living. Assisted living care promotes maximum independence and dignity while encouraging the involvement of a resident's family, neighbors, and friends" (ALFA n.d.). Basic services most often provided include: 24-hour staffing; personal care; meals and snacks; housekeeping, laundry, and maintenance services; a personalized care plan describing how health care needs may be addressed; and activities and transportation resources that are available (Gorshe 2000, 20). Gorshe (2000) also notes that models of assisted living may have "universal workers" who provide a range of personal care and housekeeping services, and may also include nursing staff who assess residents, assign tasks to the universal workers, and train and monitor these workers.

There is an emerging body of evidence from several countries on the cost-effectiveness of assisted living. Most studies compare the costs (or costs as well as outcomes) of assisted living with residential long-term care. In Sweden, Wimo and colleagues (1995) conducted a cost-utility analysis of group living for dementia patients. They compared patients in group living arrangements with those receiving home care and with institutionalized patients. Their overall finding indicated that the cost per quality-adjusted life year gained was most favourable for the group living alternative. In a static model, home care was the most favourable outcome. However, in examining changes over time, group living was the most favourable outcome for people with intermediate to high-level dementia. The difference in outcomes is, at least in part, attributable to the fact that patients in group living deteriorated at a slower rate than those receiving home care.

In the US, Schinka and colleagues (1998) compared the costs and outcomes of inpatient care and supportive housing for substance-dependent veterans. There were two groups of clients: one group was located in a hospital while the other clients resided in assisted-living apartments and walked four blocks to the hospital each day. The clients in both groups were similar at baseline. The treatment outcomes were also similar. However, the cost for the inpatient group was $9,524, compared to $4,291 for the supportive housing group. Most of the differential in costs was related to the cost of housing—that is, hospital versus assisted living residence.

In another American study, Leon and Moyer (1999) compared the costs of assisted living versus nursing homes for patients with Alzheimer's disease. Combining all levels of severity, the authors found that the annual costs of assisted living were 13.9 percent less than the costs for nursing homes. However, in a British study of different types of assisted living, Emerson and colleagues (2001) analyzed the comparative quality and costs of supported living residences and group homes while adjusting for client characteristics. This study found that there were no significant differences in service costs and relatively few differences in outcomes between groups. Thus, while the evidence is somewhat mixed, it suggests that assisted living can be cost-effective compared to residential care.

Palliative care (care to provide comfort rather than a cure in various circumstances, but most often in regard to care for the dying) is another emerging area. Two systematic reviews of hospice care (Candy et al. 2011; Higginson et al. 2003) concluded that hospice care at home (as compared to nursing homes and hospice facilities) reduced general health care use and increased patient and family satisfaction with care.

The National Hospice Study, conducted in the early 1980s in the US, compared the costs of home-based hospice care, conventional care, and hospital-based hospice care for patients with cancer (Bosanquet 2002). On average, home-based hospice costs were $4,000 lower than conventional care, and hospital-based hospice costs were $1,300 lower than conventional care. However, most of the cost difference was in the final month of life and, in fact, the costs for people with long hospice stays (over 3–4 months) were higher than the costs of conventional care. There were also differences in what care was provided. Home-based hospice patients had 10 times more home care services than patients receiving conventional care; and the patients receiving conventional care, in turn, were seven times more likely to receive aggressive anti-tumor intervention near death (Robinson and Pham 1996). In a reanalysis of the data, the authors note the "quality of the death" was better in home-based care. Another American study (Vinciguerra et al. 1986) compared the costs of caring for terminal cancer patients in the hospital and at home; the result was a per diem cost-benefit of $256 for in-home treatment.

More recently, Deans (2004) provides an overview of hospice service costs in the US. The author notes that for 2001, the per diem charge for hospital-based hospice care was $3,069. The comparable daily costs for hospice in a long-term care facility and at home were $422 and $125, respectively. In another American study, Lewin and colleagues (2005) found significant differences for similar individuals in hospital-related costs for those enrolled in a hospice compared to people not enrolled in a hospice over the final 60 days of life. The comparative costs were $59,319 for the non-hospice group compared to $15,164 for the hospice group. Major factors related to this cost differential were the number of hospital days and costs for radiology and laboratory services, drugs, and the costs of physician services. Other studies have also noted that hospital care is more expensive than residential or home-based palliative care (Maltoni et al. 1998; Lane et al. 1998; Coyle et al. 1999).

Some research examines outcomes other than costs. Aiken et al. (2006) conducted a RCT of an American palliative care intervention for seriously chronically ill patients. The researchers noted that, compared to the control group, the patients receiving palliative care intervention exhibited better outcomes on "self-management of illness, awareness of illness-related resources, and legal preparation for end of life." They also reported lower symptom distress, greater vitality, better physical functioning, and higher self-rated health than randomized controls. In contrast, a review paper concludes that there was little evidence of better outcomes for quality of life for coordinated care compared to conventional home care (Salisbury et al. 1999).

The cost-effectiveness literature on palliative care is still emerging but so far the weight of the evidence seems to indicate that there is a gradation of decreasing costs from hospice care in hospitals to residential settings to home care.

There also appears to be a growing literature on the cost-effectiveness of the *hospital-at-home* as a substitute for inpatient hospital care, an option emerging in a range of jurisdictions. Both Jester and Hicks (2003) and Coast et al. (1998), in the UK, found that hospital-at-home care was more effective and less costly than care in an acute care hospital. The lower costs were attributable to the shorter stay in an acute care hospital and the lack of hospital overhead costs. Similarly, in Australia, Board and colleagues (2000) report lower costs for the group receiving hospital-at-home care ($1,764) compared to the standard care group ($3,614), without any differences in clinical outcomes and with higher patient satisfaction.

In a Spanish study, Hernandez and colleagues (2003) analyzed a hospital-at-home option as an alternative to hospitalization for chronic obstructive pulmonary disease (COPD) patients admitted to a hospital emergency department. Patients who came to emergency with similar symptoms were randomized into two groups: hospital-at-home care and standard inpatient hospital care. There were no differences in mortality or hospital readmissions, but the hospital-at-home group had lower subsequent use of the emergency department and better quality of life. The costs for the hospital-at-home option were 62 percent lower than for standard care. In an Italian study, Aimonino and colleagues (2008) evaluated a hospital-at-home model of care versus inpatient care also for COPD patients within a RCT. The researchers found that the hospital-at-home group had a lower incidence of hospital readmissions during the six months after discharge. Also, while the hospital-at-home group had longer stays compared to patients in the acute care hospital, they experienced improvement in depression and quality of life scores, and there were lower overall costs.

In Canada, we also have some positive experience in regard to the hospital-at-home option from the program in New Brunswick (New Brunswick, Department of Health and Wellness 2006). For example, Robb (1994) notes that, in the early to mid-1990s, the Extra Mural Hospital (hospital-at-home) cost $30 per day compared to a per diem rate of $350 to $500 for hospitals. Robb also presents a number of case studies to demonstrate the benefits of the Extra Mural Hospital.

While more research is required on the hospital-at-home care concept, it may have merit for cost savings at least in some situations. Recall that the acute care hospital became the institution of choice for the practice of medicine when the federal government began its support for hospital construction in the 1950s. With their subsidization, hospitals became an attractive choice for the provinces. The hospital-at-home concept moves hospital services into the community. Policy-makers may wish to review the New Brunswick experience, which now has a long track record.

There are an increasing number of papers on the effectiveness of *telehealth*. Telehealth consists of supportive and medical care provided by telephone and/or video; clients may also have some medical equipment in the home, such as blood pressure monitors to assist doctors and nurses who use this approach. Cardozo and Steinberg's (2010) observational study examined home-based, case-managed telemedicine for a two-month period post-discharge for patients with congestive heart failure, COPD, diabetes, and hypertension. The patients received nursing visits up to three times per week and daily home telemedicine monitoring for weight, blood pressure, pulse rate, and blood glucose recordings. Patient education was also provided. Treatment goals were met for 67 percent of patients and 66 percent had improvements in nine quality indicators. The model of care was well accepted and produced excellent short-term clinical outcomes. IADLs such as shopping, motor function, and cognition were improved among frail elderly persons who received telehealth over a one-year period compared to those who did not (Chumbler et al. 2004). In a study of high-risk American veterans, home care plus telehealth and monitoring devices reduced hospital admissions, bed days of care, emergency room visits, and prescriptions compared to the control group; in this case, the telehealth group also showed high satisfaction for patients and providers (Kobb et al. 2003). In conclusion, telehealth is a technological advance that has much promise; more research is required, especially on its cost-effectiveness.

Another service of interest is *falls prevention*. This is an important preventive and supportive program for older adults. Rizzo and colleagues (1996) conducted a cost-effectiveness study of a multifactorial, targeted prevention program for falls among elderly persons living in the community. Participants randomly assigned to the treatment group received a combination of medication adjustment, behavioural recommendations, and exercises, which were determined by their baseline assessment. The remaining participants were randomized to a control group and received a series of home visits by a social work student. Overall, the mean health care cost was $2,000 (US) less for the treatment group than the control group due to lower overall health care costs and fewer falls. Subgroup analysis indicated that, within the treatment group, the strongest effects were for individuals at high risk of falling. High risk was defined as having at least four of the eight targeted risk factors.

Salkeld and colleagues (2000) studied a program to reduce home hazards (through home modifications) in order to prevent falls. The clients all had a history of falls and were to be discharged from hospital into two randomized groups: one that received the hazard-reduction program and a control group that did not. The researchers concluded that the hazard-reduction program was cost-effective for older people with a history of falls. A Canadian study found that the Strategies and Actions for Independent Living (SAIL) program in BC, while not reducing the number of falls, did reduce the number of fractures over a six-month period (Scott, Votova, and Gallagher 2006).

Falls prevention makes intuitive sense, both from a cost savings point of view and in terms of quality of life. Nevertheless, more studies on the cost-effectiveness of different programs could add to our confidence in their worthiness.

Assistive technology (which provides technological assistance to allow clients to function more effectively) is another important area. Mann and colleagues (1999) conducted a study of the effectiveness of assistive technology and environmental interventions in maintaining independence and reducing home care costs for the frail elderly. In this RCT, home-based frail elderly persons received a comprehensive functional assessment followed by either assistive devices and environmental interventions or usual care services. After 18 months, scores for the Functional Independence Measure were reduced for both groups, but there was a significantly greater decline for the control group. While the costs of assistive devices and environmental interventions were higher for the treatment group ($2,620) than the control group ($443), the control group had significantly greater expenditures for institutional care ($21,846 versus $5,630) and for nurse and case manager visits ($1,035 versus $536).

In sum, much of the literature on cost-effectiveness in continuing care has focused on home care, but there are other components of a broader continuing care system that also appear to be cost-effective. Taken together, the potential to increase value for money in the continuing care sector appears to be even greater than originally thought when the focus was only on home care. To capitalize on the full potential of continuing care, policymakers may wish to take note of these new and emerging approaches to increase the cost-effectiveness of our health care system.

Discussion

Several key findings emerge on the cost-effectiveness of continuing care. There is a small but reasonable body of evidence to indicate that it can be cost-effective to provide more basic home support services as a means of delaying institutionalization. Moreover, there is evidence that well-planned and executed preventive initiatives can have a positive impact in delaying institutionalization; in other words, home care can be a cost-effective alternative to residential long-term care and it can have a substitution effect for hospital services. In addition, there is mounting evidence that a wide range of new initiatives could reduce future hospital admissions and/ or readmissions.

Thus, it appears that home care is not only an important program in its own right, but can also be a key vehicle for increasing the efficiency and effectiveness of the broader health care system. A corollary is that there are a number of more "medical" preventive interventions or programs that may also be able to bring about greater program efficiencies. From a program development perspective, it may be useful to increase both the "high tech" and "high touch" aspects of home care to the extent that such services can increase the overall efficiency of the health care system. It is also clear that assisted living/supportive housing is beginning to emerge as a major component of the continuing care system. However, this process is still evolving and there is currently relatively little research on the cost-effectiveness of this model of care.

As always, one must be aware that investments in greater efficiencies can only achieve positive results if there are real and tangible substitutions or trade-offs that occur at the front lines, or if blockages in the efficient flow of services can be relieved. For example, in theory it may be possible to reduce hospital stays by 20 beds per year, at one-third the cost of such days, using a new home care service. However, unless such trade-offs occur, the new home care program will be an add-on cost. Unless the efficiencies gained are incorporated into a given analysis, and recognized as pro-active trade-offs between types of services, outcomes such as reduced alternate level of care (ALC) bed days due to enhanced home care may not be self-evident.

In summary, existing evidence suggests it is possible to obtain increased efficiencies in continuing care, and the overall health care system, with well-developed strategic plans that focus on the following: the cost-effective substitution of services; targeted preventive care initiatives; a focus on supportive services; and a focus on expanding both the caring and technological aspects of continuing care. The challenge is to move from findings such as those discussed here to developing and testing new, and potentially more effective, models of care delivery. This requires a recognition that continuing care, including home care, is both appropriate and essential for many of the chronic conditions and functional disabilities that are prevalent in old age. A return to only medical care for an ageing society will lose the opportunity to implement the potential value for money of continuing care services.

It is essential that action is forthcoming quickly. Already within health reform, the move has been to "hollow out" medicare as we knew it in the

1970s and 1980s in Canada (Williams et al. 2001). While the public funds approximately 70 percent of health care costs in this country, only between 2 and 4 percent of that money is allocated to home care. While the late 1990s saw modest increases to these budgets, they were followed by decreases, and at the same time, there was about a 20 percent increase in private expenses for home care services during the same period (CIHI 2007). Meanwhile, research in Ontario and BC (Penning et al. 2009; Le Goff 2002; CIHI 2007) was documenting shorter hospital stays, resulting in increased demand for short-term (intensive, post-acute hospital) care. This in turn has resulted in fewer public dollars being available for long-term home care to meet the needs of older adults suffering from chronic conditions and functional declines. This is not to argue that more outpatient surgeries and shorter lengths of hospital stay are inappropriate; however, it does suggest that those needs should be met *without* draining needed resources from long-term community care for older adults.

Home and continuing care has been increasing its concentration on high-needs clients and on the health components of the community care system (such as nurses and physiotherapists), leaving lower-level clients to pay for the services they need and removing many of the social components of home care (such as home support). These latter aspects are often where cost-savings come from, and where the maintenance and preventive function of home care services becomes evident. That is, shifting the home care/continuing care aspects of the health care system to the private sector outside of the public health care system will not afford the opportunities for the types of cost effectiveness demonstrated in the research reviewed here. Rather, it will represent lost opportunities at the expense of meeting the needs of older adults, other than those with sufficient resources to purchase services on their own. It will also further exacerbate the demands on families and friends who are already providing care to the best of their abilities.

Chapter 6

Models and Frameworks for Integrated Care

Introduction

We saw in Chapter 5 that home care (including home support) and other components of the continuing care system often cost less than residential long-term care and/or hospital care for people with similar care needs. This is a necessary, but not sufficient, condition for cost-effectiveness. Adding resources to home care (by way of an example) may simply result in an add-on cost if all other components remain the same. In order for home care to be cost-effective, less expensive home care must be substituted for more expensive residential and/or hospital care. We argue that the best way to achieve cost-effective substitutions is within a broad and comprehensive integrated system of care where proactive policy choices can be made to substitute lower cost home care for higher cost residential and/or hospital care. This can be accomplished directly by closing beds or indirectly by reducing the rate of growth of future bed construction and building capacity for home care.

The ability to achieve substitutions is made possible either by purchasing needed bed days in a capitated system (where a fixed amount of funds is provided to pay for both home and community care and residential and/or hospital care for a given population), or by a single administration and budget for the whole system of care. In the capitated models, there is an incentive for the care provider organization to care for older adults in the lowest cost setting (while ensuring adequate care provision) by avoiding the use of residential or hospital beds. In other words, the organization has the ability to substitute lower cost care with higher cost care on the basis of value and outcomes within a broader care framework that includes a full range of home/community and residential/hospital services. This model of integration has been used in the US for its Program for All-Inclusive Care for the Elderly (PACE) and in the Arizona integrated care model, both of which are discussed below. In some approaches to continuing care used in western Canada, such as the BC model used in the early 1990s, all services come under one umbrella department of the provincial government; in this case, there was also a single budget for all related services.

The ability to provide better, more cost-effective, and more continuous care for clients has been an ongoing challenge. The response has been to develop integrated models of care but there is no consensus on what the term "integrated care" means nor what services are included (Low et al. 2011; MacAdam 2008; Goodwin 2013). In some instances only services within a hospital are integrated, sometimes only home care services, etc. And not all attempts have had positive outcome evaluations; this reality highlights the complexity of designing and implementing successful systems of care.

In addition to the various efforts to develop integrated systems, there have also been efforts to develop broader frameworks that capture the essential features of successful integrated models of care. This chapter provides an overview of integrated systems with positive (or at least neutral) outcomes and of broader frameworks that can provide guidance based on best practices for developing models of integrated care.

Examples of Successful Integrated Systems of Care

Low and colleagues (2011), MacAdam (2008), and Béland and Hollander (2011) have conducted comprehensive reviews of integrated models of care and note evaluations of their effectiveness. The models with positive evaluations are documented in Table 6-1. They can be organized into three groups: larger provincial or state models; more local models where home/community and residential/hospital components are included; and integration at the local community level. There is a fourth community model that has typically not been seen to be part of continuing care but is gaining interest, the chronic care model from primary care.

Larger provincial and state models

From the late 1970s to the mid-1990s, BC had an integrated model of continuing care administered by its Continuing Care Division. This was a broad comprehensive system of care delivery that included a wide range of home/community and residential care services. It also funded geriatric

Table 6-1   Overview of Integrated Models of Care for Older Persons with Positive Evaluations

Model of Care	Studies that Evaluate the Model Positively		
	Low, Yap, and Brodaty (2011)	MacAdam (2008)	Béland and Hollander (2011)
System of Integrated Care for Older Persons (SIPA)	✓	✓	✓
Program for All-Inclusive Care for the Elderly (PACE)	✓	✓	✓
Rovereto Model (Rovereto has its own row)	✓	✓	✓
Hospital Admission Risk Program (HARP) Australia	✓	✓	n/a
Program of Research to Integrate Services for the Maintenance of Autonomy Model (PRISMA)	n/a	mentioned but evaluation not completed at the time of writing	✓
Hong Kong Model	n/a	n/a	✓
Arizona Model (early 1990s)	n/a	n/a	✓
BC Continuing Care Model (early 1990s)	n/a	n/a	✓

Sources: Low, Yap, and Brodaty 2011; MacAdam 2008; Béland and Hollander 2011

assessment units in some hospitals. The system was both horizontally and vertically integrated across primary care, secondary care (long-term care facilities), and tertiary care (geriatric units in hospitals). Care within the system, and links to other parts of health and community care, were co-ordinated by system-level case managers who conducted standard client assessments and reassessments, and who stayed with the clients irrespective of their site of care. One of the unique aspects of this system was the inclusion of a full range of clients from those with legitimate but low-level care need to high-level chronic care patients (Hollander and Pallan 1995). As Figure 5-1 demonstrated, this system allowed for cost-effective, proactive substitutions of home care for residential care (Hollander and Chappell 2007; Chappell and Hollander 2011).

The Arizona model of the early 1990s was in many ways similar to the BC model. In 1989, the state obtained federal funding for a demonstration project, the Arizona Long Term Care System, which allowed it to have a pool of funds for the care of older adults. These funds were disbursed to local agencies, usually organized on a geographic basis. For the elderly people in their geographic catchment area, the agencies received a capitated budget to use for home/community, residential, and acute care services. The agencies were responsible for covering the cost of bed days in long-term care facilities and hospitals on behalf of their clients. There was a clear incentive for these agencies to provide a reasonable quality of care in the lowest cost setting. This system also had case management (at the local level) but, unlike the BC model, focused on clients with higher care needs, clients equivalent to those who would normally be placed into residential care. An evaluation found that this model of integrated care was cost-effective (Weissert et al. 1997).

Smaller models with home, community, and residential care components

A second category of continuing care models refers to more community-based, bottom-up models, although there is, in reality, a continuum across these systems. The On Lok (Bodenheimer 1999) and PACE (Eng et al. 1997; Kane et al. 2006; Meret-Hanke 2008; Mukamel et al. 2007) models have community-based care and have to pay for residential and acute care services for people covered by their capitated budgets. There is a clear incentive to make cost-effective trade-offs. The PRISMA model in Quebec (Hébert et al. 2003a; Hébert et al. 2003b; Hébert et al. 2005) relies on voluntary coordination of all community-based providers, including providers of residential care. It is essentially a consensus-based model in which care providers co-operate to provide the best and most cost-effective care for their clients in a given community. Through co-operative activity it would be possible to substitute lower-cost home care services for residential care services.

The PACE models have capitated budgets and are responsible for the provision of home/community and institutional services for their roster of clients. PACE models usually serve clients with higher needs and who are deemed eligible for long-term residential care. While PACE is not a Canadian model, it has influenced Canadian thinking about integrated home/community services. It emerged as a comprehensive service delivery system for seniors with high care needs in the US in the early 1980s (Eng et al. 1997). In 1986, the model was replicated by other non-profit organizations. By 2001, there were 36 PACE sites in 19 states (Greenwood 2001). The programs are run by non-profit organizations. Key program components are: multidisciplinary teams, an adult day health centre and medical clinic, capitated funding, and transportation. PACE centres usually include the following services: primary care, social services, restorative therapies, personal care and supportive services, nutritional counselling, recreational therapy, and meals. Transportation of clients to and from PACE centres, and to other appointments, is provided by PACE site staff.

PACE physicians operate differently from both fee-for-service and health maintenance organization practice models. Clients who are enrolled in a PACE program are required to use only the services of PACE physicians and these physicians share decision-making with other members of the multidisciplinary team. Kane and colleagues (2006) documented the cost-effectiveness of PACE compared to a similar model called the Wisconsin Partnership Program, in which clients were allowed to use their own family physician. The authors found that the PACE model resulted in fewer hospital bed days and fewer emergency room visits. Given that the main difference in the models was the use of PACE physicians compared to the clients' own family physicians, the authors conclude that the PACE physicians were more actively engaged in the care of their clients and that the PACE model was more effective in controlling emergency room and hospital admission rates.

The Quebec model called PRISMA is quite different from PACE. It combines researchers, managers, and policy-makers (Hébert, Tourigny, and Gagnon 2005) (See Figure 6-1). It was created to help develop the mechanisms, processes, and tools necessary for the implementation and analysis of Integrated Services Delivery (ISD) in Quebec. PRISMA offers the full spectrum of geriatric care and services to the senior client, from health promotion/prevention to treatment, rehabilitation, home or residential care, and palliative care. It has six key components: coordination between decision makers at the regional and local levels; a single entry point for access to care and services; case management for service coordination; individualized service plans; a single assessment instrument (with an embedded client classification system called the SMAF[1]); and an electronic clinical chart.

PRISMA was developed on the principle of coordination among organizations. This coordination must be present at all three levels of each organization: strategic, tactical, and clinical. At the strategic or governance level, a joint governing board coordinates policy development and resource allocation. At the tactical or management level, the service coordination committee includes managers from health care and social services organizations and from community agencies. The committee members are responsible for facilitating and monitoring the continuum of service delivery and submitting recommendations to the joint governing board on resource requirements and allocation. At the clinical or operational level, the developers of PRISMA instituted a number of committees comprised of clinical staff and managers that assess and propose improvements to the PRISMA model or to specific services that provide care to frail elderly clients. While the PRISMA model can include people at all levels of care need, the main focus

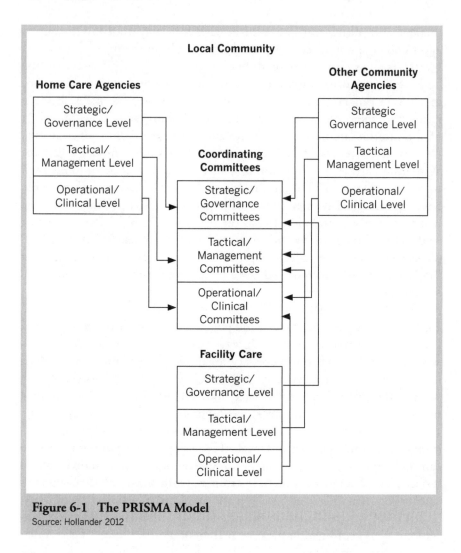

Figure 6-1 The PRISMA Model
Source: Hollander 2012

of PRISMA has been on those identified as frail elderly (in other words, people who would be eligible for placement in long-term care facilities). This local model could form the basis for a broader provincial level system.

There is an ongoing evaluation of the PRISMA model. Hébert and colleagues (2008) found that the model reduced the prevalence and incidence of functional decline, improved satisfaction and empowerment, and decreased visits to emergency rooms compared to a comparison group. Dubuc et al. (2011) found that, in communities with PRISMA, fewer people had unmet needs than in communities without PRISMA.

With the BC, Arizona, and PACE models, the potential for substituting lower-cost home care for higher-cost residential care is clear. In BC, the substitution was facilitated by policy choices made by senior continuing care administrators. In the Arizona and PACE models, cost-effectiveness is achieved by choices to purchase fewer bed days in long-term care facilities and hospitals when care can be provided in the community.

The PRISMA model has the capacity to make cost-effective trade-offs, but here it is more difficult because all community partners must arrive at a consensus about substituting home/community care for residential care in such a way that the overall bed supply is reduced over time and as more clients are looked after in the community. The ability to proactively substitute community care for residential care through coordination, such as is the case for the PRISMA model, may be less than in more structured or capitated models.

Smaller, integrated community-based models

This third category is focused on smaller models that coordinate a wide range of community resources, but do not have administrative or financial control over long-term care facilities or hospitals as part of their system of care. The System of Integrated Care for Older Persons (SIPA) model is a Canadian variant of PACE, but with the SIPA model there was no capitated budget, so there was no financial control over residential or acute care beds. Thus, SIPA was primarily a home- and community-based model. The Rovereto model in Italy and the Hong Kong model also fall into this category. There are also a variety of other attempts to better coordinate home- and community-based services. Examples of such models have been the community health centres (CHCs) in Quebec and the Community Care Access Centres (CCACs) in Ontario. Home and community care programs that are run by provincial or regional health authorities but do not include administrative and budget control over facility care are other examples.

SIPA was a pilot project developed through a joint University of Montreal–McGill University collaboration focusing on the organization, delivery, and financing of integrated services for seniors. It aimed to optimize the use of community, hospital, and institutional resources. The SIPA team maintained clinical responsibility for services, regardless of where the client was referred from (including long-term care facilities). It used intensive case management as part of multidisciplinary teams that generally included social workers, nurses, physicians, home care workers, physiotherapists, and occupational therapists plus, as appropriate, nutritionists and pharmacists. Care was co-managed with family physicians. Each team was responsible for providing a full range of home and community care services and coordinating with hospitals and long-term care facilities. The SIPA model was found to be cost neutral but decreased the use of hospital-based services (Béland et al. 2006a; Béland et al. 2006b). Once the pilot was completed, SIPA did not receive ongoing funding even though it achieved fairly positive evaluation results.

The Rovereto model, developed in Italy, was a one-year demonstration and evaluation project informed, in part, by consultations between senior officials and researchers in BC and Italy. In Rovereto, program developers used a translated version of the BC continuing care application and assessment form (Bernabei et al. 1998, 1349). The evaluation was focused on clients already receiving home and community care. These clients were divided into a control group and an experimental group that received a program of integrated social and medical care. The goal was to determine whether the existing services of primary care—a geriatric hospital unit, a skilled nursing facility, and a home health care agency—could function more effectively if the services were coordinated and integrated. The experimental group received case management and care planning by the community geriatric evaluation unit and general practitioners. All services were provided in an integrated way based on an agreement between the municipality and the local health agency. It was found that those in the control group had greater levels of functional decline, and that on a net basis, where costs of additional services for the intervention group were included, the intervention group had an average lower cost of £1125 per person per year compared to the comparison group (Bernabei et al. 1998).

Hong Kong offers another model to consider. In the late 1990s, health and social care systems in Hong Kong were compartmentalized, with inadequate communication and collaboration across these sectors, resulting in a negative impact on the continuum of care. A health care reform proposal in 2000 focused on restructuring. A change in government financing provided the opportunity to conduct a demonstration and evaluation project on integrated care for the frail elderly. In the project, a control group received usual care, but another group received interventions from a community intervention team composed of case managers, a social worker, and a registered nurse. The team conducted assessments, made regular home visits, developed care plans, and implemented the plans by linking clients to needed services through formal referral processes and routine case conferences. Counselling, and health educational services and support groups were also available. After the intervention, there were greater reductions in hospital admissions and acute bed days for the intervention group compared to the control group. Overall, there was a savings of US$170,448 for the intervention group compared to the control group over a six-month period (Leung et al. 2004). The Rovereto and Hong Kong models were similar in design and achieved similar outcomes.

The final model in this category, the Hospital Admission Risk Program (HARP) in Australia, included frail elderly persons with complex care needs and who had made three or more visits to the emergency department in the past 12 months. HARP consisted of interventions for a 90-day period by a team comprised of a project manager, six care facilitators, and a specialist geriatrician. This was a high-intensity case management and care model. The intervention group received a comprehensive assessment, the development of a care plan, the provision of information, advice, and education, and access to a suite of community-based services. The results revealed that clients in the intervention group had far fewer visits to the emergency department and lower hospital admissions than the control group.

In the examples noted above, results were revenue neutral or showed savings in the intervention group. These types of findings should be referred to as cost avoidance rather than cost-effectiveness, given that cost avoidance refers to alternative services costing less than standard care. They demonstrate the *potential* for cost-effectiveness but do not reduce costs per se. Until there are actual commensurate, or future, substitutions of care (that is, reductions in bed supply), real cost-effectiveness is not achieved. If senior administrators wish to reduce the supply of hospital and long-term care facility beds due to findings such as those noted above, this represents a move from cost-avoidance to cost-effectiveness. However, in reality, cost-effectiveness seems to be best achieved in a system where all component parts are under one administrative umbrella with a single budget envelope, or in a capitation model of funding. If all components are not under one administrative umbrella and budget, administrators across different components (such as hospitals, residential care, and home care) will continue to try to maximize their own budgets. As long as there is pressure on hospital beds, and waiting lists for long-term care facilities, administrators of these services can argue that they continue to be underfunded and need more money, regardless of cost-avoidance arguments coming from home care.

The Chronic Care Model

The primary care literature also offers a model for integrated continuing care focusing on chronic disease management, but it differs substantially from the models we have just discussed. Two of the reasons this model has arisen are as follows: first, it enhances the quality of care doctors can provide to seniors, and, second, it begins to fill the vacuum left when the continuing care component of our health care system was disbanded in favour of other priorities. The chronic care model (CCM) emerged in the US in the late 1990s as the American response to caring for frail elderly patients. The American health care system does not appear to have had a tradition of what we refer to in Canada as *continuing care*. In practice, at least in Canada, continuing care is now also often designed for people with higher-level care needs. The CCM evolved as part of an initiative that included representatives from universities and health-related organizations from across the US (Bodenheimer 2003). It has six components related to chronic care management: community resources; health care organization; self-management support; decision support; delivery system redesign; and clinical information systems. The classic CCM is presented in Figure 6-2 (Wagner et al. 2002). Since its inception, some variations on CCM have been developed, such as the enhanced chronic care model (Barr et al. 2003). The enhanced chronic care model (ECCM) incorporates several population and public health components: build healthy public policy, create supportive environments, and strengthen community action. The BC Ministry of Health recently adopted the enhanced chronic care model

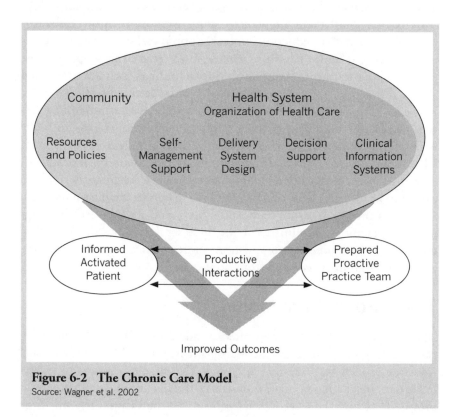

Figure 6-2   The Chronic Care Model
Source: Wagner et al. 2002

as its approach to caring for seniors with medium- to high-care needs (BC Ministry of Health, n.d.).

The CCM and ECCM formulations address a wide range of topics— such as the organization of the overall health care system, healthy public policy, building strong communities, and/or overall decision support systems and information—making it difficult to compare to the continuing care system. However, an examination of the subcomponents of the CCM and ECCM models reveals that they are focused on patient self-management, clinical practice guidelines, clinical education, group visits with family doctors, primary care teams, and case management as well as on clinical and/or disease-specific registries (Bodenheimer 2003). All of the above components except for case management are primary care activities. The chronic care model and the enhanced chronic care model can best be thought of as local, multidisciplinary primary-care organizations with case management that have links with community services. The enhanced chronic care model involves collaborations with population and public health in regard to prevention-related activities.

In the chronic care model, case managers are responsible for assessment, clinical management of care-related services, and support for behaviour change. The case managers develop care plans jointly with clients as part of the self-management component of the CCM. Case managers are also engaged in ongoing follow-up and care coordination across settings (Shaefer and Davis 2004). The local nature of the CCM model is revealed in a seminal article by Wagner and colleagues (2002). In this article, examples of CCM include the following: a multidisciplinary team to reduce readmissions to hospital for patients with congestive heart failure (Rich et al. 1993; Rich et al. 1995); and a travelling expert team that visits primary care clinics to educate front-line providers using disease-specific population-based "Roadmaps" for the delivery of planned care (McCulloch et al. 1998). Other projects include redesigning the structure of a typical office-based group visit (Beck et al. 1997) and protocols for enhanced case management that include client behavioural change and education and that provide reminders and feedback to the primary care team (Aubert et al. 1998). It will take some time to see if the chronic care model gains traction in Canada and how cost-effective it is here.

The primary care chronic disease management approach has been embraced, by some, as the new and preferred alternative to dealing with care for older adults. Chronic disease management is a welcome new development that provides family doctors with the skills to improve care and deliver more appropriate care for their elderly patients. However, it is more of a complement to—rather than a substitute for—a comprehensive, integrated system of continuing care. Thus, a combination of continuing care and chronic disease management can significantly increase the quality of care. The CCM can be a welcome addition, as a type of care for clients with high care needs, within a broader continuing care system that has a range of services and provides care for clients with a range of care needs, from low to high.

Chronic disease management models can improve the quality of care at the home and community level. However, they have several shortcomings when compared to continuing care. Family doctors prefer to focus on medical care—their area of expertise—and most would rather do what they do best than become case managers, arranging for meals programs or fighting with facility administrators regarding admissions and/or the care-related concerns of their clients. If the case management functions are carried out by the staff of the family doctor, considerable additional training would be required. However, a collaborative approach—in which continuing care case managers can be co-located in larger practice settings with a high case load of senior patients—could work well. It could also enhance the quality and continuity of care for clients with high needs.

Chronic care management approaches do not have administrative authority over residential settings or specialty geriatric services in hospitals. They cannot set, nor can they enforce, admission policies. Furthermore, they are not in a position to bring about cost-effectiveness because they cannot proactively substitute home care for residential care. Because major service components are splintered, each component will compete with the other for new funding. One way to deal with this would be to establish a form of general practitioner (GP) fundholding; however, this approach does not yet seem to have been accepted in Canada. The benefits of integrating both horizontal and vertical care through system-level case management may not be adequately realized in a chronic care management model because the focus is on horizontal integration at the community level. In addition, clients will not have a system-level case manager to ensure that their needs are met and that the most appropriate set of services are provided. (Case managers can only do this when they are able to directly authorize services for their clients.)

There are many excellent opportunities for collaboration between family doctors and continuing care staff. To date, though, there does not appear to be data indicating that the chronic care model is at least as, or more effective than, continuing care. In sum, adopting a chronic disease model as a substitute for continuing care would seem to be inappropriate.

Frameworks to Inform the Development of Integrated Systems of Care Delivery

Researchers have developed frameworks for integrated care that can be used as diagnostic tools to determine the effectiveness of existing integrated systems or as guidelines for best practices and to inform the development of new models of integration. The following examines three highly regarded frameworks for these purposes.

Three highly regarded frameworks

One of the best-known frameworks for integrating care delivery was developed by Leutz (1999), who was particularly interested in integrating medical and social care. He focused on the nature of integration, outlining three approaches that are part of a continuum from low-level integration to high-level integration:

- The lowest level is linkage, a population-based approach that begins with screening to identify emerging needs. At this level of integration, people can be cared for in a system that serves the whole population. Thus, the focus for linkage is primarily on clients with low care needs.
- The second level of integration is coordination, which envisions people such as case managers who coordinate care and benefits across services in the existing health and social care system.
- The third level is full integration, which is for individuals with high care needs. At this level of integration, new programs or units are created to provide care, and resources from multiple systems are pooled. The PACE model would be an example of full integration.

For Leutz (1999), various types of activities should be addressed in each of the levels of integration: these include screening, clinical practice, transitions/service delivery, information, case management, finance, benefits, and response to need. The following provides examples of clinical practice at three levels of need:

- At the linkage level, clinical practice would focus on understanding and responding to the needs of persons with disabilities from the existing systems (such as health, social, educational, etc.). There would be no case managers involved at this level of integration.
- At the coordination level, clinical practice would require using key workers such as case managers and discharge planners to coordinate care.

- At the full integration level, a multidisciplinary care team would manage all aspects of care for clients with high care needs. At this level, there would be teams or "super" case managers (e.g., high-intensity case managers) to manage all care.

The focus on level of care needs per se is a relatively unique aspect of this framework.

A second well-known framework for analyzing and guiding the development of integrated systems of care is that of Kodner and Spreeuwenberg (2002). The authors adopted a patient-centric view, with strategies designed to facilitate high-quality, cost-effective care for clients. Their framework consists of five aspects: funding, administration, organization, service delivery, and clinical practice. Funding relates to how the budget operates—for example, by pooling funds (similar to a global budget in Canada) or prepaid capitation. A system's administration relates to such issues as the degree of centralization, whether it is structured like a provincial model that is based on centralization, for example, or a more decentralized regional model. The third aspect is how a system is organized. For example, are staff from different providers co-located? Are discharge and transfer agreements in place? Are programs and/or services jointly managed? The fourth aspect relates to service delivery and covers issues such as the types of case management, integrated information systems, and on-call coverage. The final aspect relates to clinical issues, such as the degree of uniform, comprehensive assessment procedures, continuous patient monitoring, and regular care and support for patients and family members.

A third framework for integrated care was developed by the Care and Management Services for Older People in Europe Network (CARMEN) and is outlined by Banks (2004). The framework "offers a checklist for national and regional policy makers concerned with improving the integration of services for older people" (Banks 2004, i). The CARMEN formulation also has several aspects or components. The first two relate to a clear vision, goals, and rationale, as well as clearly enunciating and integrating the principles and values that guided its development and that continue to guide ongoing service delivery. These components set both the conceptual and value basis for the integrated system. (As well, it should be noted that they are not evident in the Leutz nor Kodner and Spreeuwenberg frameworks.) The next component is "criteria for operational success," which notes that services should be flexible and that there should be appropriate responsibilities and accountabilities. However, while these general statements say what should be, they do not say how to do it. There is less detail here than in the Kodner and Spreeuwenberg framework in terms of specific types of organizational responses and key aspects of service delivery and clinical practice.

The CARMEN framework also notes the importance of coherence with other policies relating to integrated information systems, coherent funding, and support for family caregivers. The other two frameworks also cover funding and financing issues and information systems. CARMEN, however, also includes "active promotion and incentives," such as integration of resources. Although resource issues are also covered in the other two models, they do not appear to have a component that relates directly to the promotion of integrated care. The next component for CARMEN is "evaluation and monitoring." While the other two frameworks refer to integrated information systems and patient monitoring for issues such as care and eligibility, evaluation per se does not seem to appear as a major topic. CARMEN also notes the importance of regulation and inspection, a feature that does not appear in the other two frameworks. The final component is "support for implementing policy" including matters such as input from the broader community, workforce and leadership development, and information systems.

The enhanced continuing care framework

A fourth framework is the Hollander and Prince framework (2007). In an independent review of the four broader frameworks, MacAdam (2008) concludes that the Hollander and Prince (2007) framework of enhanced continuing care is the most comprehensive. For this reason, we provide a more extended overview of this framework, summarizing it with a comparative table from the MacAdam report.

In 2001, Hollander, Prince, and colleagues conducted a comprehensive review of systems of care delivery across Canada for elderly persons and those with disabilities, chronic mental health clients, and children with special needs (in other words, a wide range of people with ongoing care needs). Overall, some 270 senior policy-makers and experts from across Canada were interviewed for the project. There was considerable similarity between the types of services used and the challenges faced in existing systems of care delivery for these four population groups. As a result, Hollander and Prince (2007) developed a framework of best practices for the organization of systems of care delivery, which is referred to as the Enhanced Continuing Care Framework (ECCF). This framework allows for the development of integrated care models that are consistent with local circumstances while still using the broader framework. In this way, it can inform the development of customized service delivery systems for each of the four population groups noted earlier.

The framework was developed based on a combination of previously existing models (such as the BC continuing care model of the early 1990s), interviews with policy-makers (noted earlier), and an analysis of challenges that an integrated system of care should be designed to overcome. The framework, which is presented in Figure 6-3, can be understood as an enhanced and updated approach to organizing continuing care relevant to current circumstances.

In terms of *philosophy and policy*, a belief in the benefits of an integrated system is desirable. There needs to be a commitment to a full range of services to meet care needs and ongoing, sustainable funding. As noted previously, even good systems can fail if they are starved of resources. Older adults have both medical and supportive needs, so that a psychosocial model of care is appropriate. A strictly medical model will not fully address the care needs of seniors for support with ADL and socialization to reduce the deleterious effects of social isolation, for example. A fundamental prerequisite in developing policy and programs is a clear, ongoing proactive review of all care activities and policies to determine how much they benefit the client. Finally, in order to improve care delivery a commitment to an ongoing program of research and evaluation is critical.

With regard to *administrative best practices*, philosophical and policy prerequisites need to be enshrined in a policy document to provide overall guidance for staff and administrators in relation to meeting daily challenges. A single or coordinated administrative structure will reduce the negative impact of service silos on user fees, eligibility requirements, and so on. A single administrative structure also allows for the allocation of resources, development of strategic plans, rationalization of human resources, and the development of an information system for the whole system of care. It is also of benefit clinically given that case managers develop a greater understanding of the nature and scope of the wide range of services in the system.

A single funding envelope is critical for the ability to move money across types of care and service providers in order to maximize value for money. In a segmented or splintered system, problems arise as each type of service (e.g., residential care, home care) tries to maximize its own budget.

An integrated information system also has benefits. It allows for more sophisticated knowledge development, it eliminates the need for multiple assessments, it facilitates strategic planning and accreditation, and it aids the development of, and reporting on, key indicators. This, in turn, facilitates evidence-based management.

With regard to *clinical best practices*, a single or coordinated entry system allows for a smooth entry of clients into the system of care with eligibility and other requirements that are the same for everyone. Single entry also ensures that only those with appropriate care needs enter the system, and the

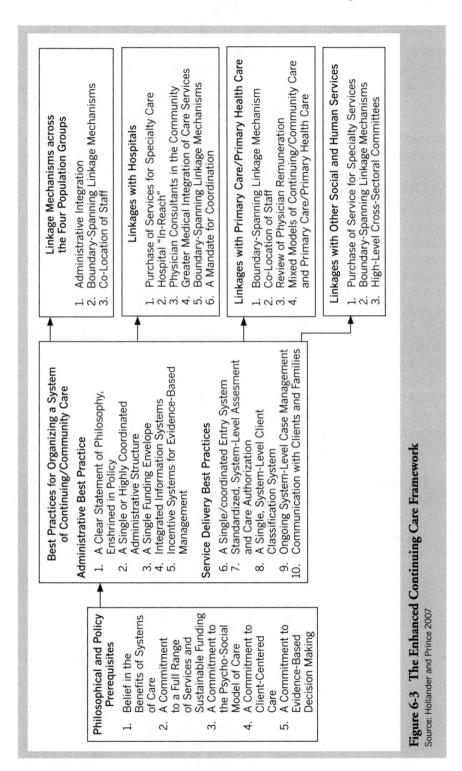

Figure 6-3   The Enhanced Continuing Care Framework

Source: Hollander and Prince 2007

system provides "one-stop shopping" for all applicants. System-level assessment, care authorization, and case management ensure appropriate assessments of need and ongoing reassessments. Case managers can serve as advocates and advisors for care delivery across a wide range of services in the integrated systems of care, and with other components of the health care system. In certain systems they can also provide an independent assessment of care levels that are linked to reimbursement, rather than, for example, residential care facilities determining funding-linked care levels themselves.

A client classification system embedded in a system-level assessment tool is critical to making apples-to-apples comparisons across sites of care in relation to future planning and value-for-money analyses. For example, if cost-effectiveness evaluations are required, the level of care need must be standardized across sites of care on a consistent basis. In terms of planning, identifying less expensive services that provide the same or better quality of care helps in planning the extent and mix of services going forward.

Finally, a greater involvement of clients and families in the care process is both beneficial and highly appreciated by clients and family members. Case managers can involve family members in developing care plans, refer them to helpful information, and act as advocates and advisors if they have questions or complaints on a range of issues.

There are a number of *linkage mechanisms* that can be developed to facilitate care between continuing care services and other components of the health care system. Developing these linkages can serve to facilitate more seamless care for clients across the health care system. Several key types of linkage mechanisms can be used:

- Boundary-spanning linkage mechanisms refer to the proactive designation of key staff to develop relationships or "linkages" with other parts of the health and social care systems. For example, case managers, by the nature of their work, work with family physicians in relation to care planning, and with hospitals in relation to admissions and discharges. Continuing care administrators can also develop linkages with their counterparts in hospitals, public health, and primary care organizations. Finally, home care physician consultants can build relationships with family doctors and hospital-based physicians to facilitate care transitions for home care clients.
- Co-location of staff refers to continuing care staff being located in the same physical space as, for example, public health staff, hospital emergency departments (as part of quick response teams), and/or primary care health centres or larger physician group practices.
- Purchase of service agreements refers to the ability of continuing care staff to purchase needed services within the system from third-party

providers (for example, care authorization for home care agencies and geriatric assessments) or to fund such services directly (for example, funding a geriatric unit in a hospital). It can also refer to authorizing purchases from outside the system (such as medical equipment) and appropriate services provided by local community centres.

- High-level cross-sectoral committees refers to committees where senior administrators from various components of the health care system exchange information, resolve cross-sectoral issues, and work to develop policies to facilitate the continuity of care across sectors.

The ability to make cost-effective substitutions is provided by the structure of the service delivery system. Chappell and Hollander (2011) show how lower-cost home care can be substituted for higher-cost residential care. As noted in Chapter 5, the ability to substitute home care for residential care in BC resulted in annual cost avoidance of some $150 million per year in 1995 compared to what the costs would have been if 1985 utilization rates had remained in place until 1995.

It is interesting to compare international perspectives on integrated care. One feature of the American literature on systems of care delivery is that much of it focuses on vertically integrated systems that include services from home care and primary care to acute care. Managed care organizations, health maintenance organizations (HMOs), and PACE are examples. Writing on the PRISMA model in Quebec, Hébert and colleagues (2010) specifically note that their approach is an Integrated Service Delivery (ISD) system that is, in fact, vertically integrated. In contrast, much of the Canadian literature has focused on enhanced, horizontally integrated systems such as the chronic care model, SIPA, and other models that primarily focus on home and community-based care, including primary care. In contrast, the ECCF is both horizontally *and* vertically integrated where the integration of all services is achieved by system-level case managers who can facilitate care and care trajectories from simple home support activities to specialized care in acute care geriatric centres. The horizontal and vertical aspects of continuing care, and the wide range of associated services that would be appropriate for older adults, is demonstrated in Figure 6-4.

Finally, it is instructive to follow what could happen to clients in an updated continuing care system. This is demonstrated in Figure 6-5. Here, we see older persons entering the system, being given an assessment and care plan, and admitted to appropriate community, residential, or hospital-based care.

MacAdam (2008) compared the three frameworks noted previously with the best practices contained in the Enhanced Continuing Care Framework. Table 6-2 reveals commonalities across the four frameworks,

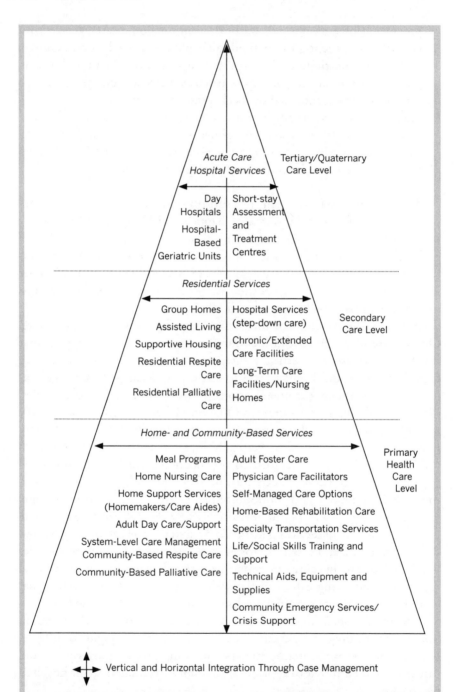

Figure 6-4   Application of the Enhanced Continuing Care Framework to Older Persons
Source: Hollander and Prince 2007

e

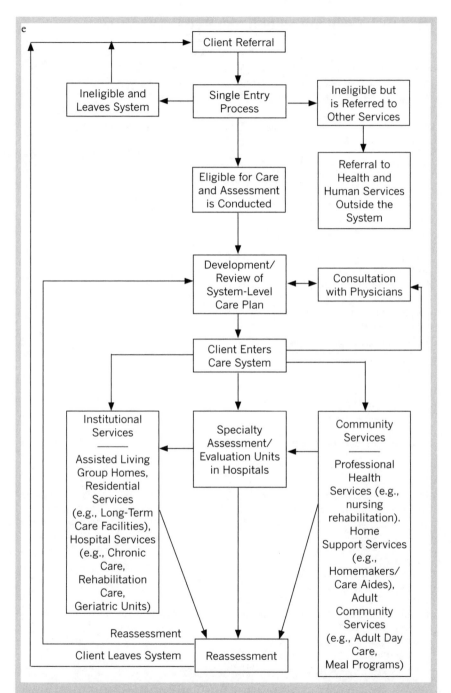

Figure 6-5   A Schematic of Client Flow through the System of Care for Older Persons
Source: Adapted from Hollander and Prince 2007

Table 6-2 Comparison of Integrated Frameworks

	Frameworks		
Enhanced Continuing Care Framework—Hollander and Prince (2007)	**Leutz (1999)**	**Kodner and Spreeuwenberg (2002)**	**Care and Management Services for Older People in Europe (CARMEN)— Banks (2004)**
Philosophical and Policy Prerequisites			
1. Belief in the benefits of systems of care 2. A commitment to a full range of services and sustainable funding 3. A commitment to the psycho-social model of care 4. A commitment to client-centred care 5. A commitment to evidence-based decision-making	No mention	No mention	Yes
Administrative Best Practices			
1. A clear statement of philosophy, enshrined in policy	No mention	No Mention	Not mentioned as such but implied
2. A single or highly coordinated administrative structure	No mention	Yes	No mention
3. A single funding envelope	No mention	Yes	Coherent funding systems
4. Integrated information systems	Yes	Yes	Yes
5. Incentive systems for evidence-based management	No mention	Common decision support tools	Yes, incentives and sanctions
Clinical Best Practices			
1. A single/coordinated entry system	Yes	Yes	No mention
2. Standardized system-level assessment and care authorization	Yes	Yes	No mention
3. A single, system-level client classification system	No mention	No mention	No mention
4. Ongoing system-level case management	Yes	Yes	No mention
5. Communication with clients and families	No mention	Yes	Support for caregivers

Table 6-2 (cont'd)

| | Frameworks | | |
Enhanced Continuing Care Framework—Hollander and Prince (2007)	Leutz (1999)	Kodner and Spreeuwenberg (2002)	Care and Management Services for Older People in Europe (CARMEN)— Banks (2004)
Linkage Mechanisms across the Four Population Groups			
1. Administrative integration	No mention	Consolidation/ decentralization of responsibilities	No mention
2. Boundary-spanning linkage mechanisms	Yes	Yes	No mention but implied
3. Co-location of staff	No mention	Yes	No mention
Linkages with Hospitals			
1. Purchase of services for specialty care	No mention	Yes	No mention
2. Hospital "in-reach"	No mention	No mention	No mention
3. Physician consultations in the community	No mention	Jointly managed care services	No mention
4. Greater medical integration of care services	No mention	Jointed managed care services	Awarding responsibilities to integrate services
5. Boundary-spanning linkage mechanisms	Yes	Yes	No mention
6. A mandate for coordination	No mention	Strategic alliances or care networks	Awarding responsibilities to integrate
Linkages with Primary Care/Primary Health Care			
1. Boundary-spanning linkage mechanisms	No mention	Yes	No mention but implied
2. Co-location of staff	No mention	Yes	No mention
3. Review of physician remuneration	No mention	No mention	Resourcing integration
4. Mixed model of continuing/ community care and primary care/primary health care	No mention	Strategic alliances or care networks	No mention
Linkages with Other Social and Human Services			
1. Purchase of service for specialty services	No mention	Joint purchasing commissioning	Resourcing integration
2. Boundary-spanning linkage mechanisms	No mention	Yes	No mention but implied
3. High-level cross-sectoral committees	Yes	Inter-sectoral planning	No mention

Source: MacAdam 2008

but the ECCF is the most comprehensive. MacAdam does, however, point out that capitated funding and joint or coordinated planning are not noted in the Hollander and Prince framework. Nevertheless, although they are not stated, they are implied. Continuing care usually has a clear and fixed budget allocation that functions like capitation to the extent that administrators have the freedom to reallocate resources as appropriate. At senior levels there is usually coordinated planning with leaders from other parts of the health sector.

Discussion

While all of the aspects noted above are relevant, there are four critical success factors for achieving cost-effectiveness in integrated systems of care.

- The first is to include under one administrative structure all of the major components of professional and supportive services in home/community settings, sheltered housing, long-term care facilities, and specialty services in acute care settings (such as geriatric assessment and treatment units). One administrative structure enables policy-making and resource allocation to take place within a broad systems perspective.
- The second is to create one budget envelope for all of these services, thus enabling resources to be adjusted to lower cost settings (while maintaining an equal or better quality of care).
- The third is to use an assessment and classification system that can be used at a system level to determine care needs and that applies to all clients irrespective of their site of care. At present, the only Canadian tool that meets these criteria is the SMAF, used in Quebec. In contrast, there are separate tools and classification systems known as the InterRAI for each major type of service. In other words, the tools are limited to the type of care for which they were designed. To meet our criteria, InterRAI would have to develop an overarching system-level assessment and classification tool.
- A fourth factor is case management at the system level, where the case manager, or care coordinator, has the authority not only to navigate and coordinate care, but also to authorize needed care for clients. In this system-level approach, the case manager functions as an advisor and advocate for the client and his or her family wherever the client goes in the system. In most jurisdictions, case managers have traditionally transferred case management responsibilities to facility staff when a client is admitted to residential care. However, case managers at the system level are essential for several reasons. Because the case managers go into supportive housing and residential care, they can provide an early

warning system for potential issues or declines in the quality of care. They can also build relationships with administrators and clinicians in residential and community settings that allow them to more effectively deal with potential issues and concerns their clients and/or family caregivers may have. Clients are not static: they can go from home to facility, from supportive housing to residential care, from residential care to hospitals and, in some cases, back again from more expensive to less-expensive settings. Transitions are often complex, and can be handled well or handled poorly. A systems level case manager should significantly improve the continuity of care and the odds of transitions being handled well.

With these four success factors, continuing care administrators can go a long way to bringing about value for money by substituting lower-cost care for higher-cost care, while maintaining or improving care quality. They can also better plan for future needs by making robust cost comparisons because people are classified in the same way irrespective of the care setting. Clients and their family members can have good continuity of care if they are aided by a case manager providing assistance at every step of their journey.

Conclusion

In this chapter, several models and frameworks of integrated care were discussed. The ECCF model is different from most other models considered for aging populations: it envisions a system that addresses all levels of legitimate care needs and a professional assessment determines a client's needs. At the lowest level of care need, this could mean as little as five to six hours of assistance per month to carry out activities that clients find difficult to do by themselves, such as household chores, shopping for food, and so on. As light as this care might seem, it matters and is preventive; failure to provide this type of care can lead to more rapid deterioration in client function and increased costs to the health care system. At the highest care levels, clients might need long-term care and acute care. In most of the other approaches discussed earlier in this chapter, the focus is only clients with higher care needs, such as those who would otherwise be admitted to a long-term care facility, or assisted living/sheltered housing setting.

Policy-makers today have established models designed for clients with higher care needs and/or reallocated funds to those with greater care needs. However, this results in raising the eligibility floor for who is, and is not, eligible for care. This results in a system where everyone other than high-needs individuals have to find their own ways to cope, placing more demands on informal caregivers. Those who cannot afford to pay privately will have no option but to turn to families or to go without. In all likelihood, this will further exacerbate an increasing cost spiral as people who are no longer eligible for care have accidents or wear themselves out, leading to more rapid and/or frequent admissions to hospitals or long-term care facilities. However, focusing on *all* levels of care needs can overcome this trend toward still higher costs by providing preventive care that reduces the rate of admissions to hospitals and long-term care facilities, facilitating the cost-effectiveness of continuing care.

Chapter 7

A Path Forward

Introduction

This book began with an outline of the facts about Canada's aging population. Virtually all people in Canada can now expect to live to old age. With the baby boomers entering later life, there will be a swell in both the numbers of people who are elderly and their proportion within the Canadian population. This has raised alarms that the public health care system will go bankrupt.

The purpose of this book is twofold. One purpose is to examine the facts and present a reasoned argument that future demands on the health care system are not primarily fuelled by older adults per se (demographic determinism), but there are needs for care that will likely increase. That is, there is an issue, but it is not insurmountable and not primarily attributable to older adults. The second purpose is to describe how health care is provided and how it *could* be in an appropriate and cost-effective health care system. While there are cost pressures and potential solutions in the broader health care system, our analysis focuses on how to enhance value for money. These suggestions have the potential to improve the cost-effectiveness of the broader health care system. Clearly, however, this is just one part of the puzzle. If cost increases continue to escalate in other parts of the system (for example, prescription drugs), this will dampen the benefits of any efficiencies achieved in continuing care.

We began by examining the numbers and needs of older adults. Numbers are increasing, but it is worth remembering that not everyone requires care, and those who do need care do not require it all of the time or at the same level. A closer examination of the health status of older adults reveals that we develop more chronic conditions and functional disabilities as we age, but a diagnosis of a chronic condition does not necessarily translate into functional difficulties. Typically, it is when we have trouble with functioning that care is needed and this varies from individual to individual even among those with similar chronic conditions. It is those individuals who are old elderly, living alone, isolated, and in poverty who are the most likely to require the most care. Intriguingly, we saw that subjective well-being or life satisfaction does not seem to decline and most certainly does not do so in correspondence to declines in physical health. Rather, older adults as a group reveal high levels of happiness.

For those older adults who do experience sufficiently poor health to require assistance, the most prevalent source of care, by far, is the informal network of family and friends. This is true across cultures, irrespective of cultural beliefs in filial responsibility, irrespective of changing times and changing family forms, and irrespective of the demands and burdens of providing that care. Informal caregivers typically provide care willingly and want to continue helping, but the caregivers themselves may at times also require assistance. However, like older adults, it is only a portion of caregivers who require assistance. Not all do, and not all who do require assistance permanently or continuously.

Projecting from what we know about those who are elderly today suggests there will be more older adults in need of care in the future. And if more people in poor health survive longer, care needs could increase even more, which could then increase the demands on informal networks and the care these caregivers need themselves. However, we do not know what the health of baby boomers will be as they age and consequently their care needs, nor do we know how their informal networks will evolve as time goes by. If health in old age improves over what it has been for previous generations, and the formal system does not provide unproven interventions, then costs for the formal system could go down.

How do the informal network and the formal system combine to care for older people, and how could they? In Canada, we have a complex provincial and federal interplay that has developed a formal system with a focus on medical care (physicians and acute care hospitals); these are the two most expensive forms of care. Only these forms of care have universal coverage. However, as noted earlier, the informal network provides more care for older people than does the formal system. There is research indicating that the public provision of support services does not lead to families abandoning care, and we also know that several countries around the world are providing substantially more formal support for caregivers than Canada provides. Both compassion (assisting those who are in need as a result of assisting others) and logic (supporting those who are providing the care without payment so they can prolong their involvement) dictate that caregivers should be supported. This can occur through both formal services for older adults and for caregivers themselves. To do this, we do not have to start from scratch. We are dealing with an existing formal system (or assortment of systems) with a particular history and idiosyncratic characteristics, and we also know much from the experience of other countries.

In older age, it is chronic conditions and functional disability that we tend to suffer from—ailments for which there are no cure, and for which medicine has no magic bullet. Rather, in older age, the goal is to maximize functioning, independence, and quality of life to the extent possible. This may mean maintenance of the status quo and hopefully prevention of further declines in functioning. This typically requires support with day-to-day living, not medical intervention. This is *not* to deny the importance of physicians and acute care hospitals, nor does it deny that older adults sometimes suffer from diseases and conditions that benefit from medical care. What this does mean is that medicine is not always—and very often is not at all—the appropriate form of care to assist individuals coping with chronic conditions. And medicine is typically not the type of assistance that informal caregivers require with their caregiving.

Rather, it is those services encapsulated within a continuing care system that most older adults require, particularly those with chronic conditions and functional difficulties. Typically such help is needed in order to maintain independence in the community. These services, at present, are not universal in Canada and with recent health care reforms have been drastically altered over the last 20 years to focus much more on short-term post–hospital care at the expense of long-term care. It is these services, especially long-term home care (but also other formal continuing care services) that have been our focus. The history of this sector is important because it points to the necessity of different types of services required by older adults due to medical necessity, but some of which have at times and within certain jurisdictions, been viewed more as social welfare than health services.

Canada is at a juncture. At a time when Canada's population overall is aging, do we want to provide only medical care by physicians and acute care in hospitals? In such a model, all other services would be left to the good, or bad, fortune of individuals, families, and friends.

We have provided much research evidence on the cost-effective potential of continuing care. In this system, appropriate services meet the chronic care needs of an aging society. At the same time, the system allows older adults to remain in their own homes for as long as possible—the desire of virtually all older adults. That is, not only are continuing care services appropriate in their own right to assist those requiring care, they also can be a cost-effective tool for the broader health care system if appropriately integrated and implemented.

In this chapter, we describe a series of steps to craft long-term, sustainable solutions by enhancing policy and programs in the continuing care sector. While we currently live in a somewhat politicized environment, the proposals that follow are presented in the hope that they will be considered on their merits alone rather than from an ideological, or party political, viewpoint. Enhancing the value for money of our health care system and doing right by our seniors, are goals that can be supported by all political parties in a non-partisan manner. An example of this non-partisan approach would be the 2010 multi-party committee called the Canadian Parliamentary Committee on Palliative and Compassionate Care (Chappell and Hollander 2010).

A Critical First Step

First and foremost, all levels of government should make a deliberate policy choice to recognize enhanced continuing care as a major component of our health care system. This policy choice will determine whether we can move forward with a best-practices approach rather than continue to provide suboptimal care. At present there are hospitals to assist people with acute conditions, medical care for the general population, and population and public health to address key determinants of health and ensure safe living environments but no component specifically designed to meet the needs of seniors and others with ongoing care needs. Chronic disease management, in our view, is a complement to, but not a substitute for, a comprehensive continuing care system.

The validation and recognition of continuing care as a major component of Canada's health care system is a critical first step. Recognition will set the foundation for the following advances in:

- clinical practice;
- information systems;
- the organization of service delivery; and
- achieving greater value for money in our health care system.

Twenty Years of Policy Drift

The report entitled *Future Directions in Continuing Care* prepared by the Federal/Provincial/Territorial Subcommittee on Continuing Care and published in 1992 could have been written today. If it were written today, it would still be seen as a progressive, visionary document for the future. This document presents a consolidated view of the leading administrators and policy-makers from each province and territory at the time and represents a consensus among senior officials responsible for continuing care service delivery across Canada in the early 1990s. The principles proposed to guide reform appear in Table 7-1, and the strategic policy and program directions proposed to improve continuing care services appear in Table 7-2. Unfortunately, just after the report was released, the Subcommittee on Continuing Care was disbanded as part of a major restructuring, leaving little time or impetus to bring about the recommended changes. This was particularly true in a policy climate focused on regionalization and primary care.

Why are we talking about a 20-year-old report? How can it be relevant to today's realities? The reason is that this report still has the potential to help move us forward and to facilitate positive change for a future with a larger population that is elderly and that includes individuals with ongoing care needs. The same thinking that is found in the *Future Directions* report is reflected in current opinion in the continuing care sector. The *Future Directions* report is as insightful and progressive as any of the recent reports noted at the end of Chapter 4.

This report also shows how our ideas today are an extension of previously existing, made-in-Canada solutions to developing a complex health and social services delivery system. Federal and provincial officials regularly search for international solutions for improving the delivery of services for seniors. However, in the early 1990s, the world was looking to Canada for solutions, and enhanced versions of some of the practices being used at that time are applicable today. In the late 1980s and early 1990s, an Italian expert task force was commissioned by Italy's president to study the best systems of care delivery in the world in order to inform the development of care for older adults in that country. After examining the systems in a number of countries, that task force was impressed by the BC system— what could also be referred to as the western Canadian model of continuing care. The task force concluded that the BC system was one of the best in the world. Subsequently a series of consultations took place in Italy at which leading academics, senior administrators, and policy-makers from across the country met with a senior BC representative to discuss what could be learned and potentially applied to Italy. As was seen in Chapter 6, in the section entitled "Larger Provincial Models," the example of the BC continuing care model from the 1990s is still robust, even from an international perspective.

The same thinking that is found in the *Future Directions* report is reflected in current opinion in the continuing care sector. Since the release of the *Future Directions* report, there have been 20 years of policy drift and lost opportunities to improve care for seniors. Will we continue to drift?

Will policy-makers recognize that the care of older adults should be a high priority issue, and implement an optimal model for care delivery?

To describe the last 20 years as we have is not to suggest that good efforts at the provincial level have been absent; there have indeed been good efforts, which deserve to be recognized and applauded. However, there have been at least two major headwinds inhibiting such efforts. One is the absence of national policy recognizing, or supporing, the development of

Table 7-1 Proposed Continuing Care Principles

The following principles are recommended to guide the development of continuing care:

- The continuing care system should be planned, developed, funded, and managed to contribute to the health and well-being of Canadians.
- Each component of the continuing care system, as well as its purpose and interaction with other components, should be defined clearly to allow it to function as an integral part of the overall health system and social service systems.
- Communities should be enabled to plan, develop services, and set priorities for effective continuing care in the context of the overall health system and, by so doing, assume greater responsibility for their health.
- Community-based care should be the service of first option where appropriate; public and professional attitudes consistent with this shift should be fostered.
- Every effort should be made to maximize the autonomy and independence of individuals; the service system should be designed to respond to unmet needs.
- The purpose of continuing care should be to supplement or support, not replace, family and community caregiving.
- There should be a rationalization of resources used, both provincially and locally as well as across all sectors.
- Continuing care services should be developed to support the lowest cost alternative appropriate to the needs of the individual.
- Funding for continuing care programs should be sufficiently stable and flexible to ensure the appropriate development of the sector, specifically in the area of home care and compressed demands in institutions.
- Funding policies at both the federal and provincial levels should provide incentives to shift the focus from institutional to community care.
- There should be a balance between generic and specialized services, to address differing needs and to provide an appropriate range of options.
- Professionals should be encouraged to utilize the appropriate resources in keeping with the needs of the client.
- Appropriate care services should be reasonably accessible to all Canadians and should be provided in the home or as close to home as possible and whenever possible in the language of choice of the client.
- Eligibility policies for the provinces should recognize the reality of the mobility of Canadians.
- All continuing care programs should establish quality assurance mechanisms and be subject to monitoring and evaluation.

Source: Based on Federal/Provincial/Territorial Subcommittee on Continuing Care, 1992 , iv, v

Table 7-2 Future Directions for Continuing Care

In order to deal with the challenges facing continuing care, it is recommended that the following eleven strategies be adopted as broad directions for its development:

- **Adopting a systems perspective:** A systems perspective promotes the reduction of historical barriers between service categories in government and in industry. An integration of services using a flexible budgeting process is recommended to facilitate the transfer of priority for new resources from residential services to community services. It may also enhance transfers of funding from the acute sector to continuing care to deal with the increasing number of elderly and disabled people requiring services.
- **Adopting a healthy public policy perspective:** This promotes greater intersectoral collaboration with related government sectors, such as housing. It also promotes local empowerment and the development of partnerships at the local level.
- **Maximizing efficiency and effectiveness:** Examples of efficiency and effectiveness include removing negative or perverse utilization incentives, developing good strategic planning, and conducting cost-effectiveness studies. Funding incentives should support the provision of lower-cost, less intrusive services, where appropriate. Adopting managed entry into continuing care, through a single-entry system, can increase the efficiency and effectiveness of the system and consumer access to it.
- **Providing comprehensive, flexible, holistic, and appropriate services:** A comprehensive range of services should be developed and made available in each jurisdiction. There should be an emphasis on community-based care, and consideration should be given to the extent to which alternatives to traditional medical care should be made available.
- **Providing support for informal caregivers, volunteers, families, and communities:** Family members, friends, and other non-paid persons provide the majority of services to those in need. Their efforts should be supported.
- **Using technology efficiently:** The criteria used for client access to technology, drugs, supplies, and equipment should not contain incentives to deliver higher-cost services. Further research and evaluation should be conducted with regard to the use of new and existing technology in the home setting.
- **Addressing emerging needs:** Continuing care services are provided to a range of clients. The special service requirements of such clients, for example multicultural and multilingual clients, should be addressed.
- **Changing public and professional attitudes:** Steps should be taken to legitimize the use of community-based services in the eyes of the public, professionals, and funders.
- **Addressing human resource issues:** A comprehensive human resources strategy, which includes appropriate human resources planning and training, should be developed for continuing care.
- **Ensuring accountability:** An appropriate system to ensure accountability should be developed which incorporates quality assurance, evaluation, fiscal management, and value-for-money auditing. It should also encourage participation from the varied parties involved in the continuing care system.
- **Using research and analysis:** Strategic plans for analysis should be developed that are congruent with the overall strategic plans for the continuing care sector. Special studies should be conducted into key areas of service delivery and administration.

Source: Based on Federal/Provincial/Territorial Subcommittee on Continuing Care, 1992, v, vi

the continuing care. This is reflected in the provisions of the 2004 Health Accord and major federal reports that only focus on short-term and specialty home care. The second headwind is the current policy environment. Change is difficult most of the time but especially so in the current climate. However, if there is a national consensus, particularly among the elites, change in continuing care could happen quite quickly. Witness the rapidity and comprehensiveness of regionalization and primary care reforms once the high-level decision makers supported the initiatives.

A Response to the Skeptics

There are a number of points that could be raised against our proposal. We address them in the following.

"The cost-effectiveness data no longer apply"

The same results regarding the cost-effectiveness of home care (for people with similar care needs) emerge across time and across jurisdictions. The weight of the evidence (see Chapter 5) now clearly supports home care as a cost-effective alternative to residential care for individuals at the intermediate level of care need. Until there is a sufficient body of evidence to show that, for people with similar care needs, home care does not cost less than residential care or cannot prevent the use of higher-cost services, the current evidence supports the view that it does.

Tertiary prevention—in other words, using low levels of home support services—can also be cost-effective in reducing admissions to hospitals and long-term care facilities. This allows people to remain at home for as long as it is feasible and safe to do so. Failure to provide preventive home support services can lead to costs spiralling upward because of increased demands on hospitals and long-term care facilities (Chappell and Hollander 2011). When costs are allowed to spiral upward in this way, we are, in effect, favouring high-cost acute and residential care over low-cost home support services, thus contributing to the rise in the cost of health care as a percentage of gross domestic product.

There is another way to consider the issue of cost-effectiveness. Existing systems may already have reached a high level of cost-effectiveness because most or all of the people are optimally allocated to home care and residential care. In such a system, cost-effectiveness will already have been achieved. An appropriate way to test whether overall cost-effectiveness has been achieved would be to conduct a study of new patients destined for facility care to see how many could *not* be cared for in the community even if the same monthly costs to the government for a facility bed were put to creative use for home and community care.[1] Another approach would be to examine the extent of overlap between home care and facility care for people at the intermediate to high levels of care need in a given jurisdiction. The lower the overlap, the greater the system's efficiencies. However, this approach is problematic as even very high-level care needs clients can be cared for at home with the right resources.

"Actual savings are not possible"

Some might argue that there are no real savings because, for example, there are no bed closures to actually reduce facility costs. This is true; however, it is not the whole story. In the examples provided, if there are savings to be obtained they represent increases in systems efficiencies (i.e., greater value for money) and can best be thought of as cost avoidance. It is highly unlikely that even the most effective innovation will result in actual annual cost savings in a given year (unless one cuts services elsewhere, for example, by closing hospital or long-term care beds). This is because there are explicit, or implicit, waiting lists for services, such as admission to a long-term care facility or surgical waiting lists. Our health care system is not funded to operate at full capacity, allowing everyone to receive services immediately. Furthermore, the difference between actual operating capacity and optimal operating capacity is unknown, but significant. Thus, for any innovation to save money in a given fiscal year, the innovation would have to be sufficiently robust to eliminate the differential between actual and optimal capacity and overcome the tendency to provide more services when there is excess capacity (i.e., the "a built bed is a filled bed" phenomenon). The innovation would have to overcome both obstacles to result in actual savings.

To make the argument that savings do not exist because they cannot be realized in a given fiscal year is a spurious argument. What can be achieved is greater efficiency and effectiveness for the system as a whole. Over time, these efficiencies can be used to slow the rate of growth of future health care expenditures on hospital and long-term care beds, if such expenditures are pro-active and are made in the context of a knowledge of potential new efficiencies. It seems clear that efficiencies through innovations have a longer-term cost savings effect in relation to avoiding future costs. As noted previously this occurred over a ten-year period from the mid-1980s to the mid-1990s in BC by holding back new bed construction and reinvesting the funds into home care. This proactive approach to realizing efficiencies resulted in significant annual cost avoidance by the mid-1990s.

Finally, some may argue that budgets have been constrained and services have been cut so much that actual efficiencies can no longer be obtained. For example, they may note that current budgets only allow for care provision for medium to high care needs clients (such as those cared for in a CCM), and thus, expanding services back to lower care needs clients is not feasible. Given existing conditions this may be a reasonable position to hold. However, in our view, what has been accomplished by policy in such a situation is cost savings by budget restraints but no, or few, efficiencies have been achieved. Furthermore, this approach has reduced the overall quality of care by disenfranchising large numbers of seniors from home care. Thus, the savings have been obtained at the expense of the quality of care.

It is our view that low-level care needs clients can be added back into the mix with a temporary infusion of money. The cost-effectiveness of tertiary prevention, noted in Chapter 5, will then come into play and delay admissions to hospitals and long-term care facilities for the low-level care needs clients who are added back into the system of care. The argument for the continuing care approach rests on being able to provide care to more people, thus increasing the overall efficiency and quality of care, for roughly the same amount of money as is being spent now. This would, however, require being able to reduce, over time, the growth in facility and hospital beds, commensurate with the decrease in demand through tertiary prevention for lower care needs clients. This would be a challenge but, with good management, it is fairly readily achievable in an integrated continuing care system.

"Large scale change is not feasible"

Change is, indeed, difficult. However, if there is a clear consensus on direction combined with the political will to make it happen, change can take place quite quickly. Furthermore, there is evidence that rapid change is possible. For example, an integrated long-term care program with home/community and facility services was developed and fully implemented in less than one year in 1977 in BC. There was a well-thought-out plan and clear political direction from the government to make it happen. The program became operational on 1 January 1978. The move to regionalization in Canada was also accomplished fairly quickly (and in a climate of economic constraint in the 1990s), as was a shift in policy focus to primary care. Governments can bring about desired change under the following conditions: governments must know what is to be accomplished (that is, have a clear plan); they must have legitimacy, feasibility, and support for the plan; they must have effective change agents; and they must have the political will to bring about change.

This book outlines what could be done to simultaneously provide better care and save money. What is needed is a dialogue at senior levels of government, preferably at the federal–provincial level, to reach a consensus on how continuing care systems should be organized. Some federal–provincial vehicles such as SUFA, or the upcoming 2014 Health Accord, could be used for this purpose. Alternatively, provincial governments could restructure their service delivery systems on their own.

Finally, even the best systems can fail if overall funding is insufficient. Any system requires sustainable funding on an ongoing basis and a range of services that is extensive enough to meet client needs.

Getting It Right

The first and foremost action is for governments to validate continuing care as a major component of our health care system. This should be done at the level of the federal, provincial, and territorial First Ministers, and/ or Ministers of Health, or the Conference of Deputy Ministers of Health. Once this recognition is achieved one can develop a blueprint for action to develop and implement an enhanced continuing care system in Canada, as follows:

• Adopt the principles and strategies noted in Tables 7-1 and 7-2 as major guide posts for developing an enhanced continuing care system in Canada.
• Adopt the enhanced continuing care framework as a set of guidelines that can be adapted to local circumstances for the development of specific models of continuing care. For a more local approach, the PRISMA model has potential, particularly if there is a built-in ability to make cost-effective trade-offs. Both approaches could be enhanced by incorporating the chronic care model (CCM) as an important component for clients with high care needs.
• Categorize costs in such a way that existing costs can be easily determined within the national health expenditure accounts and Canadian Institute for Health Information (CIHI) reports. This will validate, and bring to the attention of policy-makers, the fact that a continuing care system would be the third largest component of public expenditures in health care. In fact, a recent custom examination of CIHI's National Health Expenditures database confirms that, even if one were only to consider the currently funded components of continuing care, they would indeed constitute the third largest component of public expenditures on health. A recognition of this reality would, we hope, bring about a refreshed and more robust policy focus on continuing care than has been the case over the past two decades. In other words, it would recognize that Canada is already spending the money and that better results could be achieved by coordinating existing services.

- Establish Assistant Deputy Minister and Vice-President positions responsible for continuing care, within provincial governments and regional health authorities.
- Develop a Federal/Provincial/Territorial Advisory Committee on Continuing Care. Continuing care is complex and evolving in many different directions at the present time. The federal/provincial/territorial committee would provide a forum for discussion and for developing a consensus about how continuing care should evolve into the future.
- Adopt the SMAF or develop a new system-level assessment and classification instrument at CIHI that will allow for apples-to-apples comparisons of clients, irrespective of the site of care. In other words, develop a system-level assessment and classification tool. A new instrument based on the InterRAI tools could also fulfill this purpose.
- Recognize the dual role of unpaid caregivers—both as potential recipients in need of assistance and as partners in care for older adults. When assistance is required, ensure it is available and accessible. It is important to keep in mind the contributions of unpaid caregivers: it is estimated that caregivers age 45 and over contribute as much as $25 billion annually to health care compared to what it would cost to have paid home care staff provide services (Hollander, Liu, and Chappell 2009). Furthermore, as noted in previous chapters, there are several other factors to remember: there is no evidence indicating these caregivers can undertake more care than they are currently providing; current evidence (see Chapter 3) refutes claims that the provision of formal care to either caregivers themselves or older adults in need results in less informal care; and that caregivers themselves risk deteriorating health if they continue undertaking excessive demands over prolonged periods of time without any assistance. It makes sense to support caregivers.
- Provide funding for more focused policy research and analysis. Developing partnerships with universities to conduct the research needed to inform critical policy choices is one option (Manitoba provides an example). Developing rapid-response and policy-relevant research approaches on a contractual basis is another option. An example of this approach is the Knowledge Development System, which provides a comprehensive approach to developing new and policy-relevant knowledge using both quantitative and qualitative analysis (Hollander, Corbett, and Pallan 2010). Examples of important research topics in a Knowledge Development System for continuing care could include studies on the following:
    - the extent to which cost-effective substitution of home care for residential and acute-care services is still possible within current systems—that is, develop an estimate of the potential size of future

cost avoidance to the health care system by adopting an integrated continuing care system;

- the cost-effectiveness of tertiary prevention—that is, substituting low-cost home support services for residential and acute care, and, conversely, estimating the additional costs of current policies to exclude clients with lower care needs from eligibility for home care and home support services; and
- the development of indicators or methodologies to compare the cost-effectiveness of systems of care delivery across jurisdictions so that jurisdictions can better learn from their comparative experiences.

A structure to support the care of older adults—by having adopted a continuing care approach, designating senior officials responsible for continuing care, and establishing a federal/provincial/territorial committee to guide the evolution of continuing care and care for older adults—will facilitate the ability to address a number of other key policy issues. An integrated system of enhanced continuing care could facilitate many of the policy actions that have been called for in recent reports. With an integrated continuing care system, one could achieve the following:

- Promote a positive view of aging and combat ageism and age discrimination.
- Facilitate the portability of services across jurisdictions.
- Provide support for the voluntary sector.
- Develop healthy communities to provide livable and safe environments for seniors.
- Develop a client-focused lens for all future policy and program initiatives—in other words, review all such initiatives in light of the extent to which they will help clients and their families.
- Provide targeted service delivery options for certain populations such as First Nations and Inuit populations, people living in rural and isolated areas, new immigrants, people living in poverty, and other groups.
- Develop national standards, frameworks, or guidelines for the provision of cost-effective and high-quality care.
- Develop a health human resources strategy for the recruitment, retention, and training of care providers in continuing care.
- Develop innovative care delivery approaches for home and community care and residential care of clients with dementia.

We expect there will be those who, as a counter to our work, propose other models. Policy discourse should not become muddied by ongoing debates about competing models (although different models do need to be analyzed for their merit). Criteria for evaluating both the models we propose, and other current or future competing models, are as follows:

- To what extent, and how, can cost-effective substitutions be made in which lower-cost services can be used instead of higher-cost services? This is the primary evaluation criterion.
- Does the system include a wide range of home, community, residential, and acute care services that are specifically designed to meet the needs of elderly persons?
- Is the system designed for clients ranging from those with low-level to high-level care needs?
- How is continuity of care achieved within the system, and between the system and other components of the health care system? Is there system-level case management?
- How much discretion do senior administrators have in terms of real-locating funds between components of the care system and actual service provider organizations? That is, is there a single, or coordinated, administrative structure and a single budget envelope for all services in the system?
- Is there a system-level assessment and classification system tool that allows policy-makers, planners, and analysts to compare clients across sites of care based on the same metric of care needs?
- Is there sustainable funding for the system?

Scope of the Book

The type of system we outline can provide a more appropriate and cost-effective service system for older adults than exists at the present time in Canada. However, there are many areas not touched upon in this book, some of which have the potential to fuel cost escalation within the health care system. Unfortunately, the list is long and serious, and includes (for example) the costs of pharmaceutical prescriptions, the proliferation of expensive high medical technology, the silos within the system, and the lack of coordination and co-operation with relevant sectors outside of the health care system. This is in no way to deny the value of physician services, acute care hospitals, prescription drugs, high technology, and more; there are great benefits that flow from much that these areas offer, and those working in these areas are typically dedicated, competent, hard-working individuals. It is, however, to point out that, until we also attend to other areas within the health care system, costs are likely to continue to increase.

As the Health Council of Canada (2012), among others, has pointed out, we are servicing Canadians more and more within the medical system without evidence of the benefits of doing so; these issues must be addressed if we want to contain costs and maintain our public health care system. In other words, the solution offered in this book is not a panacea.

Even within the narrower focus of this book—informal and continuing care to address aging in Canada—there are areas that we have not discussed that are of major importance to consider. For example, human resource issues include adequate staffing, staff mix, training, and far from least compensation for the work rendered. Transportation to out-of-home services such as adult day care and the aging physical plants of some long-term care facilities also require attention.

Conclusion

Since the first of the baby boomers turned 65, there has been a noticeable increase in attention to gerontological issues both by governments and the media. Much of the attention focuses on the sustainability of our health care system. Given that old age and declining health have sparked concern, it is curious that the federal government does not appear to recognize the critical role of home support for an aging society. The provinces still fund home support, albeit at a lower level than used to be the case, and there are new intitiatives, such as the Better at Home program in BC targeted toward low-needs seniors, that are promising starts. To date, such endeavours are often time limited and lack integration within the health care system. The continued emphasis on medical care, and the relative neglect of the range of services within continuing care, speaks to the central role of the medical-pharmaceutical focus within our health care system. This is perhaps not surprising given that this is where our state-supported/universal system began half a century ago. However, it has not expanded beyond the original physician and acute care hospital embrace from which it originated. That medical system has grown, but other components, such as home care, have never been brought under the universality tent. Yet long-term home care within the community is the care required by older adults with chronic conditions. As governments grapple with the health care needs of an aging population, the lack of governmental recognition of the full spectrum of continuing care as a major component of the health care system is striking.

In this book, we considered first old age, and more specifically, health in old age and the care needs in those years. After examining how those needs are met now (primarily from family and friends), we examined the congruence between the care needs and the services provided through formal health care. We concluded that positive and constructive change to improve care for older persons can happen. The evidence base is clear. The models of care recommended are well documented and have shown they can be effective. That is, we have presented the research and then outlined the policy and program implications. We do not claim to have offered solutions for all that ails the health care system; our concern has centered on the continuing care system for those with ongoing care needs. A marked improvement in the quality and seamlessness of care provided to older persons is within reach.

In sum, recognizing enhanced continuing care as a major component of our health care system is a critical first step in caring for older Canadians, and this book is only a starting point. The challenge is for senior policymakers and administrators to implement the needed changes to ensure adequate, appropriate, and cost-effective care for our aging population.

Notes

Chapter 1

1. Baby boomers were born between the late 1940s and early 1960s; the generation is often defined as born 1946–1964.

Chapter 2

1. Mendelson and Divinsky (2002) in fact underestimated the percentage of GDP, which was 11.9 in 2009 due to decreasing GDP, discussed in a later chapter.

Chapter 4

1. All provinces had passed their own legislation to develop publicly funded medical care systems by the end of 1971.
2. British Columbia, and Peter D. Seaton, 1991; New Brunswick, E. Neil McKelvey, and Bernadette Lévesque, 1989; Nova Scotia Royal Commission on Health Care, 1989 (available online); Alberta, "Premier's Commission on Future Health Care for Albertans," 1989; Saskatchewan Commission on Directions in Health Care, 1990.

Chapter 6

1. The SMAF *(Système de measure des l'autonomie functionnelle* or *Functional Autonomy Measurement System)* is an instrument for client assessment and classification. It is possible to develop a set of profiles of different types of clients using this instrument. Thus, the Iso–SMAF profiles refer to a set of groups of clients with similar characteristics.

Chapter 7

1. Even if operational costs were equivalent, home care would still be less expensive as facilities have an additional, and significant, cost component related to their physical plant.

References

Abellan van Kan, G., Y. Rolland, H. Bergman, J.E. Morley, S.B. Kritchevsky, and B. Vellas. 2008. "The I.A.N.A. Task Force on Frailty Assessment of Older People in Clinical Practice." *The Journal of Nutrition, Health & Aging* 12 (1): 29–37.

Abellan van Kan, G., Y. Rolland, M. Houles, S. Gillette-Guyonnet, M. Soto, and B. Vellas. 2010. "The Assessment of Frailty in Older Adults." *Clinical Geriatric Medicine* 26 (2): 275–86.

Achenbaum, W.A. 1995. *Old Age in the New Land: The American Experience Since 1790.* Baltimore, MD: Johns Hopkins University Press.

Aiken, L.S., J. Butner, C.A. Lockhart, B.E. Volk-Craft, G. Hamilton, and F.G. Williams. 2006. "Outcome Evaluation of a Randomized Trial of the PhoenixCare Intervention: Program of Case Management and Coordinated Care for the Seriously Chronically Ill." *Journal of Palliative Medicine* 9 (1): 111–26.

Aimonino Ricauda, N., V. Tibaldi, B. Leff, C. Scarafiotti, R. Marinello, M. Zanocchi, and M. Molaschi. 2008. "Substitutive 'Hospital at Home' Versus Inpatient Care for Elderly Patients with Exacerbations of Chronic Obstructive Pulmonary Disease: A Prospective Randomized, Controlled Trial." *Journal of the American Geriatrics Society* 56 (3): 493–500.

Ajrouch, K.J. 2007. "Health Disparities and Arab-American Elders: Does Intergenerational Support Buffer the Inequality–Health Link?" *Journal of Social Issues* 63 (4): 745–58.

Alberta. Premier's Commission on Future Health Care for Albertans. 1989. *The Rainbow Report: Our Vision for Health.* Edmonton: The Commission.

Alexander, T. 1995. "The History and Financing of the Long-Term Care Systems." In *Continuing the Care: The Issues and Challenges for Long-Term Care,* edited by E. Sawyer and M. Stephenson, 1–43. Ottawa: Canadian Healthcare Association Press.

Anderson, C., E. Bautz-Holter, M. Dennis, P. Dey, et al. n.d. "Services for Reducing Duration of Hospital Care for Acute Stroke Patients." *Cochrane Database of Systematic Reviews* (2).

Anderson, C., C. Ni Mhurchu, P.M. Brown, and K. Carter. 2002. "Stroke Rehabilitation Services to Accelerate Hospital Discharge and Provide Home-Based Care: An Overview and Cost Analysis." *PharmacoEconomics* 20 (8): 537–52.

Andrieu, S., L. Balardy, S. Gillette-Guyonnet, H. Bocquet, C. Cantet, J.L. Albarède, B. Vellas, and A. Grand. 2003. "Informal Caregiver's Burden of Alzheimer's Patients: Assessment and Factors Associated." *Revue de Medecine Interne* October 24 (S3): 351–59.

Andrén, S., and S. Elmståhl. 2005. "Family Caregivers' Subjective Experiences of Satisfaction in Dementia Care: Aspects of Burden, Subjective Health and Sense of Coherence." *Scandinavian Journal of Caring Sciences* 19 (2): 157–68.

Antonucci, T.C., J.S. Jackson, and S. Biggs. 2007. "Intergenerational Relations: Theory, Research, and Policy." *Journal of Social Issues* 63 (4): 679–93.

Arber, S., and J. Ginn. 1993. "Class, Caring and the Life Course." In *Ageing, Independence and the Life Course,* edited by S. Arber and M. Evandrou, 149–68. London: Jessica Kingsley.

Armitage, A. 1996. *Social Welfare in Canada Revisited: Facing Up to the Future.* Toronto: Oxford University Press Canada.

Assisted Living Federation of America (ALFA). n.d. "Assisted Living." Available online.

Aubert, R.E., et al. 1998. "Nurse Case Management to Improve Glycemic Control in

Diabetic Patients in a Health Maintenance Organization: A Randomized, Controlled Trial." *Annals of Internal Medicine* 129 (8): 605–12.

Aucoin, P. 1974. "Federal Health Care Policy." In *Issues in Canadian Public Policy*, edited by G. Bruce Doern and V. S.Wilson, 55–84. Toronto: Macmillan of Canada.

Bajekal, M., D. Bland, I. Grewal, S. Karlsen, and J. Nazroo. 2004. "Ethnic Differences in Influences on Quality of Life at Older Ages: A Quantitative Analysis." *Ageing and Society* 24 (5): 709–28.

Baltes, P.B., and M.M. Baltes. 1990. "Psychological Perspectives on Successful Aging: The Model of Selective Optimization with Compensation." In *Successful Aging: Perspectives from the Behavioral Sciences* edited by P.B. Baltes and M.M. Baltes, 1–34. NY: Cambridge University Press.

Baltes, P.B., and J. Smith. 2003. "New Frontiers in the Future of Aging: From Successful Aging of the Young Old to the Dilemmas of the Fourth Age." *Gerontology* 49 (2): 123–35.

Banks, P. 2004. *Policy Framework for Integrated Care for Older People*. London: King's Fund. Available online.

Barr, V.J., S. Robinson, B. Marin-Link, L. Underhill, A. Dotts, D. Ravensdale, and S. Salivaras. 2003. "The Expanded Chronic Care Model: An Integration of Concepts and Strategies from Population Health Promotion and the Chronic Care Model." *Hospital Quarterly* 7 (1): 73–82.

Beck, A., J. Scott, P. Williams, et al. 1997. "A Randomized Trial of Group Outpatient Visits for Chronically Ill Older HMO Members: The Cooperative Health Care Clinic." *Journal of the American Geriatrics Society* 45 (5): 543–49.

Beck, U., and E. Beck-Gernsheim. 2001. *Individualization: Institutionalized Individualism and Its Social and Political Consequences*. London, UK: SAGE.

Beech, R., A.G. Rudd, K. Tilling, and C.D. Wolfe. 1999. "Economic Consequences of Early Inpatient Discharge to Community-Based Rehabilitation for Stroke in an Inner-London Teaching Hospital." *Stroke: a Journal of Cerebral Circulation* 30 (4): 729–35.

Béland, F., H. Bergman, P. Lebel, et al. 2006a. "Integrated Services for Frail Elders (SIPA): A Trial of a Model for Canada." *Canadian Journal on Aging* 25 (1): 5–42.

———. 2006b. "A System of Integrated Care for Older Persons with Disabilities in Canada: Results from a Randomized Controlled Trial." *The Journals of Gerontology. Series A, Biological Sciences and Medical Sciences* 61 (4): 367–73.

Béland, F., and M.J. Hollander. 2011. "Integrated Models of Care Delivery for the Frail Elderly: International Perspectives." *Gaceta Sanitaria* 25: 138–46.

Bengtson, V.L., R. Giarrusso, M. Silverstein, and H. Wang. 2000. "Families and Intergenerational Relationships in Aging Societies." *Hallym International Journal of Aging* 2: 3–10.

Bernabei, R., F. Landi, G. Gambassi, A. Sgadari, G. Zuccala, V. Mor, L.Z. Rubenstein, and P. Carbonin. 1998. "Randomised Trial of Impact of Model of Integrated Care and Case Management for Older People Living in the Community." *BMJ: British Medical Journal* 316 (7141): 1348–51.

Board, N., N. Brennan, and G.A. Caplan. 2000. "A Randomized Controlled Trial of the Costs of Hospital as Compared with Hospital in the Home for Acute Medical Patients." *Australian & New Zealand Journal of Public Health* 24 (3): 305–11.

Bodenheimer, T. 1999. "Long-Term Care for Frail Elderly People—The On Lok Model." *The New England Journal of Medicine* 341 (17): 1324–28.

———. 2003. "Interventions to Improve Chronic Illness Care: Evaluating Their Effectiveness." *Disease Management* 6 (2): 63–71.

Bolin, K., B. Lindgren, and P. Lundborg. 2008. "Informal and Formal Care Among Single-living Elderly in Europe." *Health Economics* 17 (3): 393–409.

Bosanquet, N. 2002. "Models of Palliative Care Service Delivery: What Is Most Cost Effective?" *Disease Management & Health Outcomes* 10 (6): 349–53.

Bonsang, E. 2009. "Does Informal Care from Children to Their Elderly Parents Substitute for Formal Care in Europe?" *Journal of Health Economics* (28): 143–54.

Braithwaite, V. 1998. "Institutional Respite Care: Breaking Chores or Breaking Social Bonds?" *Gerontologist* 38 (5): 610–17.

Brazil, K., L. Thabane, G. Foster, and M. Bédard. 2009. "Gender Differences among Canadian Spousal Caregivers at the End of Life." *Health & Social Care in the Community* 17 (2): 159–66.

British Columbia. Ministry of Health. n.d. *Expanded Chronic Care Model.* Available online.

British Columbia, and P.D. Seaton. 1991. *Closer to Home: The Report of the Royal Commission on Health Care and Costs.* Victoria, BC: The Commission.

British Columbia Law Foundation. 2009. *Grandparents Raising Grandchildren: Legal Issues and Resources.* Parent Support Services of BC. Available online.

British Columbia Law Institute and the Canadian Centre for Elder Law. 2010. *Care/Work: Law Reform to Support Family Caregivers to Balance Paid Work and Unpaid Caregiving.* BCLI Study Paper No. 4; CCEL Study Paper No. 4. Available online.

Brody, E.M., S.J. Litvin, C. Hoffman, and M.H. Kleban. 1995. "Marital Status of Caregiving Daughters and Co-residence with Dependent Parents." *The Gerontologist* 35: 75–85.

Brown, R.L. 2011. *Economic Security in an Aging Canadian Population.* Hamilton, ON: SEDAP Research Program, McMaster University. Available online.

Cade, A., and J. Puntis. 1998. "Economics of Home Parenteral Nutrition." *PharmacoEconomics* 12 (3): 327–38.

Calasanti, T.M., and K.F. Slevin. 2001. *Gender, Social Inequalities, and Aging.* Walnut Creek, CA: AltaMira Press.

Canada. Department of Finance. 2008. Canada Health Transfer. Ottawa: Department of Finance.

——. 2009. *Tax Expenditures and Evaluations.* Catalogue No. F1-27/2009E. Ottawa: Department of Finance.

——. 2011. *What Is the Canada Health Transfer (CHT)?* Available online.

——. 2012. *Canada Assistance Plan and the Canada Health and Social Transfer Statistical Tables, Special Data Runs.* Ottawa: Department of Finance.

Canada. Government of Canada. 1999. *A Framework to Improve the Social Union for Canadians: An Agreement between the Government of Canada and the Governments of the Provinces and Territories.* News release, 4 February.

——. 2006. *The Human Face of Mental Health and Mental Illness in Canada.* Ottawa: Public Works and Government Services Canada. Available online.

——. 2010. *New Horizons for Seniors Program: Federal Elder Abuse Initiative Funding Guide.*

——. 2011. *Improving Tax Support for Caregivers.* Available online.

Canada. National Seniors Council. 2009. *Report of the National Seniors Council on Low Income Among Seniors.* Ottawa: National Seniors Council. Available online.

Canada. Provincial and Territorial Ministers of Health. 2000. *Understanding Canada's Health Care Costs: Interim Report.* St. John's, NL: Government of Newfoundland and Labrador.

Canadian Agency for Drugs and Technologies in Health. 2006. *Guidelines for the Economic Evaluation of Health Technologies: Canada.* Ottawa: Canadian Agency for Drugs and Technologies in Health.

Canadian Cancer Society. n.d. "Fight Back to Support Caregivers," "Handy Facts about Caregivers." Available online.

The Canadian Caregiver Coalition (CCC). 2008. *A Framework for a Canadian Caregiver Strategy*. Available online.

Canadian Doctors for Medicare. 2011. *Neat, Plausible, and Wrong: The Myth of Health Care Unsustainability*. Toronto: Canadian Doctors for Medicare. Available online.

Canadian Health Services Research Foundation (CHSRF). 2001. "Myth: The Aging Population Will Overwhelm the Healthcare System." *Journal of Health Services Research and Policy* 8 (3) 189–90.

———. 2007. "Myth: Canada's System of Healthcare Financing Is Unsustainable." Ottawa: CHRSF. Available online.

———. 2011a. *Better with Age: Health Systems Planning for an Aging Population: Synthesis Report*. Ottawa: CHRSF. Available online.

———. 2011b. *Research Synthesis on Cost Drivers in the Health Sector and Proposed Policy Options*. Ottawa: CHRSF. Available online.

Canadian Institute for Health Information (CIHI). 2007. *Public-Sector Expenditures and Utilization of Home Care Services in Canada: Exploring the Data*. Ottawa: CIHI. Available online.

———. 2009. *Analysis in Brief: Experiences with Primary Health Care in Canada*. Ottawa: CIHI. Available online

———. 2011a. *CIHI 2010–2011 Annual Report: The Difference Data Makes*. Ottawa: CIHI. Available online.

———. 2011b. *Health Care in Canada, 2011: A Focus on Seniors and Aging*. Ottawa: CIHI. Available online.

———. 2011c. *Health Indicators 2011*. Statistics Canada Catalogue no. 82-221-XWE. Ottawa: Statistics Canada. Available Online.

———. 2011d. *National Health Expenditure Trends, 1975 to 2011*. Ottawa: CIHI. Available online.

Canadian Life and Health Insurance Association (CLHIA). 2012. *CLHIA Report on Long-Term Care Policy: Improving the Accessibility, Quality and Sustainability of Long-Term Care in Canada*. Toronto: CLHIA. Available online.

Canadian Medical Association (CMA). 1983. *Health, a Need for Redirection*, A Task Force on the Allocation of Health Care Resources. Joan Watson, Chairman.

Canadian Study of Health and Aging Working Group. 1994. "Canadian Study of Health and Aging: Study Methods and Prevalence of Dementia." *Canadian Medical Association Journal* 150 (6): 899–913.

Candy, B., A. Holman, B. Leurent, S. Davis, and L. Jones. 2011. "Hospice Care Delivered at Home, in Nursing Homes and in Dedicated Hospice Facilities: A Systematic Review of Quantitative and Qualitative Evidence." *International Journal of Nursing Studies* 48 (1): 121–33.

Capitman, J.A. 1986. "Community-Based Long-Term Care Models, Target Groups, and Impacts on Service Use." *The Gerontologist* 26 (4): 389–97.

Caplan G., N. Board, A. Paten, J. Tazelaar-Molinia, P. Crowe, et al. 1998. "Decreasing Lengths of Stay: The Cost to the Community." *The Australian and New Zealand Journal of Surgery* 69 (6): 433–37.

Cardozo, L., and J. Steinberg. 2010. "Telemedicine for Recently Discharged Older Patients." *Telemedicine Journal and E-Health: The Official Journal of the American Telemedicine Association* 16 (1): 49–55.

Carrière, Y., J. Légaré, X. Lin, and G. Rowe. 2007. "Population Aging and Immediate

Family Composition: Implications for Future Home Care Services." *GENUS* 63 (1–2): 11–31.

Carstairs, S., and W.J. Keon. 2009. *Special Senate Committee on Aging Final Report: Canada's Aging Population—Seizing the Opportunity.* Ottawa: Special Senate Committee on Aging.

Chappell, N.L. 2007. "Ethnicity and Quality of Life." In *Quality of Life in Old Age*, edited by H. Mollenkopf and A.Walker, 179–94. Dordrecht: Springer.

———. 2008. "Comparing Caregivers to Older Adults in Shanghai." *The Asian Journal of Gerontology and Geriatrics* 3(2): 57–65.

———. 2009. "The Way Ahead." In *Health and Aging in British Columbia: Vulnerability and Resilience*, edited by Denise S. Cloutier-Fisher, Leslie T. Foster, and David F. Hultsch, 361–75. Victoria: Western Geographical Press.

Chappell, N.L., and A.A. Blandford. 1991. "Informal and Formal Care: Exploring the Complementarity." *Ageing and Society* 11 (3): 299–317.

Chappell, N.L., and H.A. Cooke. 2010. "Age Related Disabilities—Aging and Quality of Life." In *International Encyclopedia of Rehabilitation*, edited by M. Blouin, and J. Stone. NY: Center for International Rehabilitation Research Information and Exchange. Available online.

Chappell, N.L., and C. Dujela. 2008. "Caregiving: Predicting At-Risk Status." *Canadian Journal on Aging* 27 (2): 169–79.

Chappell, N.L., and L.M. Funk. 2011a. "Filial Responsibility: Does It Matter for Caregiving Behaviours?" *Ageing and Society* 1–19.

———. 2011b. "Filial Caregivers: Diasporic Chinese Compared with Homeland and Hostland Caregivers." *Journal of Cross-Cultural Gerontology* 26 (4): 315–29.

Chappell, N.L., M. Gibbens, and B. Schroeder. 2008. "Respite for Rural and Remote Caregivers." In *A Good Place to Grow Old? Critical Perspectives on Rural Ageing*, edited by N.C. Keating, 53–62. Bristol: The Policy Press.

Chappell, N.L., B. Havens, M.J. Hollander, J.A. Miller, and C. McWilliam. 2004. "Comparative Costs of Home Care and Residential Care." *The Gerontologist* 44 (3): 389–400.

Chappell, N.L., and M.J. Hollander. 2010. *Policy Challenges to Provide Compassionate Care to an Aging Population.* Canadian Parliamentary Committee on Palliative and Compassionate Care. Victoria, November.

Chappell, N.L., and M.J. Hollander. 2011. "Evidence-Based Policy Prescription for an Aging Population." *HealthcarePapers* 11 (1): 8–18.

Chappell, N.L., and K. Kusch. 2007. "The Gendered Nature of Filial Piety: A Study Among Chinese Canadians." *Journal of Cross-Cultural Gerontology* 22 (1): 29–45.

Chappell, N.L., L. McDonald, and M. Stones. 2008. *Aging in Contemporary Canada.* Toronto: Pearson Canada.

Chappell, N.L., and M. Penning. 2012. *Health Inequalities in Later Life, Differences by Age/ Stage. Final Report.* Ottawa: Public Health Agency of Canada.

Chappell, N.L., and E. Pridham. 2010. *Age Friendly Communities (AFC)—Good for Caregivers.* Ottawa: Public Health Agency of Canada.

Chappell, N.L., and R.C. Reid. 2002. "Burden and Well-Being among Caregivers: Examining the Distinction." *The Gerontologist* 42 (6): 772–80.

Chappell, N.L., R.C. Reid, and E. Dow. 2001. "Respite Reconsidered: A Typology of Meanings Based on the Caregiver's Point of View." *Journal of Aging Studies* 15 (2): 201–16.

Chiu, L., and W.C. Shyu. 2001. "Estimation of the Family Cost of Private Nursing Home

Care Versus Home Care for Patients with Dementia in Taiwan." *Chang Gung Medical Journal* 24 (10): 608–14.

Chiu, L., W.C. Shyu, and Y.H. Liu. 2001. "Comparisons of the Cost-Effectiveness among Hospital Chronic Care, Nursing Home Placement, Home Nursing Care and Family Care for Severe Stroke Patients." *Journal of Advanced Nursing* 33 (3): 380–86.

Christakis, N.A., and P.D. Allison. 2006. "Mortality after the Hospitalization of a Spouse." *New England Journal of Medicine* 354 (7): 719–30.

Crichton, A. 1993. "A Critical Analysis of Recent Canadian Health Policy: Models for Community-Based Services." *International Journal of Health Planning and Management* 8 (4): 295–314.

———. 1997. *Health Care: A Community Concern? Developments in the Organization of Canadian Health Services.* Calgary: University of Calgary Press.

Crichton, A., D. Hsing-Sheng Hsu, and S. Tsang. 1994. *Canada's Health Care System: Its Funding and Organization.* Ottawa: CHA Press.

Chumbler, N.R., W.C. Mann, S. Wu, A. Schmid, and R. Kobb. 2004. "The Association of Home-telehealth Use and Care Coordination with Improvement of Functional and Cognitive Functioning in Frail Elderly Men." *Telemedicine Journal and E-Health: The Official Journal of the American Telemedicine Association* 10 (2): 129–37.

CIA World Factbooks. 2011. *Age Structure > 65 Years and over by Country, CIA World Factbooks 18 December 2003 to 28 March 2011.* Available online.

Ciment, J. 1999. "Life Expectancy of Russian Men Falls to 58." *British Medical Journal* 319 (7208): 468.

Clarke, L.H., and M. Griffin. 2008. "Visible and Invisible Ageing: Beauty Work as a Response to Ageism." *Ageing & Society* 28 (5): 653–74.

Cloutier-Fisher, D.S., L.T. Foster, and D.F. Hultsch, eds. *Health and Aging in British Columbia: Vulnerability and Resilience.* Victoria: Western Geographical Press.

Coast, J., S.H. Richards, T.J. Peters, D.J. Gunnell, M-A. Darlow, and J. Pounsford. 1998. "Hospital at Home or Acute Hospital Care? A Cost Minimisation Analysis." *British Medical Journal* 316 (7147): 1802–6.

Cohen, M. 2012. *Caring for BC's Aging Population. Improving Health Care for All.* Vancouver: Canadian Centre for Policy Alternatives. [e-book]

Colombo, F., et al. 2011. *Help Wanted? Providing and Paying for Long-Term Care.* Paris: Organisation for Economic Co-operation and Development Health Policy Studies, OECD Publishing.

Contandriopoulos, A., G. Tessier, and D. Larouche. 1986. "The Effects of Quebec Home Aid Services on the Utilization Profile of Sociosanitary Resources: A Substitution Study." *Social Science and Medicine* 22 (7): 731–36.

Cott, C.A., and M.T. Fox. 2001. "Health and Happiness for Elderly Institutionalized Canadians." *Canadian Journal on Aging* 20 (4): 517–36.

Covinsky, K.E., C. Eng, L. Lui, L.P. Sands, A.R. Sehgal, L.C. Walter, D. Wieland, G.P. Eleazer, and K. Yaffe. 2001. "Reduced Ehmployment in Caregivers of Frail Elders: Impact of Ethnicity, Patient Clinical Characteristics, and Caregiver Characteristics." *Journal of Gerontology,* Series A 56: M707–M713.

Coyle, D., N. Small, A. Ashworth, S. Hennessy, S. Jenkins-Clark, et al. 1999. "Costs of Palliative Care in the Community, in Hospitals and in Hospices in the UK." *Critical Reviews in Oncology-Hematology* 32 (2): 71–85.

Coyte, P.C., M.J. Dobrow, and L. Broadfield. 2001. "Incremental Cost Analysis of Ambulatory Clinic and Home-Based Intravenous Therapy for Patients with Multiple Myeloma." *Pharmacoeconomics* 19 (8): 845–54.

Coyte, P.C., W. Young, and R. Croxford. 2000. "Costs and Outcomes Associated with Alternative Discharge Strategies Following Joint Replacement Surgery: Analysis of an Observational Study Using a Propensity Score." *Journal of Health Economics* 19 (6): 907–29.

Cranswick, K. 2003. *General Social Survey, Cycle 16: Caring for an Aging Society.* Statistics Canada Catalogue no. 89-582-X1E. Ottawa: Statistics Canada. Available online.

Cranswick, K., and D. Dosman. 2008. *Eldercare: What We Know Today.* Canadian Social Trends. Component of Statistics Canada Catalogue no. 11-008-X, No. 86. Ottawa: Statistics Canada. Available online.

Crimmins, E.M. 2004. "Trends in the Health of the Elderly." *Annual Review of Public Health* 25: 79–98.

Cutt, J. 1989. "Budgeting in British Columbia, 1976–1986: Coping and Caring in Tough Times." In *Budgeting in the Provinces: Leadership and the Premiers*, edited by A.M. Maslove, 143–69. Toronto: Institute of Public Administration of Canada.

Daatland, S., and A. Lowenstein. 2005. "Intergenerational Solidarity and the Family–Welfare State Balance." *European Journal of Aging* 2 (3): 174–82.

Daly, M., and K. Rake. 2003. *Gender and the Welfare State: Care, Work and Welfare in Europe and the USA.* Cambridge, UK: Polity Press.

Dannefer, D., R. Siders, R.S. Patterson, and P. Stein. 2008. "Is That All There Is? The Concept of Care and the Dialectic of Critique." *Journal of Aging Studies* 22 (2): 101–8.

Darby, P. W. 1992. "Quick Response Teams: A New Approach in Utilization Management." *Leadership in Health Services* 1 (5): 27–31.

Dautzenberg, M.G.H., J.P.M. Diederiks, H. Philipsen, F.C.J., Stevens, F.E.S. Tan, and M.J.F.J. Vernooij-Dassen. 2000. "The Competing Demands of Paid Work and Parent Care: Middle-Aged Daughters Providing Assistance to Elderly Parents." *Research on Aging* 22 (2): 165–87.

Deans, C.T. 2004. "The State of Hospice in America: Looking Back, Looking Forward." *Caring* 23 (2): 44–57.

Deaton, A. 2008. "Income, Health, and Well-Being around the World: Evidence from the Gallup World Poll." *Journal of Economic Perspectives* 22 (2): 53–72.

de Jong Gierveld, J., T. Van Tilburg, and L. Lecchini. 1997. "Socio-Economic Resources, Household Composition and the Social Network as Determinants of Well-Being among Dutch and Tuscan Older Adults." *Genus* 53 (3–4): 75–100.

Delbès, C., J. Gaymu, and S. Springer. 2006. "Les femmes vieillissent seules, les hommes vieillissent à deux. Un bilan européen." *Population et Sociétés* 419: 1–4.

Denton, F.T., C.H. Feaver, and B.G. Spencer. 1998. "The Future Population of Canada, Its Age Distribution and Dependency Relations." *Canadian Journal on Aging* 17 (1): 83–109.

Denton, F.T., and B.G. Spencer. 1999. "Population Aging and Its Economic Costs: A Survey of the Issues and Evidence." *Social and Economic Dimensions of an Aging Population (SEDAP) Research Paper No. 1.* Hamilton, ON: McMaster University. Available online.

———. 2010. "Chronic Health Conditions: Changing Prevalence in an Aging Population and Some Implications for the Delivery of Health Care Services." *Canadian Journal on Aging* 29 (1): 11–21.

DesMeules, M., D. Manuel, and R. Cho. 2004. "Mortality: Life and Health Expectancy of Canadian Women." *BMC Women's Health* 4 (Suppl. 1): S1–S9.

Detsky, A.S., J.R. McLaughlin, H.B Abrams, J.S. Whittaker, J. Whitwell, K. L'Abbé, and K.N. Jeejeebhoy. 1986. "A Cost-Utility Analysis of the Home Parenteral Nutrition Program at Toronto General Hospital: 1970–1982." *Journal of Parenteral and Enteral Nutrition* 10 (1): 49–57.

Dillaway, H., and M. Byrnes. 2009. "Reconsidering Successful Aging: A Call for Renewed and Expanded Academic Critiques and Conceptualizations." *Journal of Applied Gerontology* 28 (6): 702–22.

Di Matteo, L. 2005. "The Macro Determinants of Health Expenditure in the United States and Canada: Assessing the Impact of Income, Age Distribution and Time." *Health Policy* 71 (1): 23–42.

Dodge, D.A., and R. Dion. 2011a. *Chronic Healthcare Spending Disease: A Macro Diagnosis and Prognosis.* Toronto: C.D. Howe Institute.

———. 2011b. *Chronic Healthcare Spending Disease: Background and Methodology.* Toronto: C.D. Howe Institute.

Donorfio, L.M. 1996. "Filial Responsibility: Widowed Mothers and Their Caregiving Daughters, a Qualitative Grounded Theory Approach." PhD diss., University of Connecticut, 1996. (Dissertation Abstracts International Section A: Humanities & Social Sciences. US, University Microfilms International 57: 2158.)

Dosman, D., J. Fast, N. Keating, et al. 2005. *Care Networks of Frail Seniors and the Formal-Informal Interface.* Paper presented at Conférence "Familles canadiennes sous tension?" Montreal, 20 May, 2005. Centre interuniversitaire québécois de statistiques sociales. Available online.

Driedger, L. 2003. *Race and Ethnicity: Finding Identities and Equalities.* Toronto: Oxford University Press.

Drummond, D., and D. Burleton. 2010. *Charting a Path to Sustainable Health Care in Ontario: 10 Proposals to Restrain Cost Growth without Compromising Quality of Care.* TD Economics Special Reports. Toronto: TD Economics. Available online.

Drummond, M.F., G. Stoddart, and G.W. Torrance. 1987. *Methods for the Economic Evaluation of Health Care Programmes.* Toronto: Oxford University Press.

Dubuc, N., M-F. Dubois, R. Hébert, M. Raîche, and N. Gueye. 2011. "Meeting the Home-Care Needs of Disabled Older Persons Living in the Community: Does Integrated Services Delivery Make a Difference?" *BMC Geriatrics* 11: 67.

Edwards, A.B., S.H. Zarit, M.A. Stephens, and A. Townsend. 2002. "Employed Family Caregivers of Cognitively Impaired Elderly: An Examination of Role Strain and Depressive Symptoms." *Aging and Mental Health* 6 (1): 55–61.

Embree, V., and M.J. Hollander. 2000. *Evaluation of the Carelinks Program.* Victoria: KPMG Consulting and Hollander Analytical Services Ltd.

Emerson, E., J. Robertson, N. Gregory, C. Hatton, S. Kessissoglou, et al. 2001. "Quality and Costs of Supported Living Residences and Group Homes in the United Kingdom." *American Journal on Mental Retardation* 106 (5): 401–15.

Eng, C., J. Pedulla, G.P. Eleazer, R. McCann, and N. Fox. 1997. "Program of All-Inclusive Care for the Elderly (PACE): An Innovative Model of Integrated Geriatric Care and Financing." *Journal of the American Geriatrics Society* 45: 223–32.

Fast, J.E., D.L. Williamson, and N.C. Keating. 1999. "The Hidden Costs of Informal Elder Care." *Journal of Family and Economic Issues* 20 (3): 301–26.

Federal/Provincial/Territorial Subcommittee on Institutional Program Guidelines. 1988. *Assessment and Placement for Adult Long Term Care: A Single Entry Model.* Ottawa: Health and Welfare Canada.

Federal/Provincial/Territorial Subcommittee on Long Term Care. 1990. *Report on Home Care.* Ottawa: Health and Welfare Canada

Federal/Provincial/Territorial Subcommittee on Continuing Care. 1992. *Future Directions in Continuing Care: Report of the Federal/Provincial/Territorial Subcommittee on Continuing Care.* Ottawa: Health and Welfare Canada. Continuing Care.

Fine, M. 2005. "Individualization, Risk and the Body: Sociology and Care." *Journal of Sociology* 41 (3): 247–66.

Finkelstein, S.M., S.M. Speedie, and S. Potthoff. 2006. "Home Telehealth Improves Clinical Outcomes at Lower Cost for Home Healthcare." *Telemedicine Journal and e-Health* 12 (2): 128–36.

Finland. Ministry of Social Affairs and Health. 2006. *Social Welfare in Finland.* Brochures of the Ministry of Social Affairs and Health (2006:11 eng.). Helsinki: Ministry of Social Affairs and Health. Available online.

Funk, L.M., and K.I. Stajduhar. 2009. "Interviewing Family Caregivers: Implications of the Caregiving Context for the Research Interview. *Qualitative Health Research* 19(6): 859–67.

Funk, L.M., N.L. Chappell, and G. Liu. 2011. "Associations Between Filial Responsibility and Caregiver Well-Being: Are There Differences by Cultural Group?" *Research on Aging* 35 (1): 78–95.

Gaymu, J., P. Ekamper, and G. Beets. 2007. "Qui prendra en charge les Européens âgés dependants en 2030? " *Population* [French Edition] 62: 789–820.

Gee, E., M. Thomas, and G.M. Gutman. 2000. *The Overselling of Population Aging: Apocalyptic Demography, Intergenerational Challenges and Social Policy.* Toronto: Oxford University Press.

Gignac, M.A., C. Cott, and E.M. Badley. 2000. "Adaptation to Chronic Illness and Disability and Its Relationship to Perceptions of Independence and Dependence. *Journal of Gerontology: Psychological Sciences* 55B(6): P362–P372.

Gilleard, C., and P. Higgs. 2007. "The Third Age and the Baby Boomers: Two Approaches to the Social Structuring of Later Life." *International Journal of Ageing and Later Life* 2 (2): 13–30.

Gilmour, H., and J. Park. 2006. "Dependency, Chronic Conditions and Pain in Seniors." *Health Reports* 16: 21–31. Statistics Canada Catalogue no. 82-003-X. Ottawa: Statistics Canada. Available online.

Glaser, K., and E. Grundy. 2002. "Class, Caring and Disability: Evidence from the British Retirement Survey." *Ageing and Society* 22 (3): 325–42.

Glaser, K., R. Stuchbury, C. Tomassini, and J. Askham. 2008. "The Long-Term Consequences of Partnership Dissolution for Support in Later Life in the United Kingdom." *Ageing and Society* 28 (3): 329–51.

Goodhead, A., and J. McDonald. 2007. *Informal Caregivers Literature Review: A Report Prepared for the National Health Committee.* Wellington, New Zealand: Health Services Research Centre, Victoria University of Wellington. Available online.

Gonçalves, D.C. 2009. "From Loving Grandma to Working with Older Adults: Promoting Positive Attitudes Towards Aging." *Educational Gerontology* 35 (3): 202–25.

Goodwin, N. 2013. Editorial: "Understanding Integrated Care: A Complex Process, A Fundamental Principle." *International Journal of Integrated Care* 13 (January–March).

Gorshe, N. 2000. "Supporting Aging in Place and Assisted Living Through Home Care." *Caring* 19 (6): 20–22.

Government of Alberta. 2009. *The Demographic Shift.* May. Edmonton, AB: Government of Alberta. Available online.

Government of Newfoundland. 2000. *Understanding Canada's Health Care Costs – Interim Report.* St. John's, NL: Government of Newfoundland.

Graham, J.E., K. Rockwood, B.L. Beattie, R. Eastwood, S. Gauthier, et al. 1997. "Prevalence and Severity of Cognitive Impairment With and Without Dementia in an Elderly Population. *The Lancet* 349 (9068): 1793–96.

Graham, J.R., K. Swift, and R. Delaney. 2012. *Canadian Social Policy: An Introduction.* Toronto: Pearson Canada.

Graves, N., M. Courtney, H. Edwards, A. Chang, A. Parker, and K. Finlayson. 2009. "Cost-Effectiveness of an Intervention to Reduce Emergency Re-admissions to Hospital Among Older Patients." *PloS one* 4 (10): e7455.

Greene, V.L., M.E. Lovely, and J.I Ondrich. 1993. "The Cost-Effectiveness of Community Services in a Frail Elderly Population." *The Gerontologist* 33 (2): 177–89.

Greenwood, R. 2001. "The PACE Model." *Center for Medicare Education, Issue Brief* 2 (10): 1–8.

Grundy, E. 2006. "Ageing and Vulnerable People: European Perspectives." *Ageing and Society* 26 (1): 105–34.

Guber, A., E. Morris, B. Chen, and S. Israeli. 2002. "First Experience with the Home-Care Management System for Respiratory Patients in Israel." *Israel Medical Association Journal: IMAJ* 4 (6): 418–20.

Guberman, N., J-P. Lavoie, and I. Olazabal. 2011. "Baby-Boomers and the 'Denaturalisation' of Care-Giving in Quebec." *Ageing and Society* 31 (7): 1141–58.

Harjai, K.J., M.R. Mehra, H.O. Ventura, Y.M. Lapeyre, J.P. Murgo, et al. 1997. "Home Inotropic Therapy in Advanced Heart Failure: Cost Analysis and Clinical Outcomes." *Chest* 112 (5): 1298–1303.

Harrow, B.S., D.F. Mahoney, A.B. Mendelsohn, M.G. Ory, D.W. Coon, S.H. Belle, and L.O Nichols. 2004. "Variation in Cost of Informal Caregiving and Formal-Service Use for People with Alzheimer's Disease." *American Journal of Alzheimer's Disease and Other Dementias* 19 (5): 299–308.

Haskins, B. 1985. *Evaluation of Coordinated Community-Oriented Long-Term Care Demonstration Projects. (Final Report, May).* Berkeley, California: Berkeley Planning Associates.

Hastings, J.E.F. 1972–73. *Hastings Report: Report of the Community Health Centre Project to the Conference of Health Ministers.* (3 volumes). Ottawa: Information Canada.

Heagerty, J.J. 1943. *Health Insurance: Report of the Advisory Committee on Health Insurance.* Ottawa: E. Cloutier, Printer to the King.

Health Canada. 2006a. *2003 First Ministers' Accord on Health Care Renewal.* Available online.

———. 2006b. *First Ministers' Meeting on the Future of Health Care 2004: A 10-Year Plan to Strengthen Health Care.* Available online.

Health Canada, Division of Aging and Seniors. 2002. *Physical Activity and Older Adults.* Ottawa: Minister of Public Works and Government Services Canada.

Health Care Innovation Working Group. 2012. *From Innovation to Action: The First Report of the Health Care Innovation Working Group.* Ottawa: The Council of the Federation. Available online.

Health Council of Canada. 2009. *Value for Money: Making Canadian Health Care Stronger.* Toronto: Health Council of Canada.

———. 2012. *Seniors in Need, Caregivers in Distress: What Are the Home Care Priorities for Seniors in Canada?* Toronto: Health Council of Canada.

Hébert, P.C., J. Coutts, D. Rosenfield, N. MacDonald, M. Stanbrook, and K. Flegel. 2011. "Sustainability Is Not the Issue: Let's Focus on Quality." *Canadian Medical Association Journal* 183 (8): 885–86.

Hébert, R., N. Dubuc, M. Buteau, J. Desrosiers, G. Bravo, L. Trottier, C. St-Hilaire, and C. Roy. 2001. "Resources and Costs Associated with Disabilities of Elderly People Living at Home and in Institutions." *Canadian Journal on Aging* 20 (1): 1–22.

Hébert, R., P.J. Durand, N. Dubuc, and A. Tourigny. 2003 "Frail Elderly Patients. New Model for Integrated Service Delivery." *Canadian Family Physician* 49: 992–97.

Hébert, R., P.J. Durand, N. Dubuc, A. Tourigny, and The PRISMA Group. 2003 "PRISMA: A New Model of Integrated Service Delivery for the Frail Older People in Canada." *International Journal of Integrated Care* 3: 1–10.

Hébert, R., M. Raîche, M.F. Dubois, N.R. Gueye, N. Dubuc, and M. Tousignant. 2010. "Impact of PRISMA, A Coordination-Type Integrated Service Delivery System for Frail Older People in Quebec (Canada): A Quasi-Experimental Study." *Journal of Gerontology B Psychology Science Social Science* 65B (1): 107–18.

Hébert, R., A. Tourigny, and M. Gagnon. 2005. *Integrated Service Delivery to Ensure Persons' Functional Autonomy.* Estrie, Quebec: Edisem.

Hébert, R., A. Veil, M. Raîche, M. Dubois, N. Dubuc, et al. 2008. "Evaluation of the Implementation of PRISMA, a Coordination-Type Integrated Service Delivery System for Frail Older People in Quebec." *Journal of Integrated Care* 16 (6): 4–14.

Heikkinen, E. 2003. *What Are the Main Risk Factors for Disability in Old Age and How Can Disability Be Prevented?* Health Evidence Network report. Copenhagen, Denmark: World Health Organization Regional Office for Europe. Available online.

Helliwell, J. 2002. "How's Life? Combining Individual and National Variables to Explain Subjective Well-being." *Economic Modelling* 20 (2): 331–60.

Henderson, J., and L. Forbat. 2002. "Relationship-based Social Policy: Personal and Social Constructions of 'Care.'" *Critical Social Policy* 22 (4): 669–87.

Hernandez, C., A. Casas, J. Escarrabill, J. Alonso, J. Puig-Junoy, et al. 2003. "Home Hospitalisation of Exacerbated Chronic Obstructive Pulmonary Disease Patients." *European Respiratory Journal* 21 (1): 58–67.

Higginson, I.J., I.G. Finlay, D.M. Goodwin, K. Hood, A.G.K. Edwards, et al. 2003. "Is There Evidence that Palliative Care Teams Alter End-of-Life Experiences of Patients and Their Caregivers?" *Journal of Pain and Symptom Management* 25 (2): 150–68.

Hirst, M. 2005. "Carer Distress: A Prospective, Population-Based study." *Social Science and Medicine* 61 (3): 697–708.

Ho, S.C., A. Chan, J. Woo, P. Chong, and A. Sham. 2009. "Impact of Caregiving on Health and Quality of Life: A Comparative Population-Based Study of Caregivers for Elderly Persons and Noncaregivers." *The Journals of Gerontology* 64A (8): 873–79.

Hogan, D.B. 2007. "Proceedings and Recommendations of the 2007 Banff Conference on the Future of Geriatrics in Canada." *Canadian Journal of Geriatrics* 10 (4): 133–48.

Hogan, D.B., H. Bergman, P.N. McCracken, and C.J. Patterson. 1997. "The History of Geriatric Medicine in Canada." *Journal of the American Geriatrics Society* 45 (9): 1134–39.

Hogan, D.B., E.M. Ebly, and T.S. Fung. 1999. "Disease, Disability, and Age in Cognitively Intact Seniors: Results from the Canadian Study of Health and Aging." *Journal of Gerontology, Medical Sciences* 54A (2): M77–M82.

Hogan, D.B., C. MacKnight, and H. Bergman. 2003. "Models, Definitions, and Criteria of Frailty." *Aging Clinical and Experimental Research* 15 (suppl. 3): 1–29.

Hollander, M.J. 1994. *Report of the Project to Review the Need for, and Feasibility of, a National Database on Continuing Care.* Statistics Canada Reference No.: 82F0012XPE. Ottawa: Statistics Canada.

———. 2001a. *Evaluation of the Maintenance and Preventive Model of Home Care.* Victoria: Hollander Analytical Services Ltd.

———. 2001b. Substudy 1: *Final Report of the Study on the Comparative Cost Analysis of Home Care and Residential Care Services.* Victoria: National Evaluation of the Cost-Effectiveness of Home Care.

————. 2012. *The Importance of Context in Care Delivery and Funding for Home Care and Home Care Information Technology: A Vision for the Business of Home Care—Tomorrow and Beyond.* Presented to the Procura Executive Forum. October.

Hollander, M.J., and N.L. Chappell. 2002a. *Final Report of the National Evaluation of the Cost-Effectiveness of Home Care.* Victoria: National Evaluation of the Cost-Effectiveness of Home Care.

————. 2002b. *Synthesis Report: Final Report of the National Evaluation of the Cost-Effectiveness of Home Care.* Victoria, British Columbia: National Evaluation of the Cost-Effectiveness of Home Care.

————. 2007. "A Comparative Analysis of Costs to Government for Home Care and Long-Term Residential Care Services, Standardized for Client Care Needs." *Canadian Journal on Aging* 26 (Supplement 1): 149–61.

————. 2010. *Enhancing Compassionate Care for the Elderly: A Systems Perspective.* Presented to the Canadian Parliamentary Committee on Palliative and Compassionate Care, Victoria. November 9.

Hollander, M.J., N.L. Chappell, B. Havens, C. McWilliam, and J.A. Miller. 2002. *Substudy 5: Study of the Costs and Outcomes of Home Care and Residential Long Term Care Services.* Victoria: National Evaluation of the Cost-Effectiveness of Home Care.

Hollander, M.J., N.L. Chappell, M.J. Prince, and E. Shapiro. 2007. "Providing Care and Support for an Aging Population: Briefing Notes on Key Policy Issues." *Healthcare Quarterly* 10 (3): 34–45.

Hollander, M.J., C. Corbett, and P. Pallan. 2010. "Time for a Paradigm Shift: Managing Smarter by Moving from Data and Information to Knowledge and Wisdom in Healthcare Decision-Making." *Healthcare Quarterly* 13 (2): 49–54.

Hollander, M.J., G. Liu, and N.L. Chappell. 2009. "Who Cares and How Much? The Imputed Economic Contribution to the Canadian Healthcare System of Middle-Aged and Older Unpaid Caregivers Providing Care to the Elderly." *Healthcare Quarterly* 12 (2): 44–51.

Hollander, M.J., J.A. Miller, M. MacAdam, N. Chappell, and D. Pedlar. 2009. "Increasing Value for Money in the Canadian Healthcare System: New Findings and the Case for Integrated Care for Seniors." *Healthcare Quarterly* 12 (1): 38–47.

Hollander, M.J., and P. Pallan. 1995. "The British Columbia Continuing Care System: Service Delivery and Resource Planning." *Aging* (Milano) 7 (2): 94–109.

Hollander, M.J., and M. Prince. 2007. "Organizing Healthcare Delivery Systems for Persons with Ongoing Care Needs and Their Families: A Best Practices Framework." *Healthcare Quarterly* 11(1): 42–54.

Hollingworth, W., C. Todd, M. Parker, J. Roberts, and R. Williams. 1993. "Cost Analysis of Early Discharge After Hip Fracture." *British Medical Journal* 306 (6909): 903–6.

Holmqvist, L.W., L. von Koch, V. Kostulas, M. Holm, G. Widsell, et al. 1998. "A Randomized Controlled Trial of Rehabilitation at Home After Stroke in Southwest Stockholm." *Stroke* 29 (3): 591–97.

Houldin, A.D. 2007. "A Qualitative Study of Caregivers' Experiences with Newly Diagnosed Advanced Colorectal Cancer." *Oncology Nursing Forum* 34 (2): 323–30.

Huguet, N., M.S. Kaplan, and D. Feeny. 2008. "Socioeconomic Status and Health-Related Quality of Life among Elderly People: Results from the Joint Canada/United States Survey of Health." *Social Science and Medicine* 66 (4): 803–10.

Ikels, C. 2004. *Filial Piety: Practice and Discourse in Contemporary East Asia.* Palo Alto: Stanford University Press.

Jester, R., and C. Hicks. 2003. "Using Cost-Effectiveness Analysis to Compare Hospital at Home and In-patient Interventions. Part 2." *Journal of Clinical Nursing* 12 (1): 20–27.

Johri, M., F. Beland, and H. Bergman. 2003. "International Experiments in Integrated Care for the Elderly: A Synthesis of the Evidence." *International Journal of Geriatric Psychiatry* 18 (3): 222–35.

Jönsson, I. 2003. "Policy Perspectives on Changing Intergenerational Relations." *Social Policy and Society* 2 (3): 241–48.

Kalache, A. 2009. "Towards Age-Friendly Societies: From Research to Policy, From Policy to Society." *International Journal of Integrated Care* 9 (Supplement): e40.

Kane, R.L., J.G. Evans, and D. Macfadyen. 1990. *Improving the Health of Older People: A World View.* Oxford: Oxford University Press on behalf of World Health Organization.

Kane, R.L., P. Homyak, B. Bershadsky, and S. Flood. 2006. "Variations on a Theme Called PACE." *Journal of Gerontology* 61A (7): 689–93.

Kane, M.N., D. Lacey, D. Green. 2008. "Investigating Social Work Students' Perceptions of Elders' Vulnerability and Resilience." *Social Work in Mental Health* 7 (4) 307–24.

Kannus, P., H. Sievänen, M. Palvanen, T. Järvinen, and J. Parkkari. 2005. "Prevention of Falls and Consequent Injuries in Elderly People." *Lancet* 366 (9500): 1885–93.

Kaplan, M.S., N. Huguet, D.H. Feeny, and B.H. McFarland. 2010. "Self-Reported Hypertension Prevalence and Income Among Older Adults in Canada and the United States." *Social Science & Medicine* 70 (6): 844–49.

Katz, R., and P. Shah. 2010. "The Patient Who Falls." *JAMA: Journal of the American Medical Association* 303 (3): 273–74.

Keefe, J., and P. Fancey. 2000. "The Care Continues: Responsibility for Elderly Relatives Before and After Admission to a Long Term Care Facility." *Family Relations* 49(3): 235–44.

Keefe, J., J. Légaré, and Y. Carrière. 2007a. "Developing New Strategies to Support Future Caregivers of Older Canadians with Disabilities: Projections of Need and Their Policy Implications." *Canadian Public Policy* 33: S65–S80.

———. 2007b. "Developing New Strategies to Support Future Caregivers of Older Canadians with Disabilities: Projections of Need and their Policy Implications." *Canadian Public Policy* 33 (supplement): S65–S80.

Keefe, J., and B. Rajnovich. 2007. "To Pay or Not to Pay: Examining Underlying Principles in the Debate on Financial Support for Family Caregivers." *Canadian Journal on Aging* 26 (suppmlement 1): 77–90.

Keefe, J., S. Vézina, J. Légaré, Y. Décarie, and G. Lefrançois. 2012. *Population Change and Lifecourse Strategic Knowledge Cluster.* London, ON: University of Western Ontario.

Kemp, C.L., and C.J. Rosenthal. 2001. *The Consequences of Caregiving: Does Employment Make a Difference.* Hamilton, ON: Research Institute for Quantitative Studies in Economics and Population, McMaster University.

Kemper, P. 1986. *The Evaluation of the National Long Term Care Demonstration: Final Report.* Washington: US Government Printing Office.

Kinsella, K., and V.A. Velkoff. 2001. *An Aging World: 2001.* US Census Bureau, Series P95/01–1. Washington: US Government Printing Office. International Population Reports, 127

Kirby, M.J. 2002. *The Health of Canadians: The Federal Role. Volume Six: Recommendations for Reform.* Ottawa: Standing Senate Committee on Social Affairs, Science, and Technology.

Kirchheimer, B. 2008. "A Grey Tsunami Cometh." ModernHealthcare.com. July 21. Availale online.

Kirsi, T., A. Hervonen, and M. Jylha. 2000. "A Man's Gotta Do What a Man's Gotta Do: Husbands as Caregivers to Their Demented Wives: A Discourse Analytic Approach." *Journal of Aging Studies* 14 (2): 153–69.

Knight, K.W., and E.A. Rosa. 2011. "The Environmental Efficiency of Well-Being: A Cross-National Analysis." *Social Science Research* 40 (3): 931–49.

Kobb, R., N. Hoffman, R. Lodge, and S. Kline. 2003. "Enhancing Elder Chronic Care through Technology and Care Coordination: Report from a Pilot." *Telemedicine Journal and e-Health* 9 (2): 189–95.

Kodner, D. 2006. "Whole-System Approaches to Health and Social Care Partnerships for the Frail Elderly: An Exploration of North American Models and Lessons." *Health and Social Care in the Community* 14 (5): 383–90.

Kodner, D., and C. Spreeuwenberg. 2002. "Integrated Care: Meaning, Logic, Applications and Implications—A Discussion Paper." *International Journal of Integrated Care* 2: e12.

Lafrenière, S.A., Y. Carrière, L. Martel, and A. Bélanger. 2003. "Dependent Seniors at Home: Formal and Informal Help." *Health Reports*. Statistics Canada Catalogue No. 82-003. 14(4): 31–40.

Lai, D. 2010. "Filial Piety, Caregiving Appraisal, and Caregiving Burden." *Research on Aging* 32 (2): 200–23.

Lan, P.-C. 2002. "Subcontracting Filial Piety: Elder Care in Ethnic Chinese Immigrant Families in California." *Journal of Family Issues* 23 (7): 812–35.

Landi, F., G. Gambassi, R. Pola, et al. 1999. "Impact of Integrated Home Care Services on Hospital Use." *Journal of the American Geriatrics Society* 47 (12): 1430–34.

Landi, F., G. Onder, A. Russo, S. Tabaccanti, R. Rollo, S. Federici, et al. 2001. "A New Model of Integrated Home Care for the Elderly: Impact on Hospital Use." *Journal of Clinical Epidemiology* 54 (9): 968–70.

Lane, M., D. Davis, C. Cornman, C. Macera, and M. Sanderson. 1998. "Location of Death as an Indicator of End-of-Life Costs for the Person with Dementia." *American Journal of Alzheimer's Disease and Other Dementias* 13 (4): 208–10.

Langa, K.M., N.H. Fultz, S. Saint, M.U. Kabeto, and A.R. Herzog. 2002. "Informal Caregiving Time and Costs for Urinary Incontinence in Older Individuals in the United States." *Journal of the American Geriatrics Society* 50 (4): 733–37.

Larson, D., R. Odegard, and N.E. Brown. 1992. "A Specialized Home Care Team Does Make a Difference." *Healthcare Management Forum* 5 (3): 38–41.

Laslett, Peter. 1996. *A Fresh Map of Life: The Emergence of the Third Age*. London: Macmillan Press.

Lee, Y-R., and K-T. Sung. 1998. "Cultural Influences on Caregiving Burden: Cases of Koreans and Americans." *International Journal of Aging and Human Development* 46(2): 125–41.

Leeson, G.W. 2004. *PEFETE (Pan-European Forum for Education of the Elderly): National Background Report for Denmark*. Oxford: University of Oxford, Oxford Institute of Ageing

Lefrançois, G., S. Vézina, J. Keefe, and J. Légaré. Forthcoming. "Trends and Characteristics Affecting Disability among Older Canadians Living in Private Households." *Canadian Studies in Population*.

Le Goff, P. 2002. *Home Care Sector in Canada: Economic Problems*. Ottawa: Library of Parliament, Parliamentary Research Branch, Economics Division. Available online.

Leon, J., and D. Moyer. 1999. "Potential Cost Savings in Residential Care for Alzheimer's Disease Patients." *Gerontologist* 39 (4): 440–49.

Leung, A., C. Lui, N. Chow, and I. Chi. 2004. "Cost-Benefit Analysis of a Case Management Project for the Community-Dwelling Frail Elderly in Hong Kong." *Journal of Applied Gerontology* 23 (1): 70–85.

Leutz, W. 1999. "Five Laws for Integrating Medical and Social Services: Lessons from the United States and the United Kingdom." *The Milbank Quarterly* 77 (1): 77–110.

Lewin, S.N., B.M. Buttin, M.A. Powell, R.K. Gibb, J.S. Rader, et al. 2005. "Resource Utilization for Ovarian Cancer Patients at the End of Life: How Much Is Too Much?" *Gynecologic Oncology* 99 (2): 261–66.

Lewis, S. 2002. *Sharing the Learning: Health Transition Fund. Synthesis Series: Supporting an Evidence-Based Future in Canadian Health Care.* Ottawa: Health Canada. Available online.

Li, Peter S. 1998. *The Chinese in Canada.* Toronto: Oxford University Press.

Lim, W.K., S.F. Lambert, and L.C. Gray. 2003. "Effectiveness of Case Management and Post-Acute Services in Older People After Hospital Discharge." *Medical Journal of Australia* 178 (6): 262–66.

Lin, I-F. 2008. "Consequences of Parental Divorce for Adult Children's Support of Their Frail Parents." *Journal of Marriage and Family* 70 (1): 113–28.

Lindsey, C. 2006. General Social Survey Matter of Fact Series No. 4. *Do Older Canadians Have More Friends Now Than in 1990?* Component of Statistics Canada Catalogue no. 89-630-X. Ottawa: Statistics Canada. Available online.

Litwak, E. 1960. "Geographic Mobility and Extended Family Cohesion." *American Sociological Review* 25 (3): 385–94.

Liu, W.T., and H. Kendig. 2000. *Who Should Care for the Elderly? An East-West Value Divide.* Singapore: Singapore University Press.

Low, L.F., M. Yap, and H. Brodaty. 2011. "A Systematic Review of Different Models of Home and Community Care Services for Older Persons." *BMC Health Services Research* 11 (1): 93.

Lowenstein, A. 2007. "Solidarity–Conflict and Ambivalence: Testing Two Conceptual Frameworks and Their Impact on Quality of Life for Older Family Members." *The Journal of Gerontology* 62A (2): S100-S107.

Lowenthal, R.M., A. Piaszczyk, G.E. Arthur, and S. O'Malley. 1996. "Home Chemotherapy for Cancer Patients: Cost Analysis and Safety." *Medical Journal of Australia* 165 (4): 184–87.

Lynch, J.W., P. Due, C. Muntaner, and G. Smith. 2000. "Social Capital—Is It a Good Investment Strategy for Public Health?" *Journal of Epidemiology and Community Health* 54 (6): 404–8.

Lyonette, C., and L. Yardley. 2003. "The Influence on Carer Wellbeing of Motivations to Care for Older People and the Relationship with the Care Recipient." *Ageing and Society* 23 (4): 487–506.

MacAdam, M. 2008. *Frameworks of Integrated Care for the Elderly: A Systematic Review.* Ottawa: Canadian Policy Research Networks.

MacEachen, A.J. 1981. *Federal–Provincial Fiscal Arrangements in the Eighties: A Submission to the Parliamentary Task Force on the Federal–Provincial Fiscal Arrangements.* Ottawa: Department of Finance.

Mac Rae, H. 1998. "Managing Feelings: Caregiving as Emotion Work." *Research on Aging* 20 (1): 137–60.

Magnus, G. 2009. *The Age of Aging: How Demographics Are Changing the Global Economy and Our World.* Singapore: John Wiley and Sons.

Maltoni, M., O. Nanni, M. Naldoni, P. Serra, and D. Amadori. 1998. "Evaluation of Cost of Home Therapy for Patients with Terminal Diseases." *Current Opinion in Oncology* 10 (4): 302–9.

Mamulo, M., and S. Scherbov. 2009. *Population Projections for Forty-Four European Countries: The Ongoing Population Ageing.* Vienna: Vienna Institute of Demography.

Manitoba. 2011. "Caregiver Recognition Act Would Recognize Caregivers' Contribution to Families, Communities: Rondeau," news release, 26 May. Available online.

Manitoba. Government of Manitoba. 2012. "Bill 42: The Caregiver Recognition Act." Winnipeg: Legislative Assembly of Manitoba. Available online.

Manitoba. Manitoba Finance. 2008. *Primary Caregiver Tax Credit. Manitoba Finance.* Available online.

Mann, W. C., K.J. Ottenbacher, L. Fraas, M. Tomita, and C.V. Granger. 1999. "Effectiveness of Assistive Technology and Environmental Interventions in Maintaining Independence and Reducing Home Care Costs for the Frail Elderly." *Archives of Family Medicine* 8 (3): 210–17.

Manton, K.G. 2008. "Recent Declines in Chronic Disability in the Elderly U.S. Population: Risk Factors and Future Dynamics. *Annual Review of Public Health* 29: 91–113.

Marks, N., J. Lambert, H. Jun, and J. Song. 2008. "Psychological Moderators of the Effects of Transitioning into Filial Caregiving on Mental and Physical Health." *Research on Aging* 30 (3): 358–89.

Marmor, T.R. 2009. "Book Review: Fads, Fallacies and Foolishness in Medical Care Management and Policy." *The International Journal of Health Planning and Management* 24 (1): 87–90.

Marsh, L. 1943. *Report on Social Security for Canada.* Toronto: University of Toronto Press.

Martel, L., and J. Légaré. 2001. "Avec ou sans famille proche à la vieillesse: une description du réseau de soutien informel des personnes âgées selon la présence du conjoint et des enfants." *Cahiers québécois de démographie* 30 (1): 89–114.

Martin, M.T. 2009. "Leveraging our Collective Investment in Canada's Healthcare System." *HealthcarePapers* 9 (4): 47–50.

Martin, T. 2011. "Private Member's Bill: Bill C-545: An Act to Eliminate Poverty in Canada." Ottawa: Parliament of Canada. Available online.

Mathematica Policy Research Inc., R.A. Applebaum, and M. Harrigan. 1986. *Channeling Effects on the Quality of Clients' Lives.* Princeton, NJ: Mathematica Policy Research Inc. Washington: US Department of Health and Human Services, Office of the Assistant Secretary for Planning and Evaluation, Division of Disability Aging and Long Term Care Policy.

McCulloch, D.K., et al. 1998. "A Population-Based Approach to Diabetes Management in a Primary Care Setting: Early Results and Lessons Learned." *Effective Clinical Practice* 1 (1): 12–22.

McGrail, K., A. Zierler, and I. Ip. 2009. "Getting What We Pay For? The Value-for-Money Challenge." *HealthcarePapers* 9 (4): 8–22.

McIntosh, C.N., P. Finès, R. Wilkins, and M.C. Wolfson. 2009. "Income Disparities in Health-Adjusted Life Expectancy for Canadian Adults, 1991 to 2001." *Health Reports.* Statistics Canada Catalogue no. 82-003-X. Ottawa: Statistics Canada. Available online.

Meilicke, C.A., and J.L. Storch. 1980. *Perspectives on Canadian Health and Social Services Policy: History and Emerging Trends.* Ann Arbor, Michigan: Health Administration Press.

Melin, A.L., and L.O. Bygren. 1992. "Efficacy of the Rehabilitation of Elderly Primary Health Care Patients After Short-Stay Hospital Treatment." *Medical Care* 30 (11): 1004–15.

Mendleson, M., and P. Divinsky. 2002. *Canada 2015: Globalization and the Future of Canada's Health and Health Care.* Toronto: Queen's University Institute of Intergovernmental Relations. Available online.

Meret-Hanke, L.A. 2008. "The Effects of the Program of All-Inclusive Care for the Elderly (PACE) on Hospital and Nursing Home Use." PhD diss., Pennsylvania State University, 2008.

Mérette, M. 2002. *The Bright Side: A Positive View on the Economics of Aging.* Montreal: Institute for Research on Public Policy.

Mhatre, S.L., and R.B. Deber. 1992. "From Equal Access to Health Care to Equitable Access to Health: A Review of Canadian Provincial Health Commissions and Reports." *International Journal of Health Services* 22 (4): 645–68.

Milan, A., and M. Vézina. 2011. *Senior Women. Women in Canada: A Gender-Based Statistical Report.* Component of Statistics Canada Catalogue no. 89-503-X. Ottawa: Statistics Canada. Available online.

Montgomery, R.J.V., E.F. Borgatta, and M.L. Borgatta. 2000. "Societal and Family Change in the Burden of Care." In *Who Should Care for the Elderly? An East–West Value Divide,* edited by W.T. Liu and H. Kendig, 27–54. Singapore: Singapore University Press

Morgan, S. and C. Cunningham. 2011. "Population Aging and the Determinants of Healthcare Expenditures: The Case of Hospital, Medical and Pharmaceutical Care in British Columbia, 1966 to 2006." *HealthCare Policy* 7 (1): 68–79.

Moriarty, J., and J. Butt. 2004. "Social Support and Ethnicity in Old Age." In *Growing Older: Quality of Life in Old Age,* edited by A. Walker and C. Hagan Hennessy, 167–87. Maidenhead, UK: Open University Press.

Morneau, W. 2011. "Canada's Health Care System: Time for an Intervention." *Vision* 14 (2): 1–11. Toronto: Morneau–Sheppell Inc.

Morrell, C.J., S.J. Walters, S. Dixon, K.A. Collins, L.M. Brereton, J. Peters, and C.G. Brooker. 1998. "Cost Effectiveness of Community Leg Ulcer Clinics: Randomised Controlled Trial." *British Medical Journal* 316 (7143): 1487–91.

Mukamel, D.B., D.R. Peterson, H. Temkin-Greener, R. Delavan, D. Gross, S.J. Kunitz, et al. 2007. "Program Characteristics and Enrollees' Outcomes in the Program of All-Inclusive Care for the Elderly (PACE)." *Milbank Quarterly* 85 (3): 499–531.

Murphy, N., C. Byrne, and R.W. Costello. 2002. "An Early Supported Discharge Programme for Patients with Exacerbations of Chronic Obstructive Pulmonary Disease (COPD) in Ireland." *All Ireland Journal of Nursing & Midwifery* 2 (6): 30–34.

National Advisory Council on Aging (NACA). 2004. *The NACA Position on Alzheimer Disease and Related Dementias.* Ottawa: Minister of Public Works and Government Services Canada.

National Forum on Health. 1997. *Canada Health Action: Building on the Legacy. Volumes 1: The Final Report, and Volume II: Synthesis Reports and Issue Papers.* Ottawa: National Forum on Health.

Navaie-Waliser, M., P.H. Feldman, D.A. Gould, C. Levine, A.N. Kuerbis, and K. Donelan. 2002. "When the Caregiver Needs Care: The Plight of Vulnerable Caregivers." *American Journal of Public Health* 92 (3): 409–13.

Navarro, Vicente. 2007. *Neoliberalism, Globalization, and Inequalities: Consequences for Health and Quality of Life.* Amityville, NY: Baywood.

Nazroo, J., M. Bajekal, D. Blane, and I. Grewal. 2004. "Ethnic Inequalities." In *Growing Older: Quality of Life in Old Age,* edited by A. Walker and C. Hagan Hennessy, 35–59. Maidenhead, UK: Open University Press.

Neugarten, B.L. 1974. "Age Groups in American Society and the Rise of the Young-Old." *The Annals of the American Academy of Political and Social Sciences* 415 (1): 187–98.

New Brunswick. Department of Health and Wellness. 2006. *Healthcare Without Walls. The New Brunswick Extra-Mural Program.* Fredericton: Department of Health and Wellness. Available online.

New Brunswick, E. Neil McKelvey and Bernadette Lévesque. 1989. *Report of the Commission on Selected Health Care Programs.* Fredericton: The Commission.

News Canada. 2012. *Poll [Revera Living Poll] Shows Boomers Not Content with Aging Prospects.* April 2012. Available online.

Nicholson, C., S. Bowler, C. Jackson, D. Schollay, M. Tweeddale, and P. O'Rourke. 2001. "Cost Comparison of Hospital- and Home-Based Treatment Models for Acute Chronic Obstructive Pulmonary Disease." *Australian Health Review* 24 (4): 181–87.

Nova Scotia. Department of Health and Wellness, Continuing Care Branch. 2010. *Caregiver Benefit Program Policy.* Halifax: Department of Health and Wellness. Available online.

Nova Scotia Royal Commission on Health Care. 1989. *The Report of the Nova Scotia Royal Commission on Health Care: Towards a New Strategy.* Halifax: Nova Scotia Royal Commission on Health Care. Available online.

Nuñez, D.E., C. Armbruster, W.T. Phillips, and B.J. Gale. 2003. "Community-Based Senior Health Promotion Program Using a Collaborative Practice Model: The Escalante Health Partnerships." *Public Health Nursing* 20 (1): 25–32.

O'Brien, S.P., V. Gahtan, S. Wind, and M.D. Kerstein. 1999. "What Is the Paradigm: Hospital or Home Health Care for Pressure Ulcers?" *American Surgeon* 65 (4): 303–6.

O'Connor, D.L. 2007. "Self-Identifying as a Caregiver: Exploring the Positioning Process." *Journal of Aging Studies* 21 (2): 165–74.

Organization for Economic Co-operation and Development (OECD). 2009a. *Achieving Better Value for Money in Health Care.* Available online.

———. 2009b. "Life Expectancy at Age 65." In *Health at a Glance 2009: OECD Indicators.* Paris: OECD Publishing. Available online.

———. 2011. OECD Health Data 2011—Frequently Requested Data. Available online.

Østbye, T., and E. Crosse. 1994. "Net Economic Costs of Dementia in Canada." *CMAJ Canadian Medical Association Journal* 151 (10): 1457–64. [erratum in 1995: *Canadian Medical Association Journal* 152 (2): 158.]

Østbye, T., B. Kristjansson, G. Hill, S.C. Newman, R.N. Brouwer, and I. McDowell. 2005. "Prevalence and Predictors of Depression in Elderly Canadians: The Canadian Study of Health and Aging." *Chronic Diseases in Canada* 26 (4): 93–99.

Parkatti, T., and P. Eskola. 2004. *EUROFAMCARE: National Background Report for Finland. Services for Supporting Family Carers of Elderly People in Europe: Characteristics, Coverage and Usage (EUROFAMCARE).* Available online.

Patterson, C., and L.W. Chambers. 1995. "Preventive Health Care." *The Lancet* 345 (8965): 1611–15.

Pearlin, L.I., J.T. Mullan, S.J. Semple, and M.M. Skaff. 1990. "Caregiving and the Stress Process: An Overview of Concepts and Their Measures." *The Gerontologist* 30: 583–94.

Pedlar, D., and J. Walker. 2004. "The Overseas Service Veteran (OSV) At Home Pilot: How Choice of Care May Affect Use of Nursing Home Beds and Waiting Lists." *Canadian Journal on Aging* 23 (4): 367–69.

Peleg, R., Y. Press, M. Asher, T. Pugachev, H. Glicensztain, M. Lederman, and A. Biderman. 2008. "An Intervention Program to Reduce the Number of Hospitalizations of Elderly Patients in a Primary Care Clinic." *BMC Health Services Research* 8: 36.

Penning, M.J. 1998. "In the Middle: Parental Caregiving in the Context of Other Roles." *Journal of Gerontology* 53B: S188–S197.

Penning, M.J., M.E. Brackley, C. Zheng, and D.E. Allan. 2009. "Geography, Home Care and Health Care Reform in British Columbia, 1991–2000." In *Health and Aging in British Columbia: Vulnerability and Resilience,* edited by Denise S. Cloutier-Fisher, Leslie T. Foster, and David F. Hultsch, 285–308. Victoria: Western Geographical Press.

Penning, M.J., and N.L. Chappell. 2010. *Health Inequalities among Adults in Later Life: Review of Issues, Promising Practices and Upstream Health Interventions in Responding to Aging and Older People in Canada.* Unpublished report for the Public Health Agency of Canada.

Phillipson, C. 2007. "Understanding the Baby Boom Generation: Comparative Perspectives." *International Journal of Aging and Later Life* 2 (2): 7–11.

Pickard, L. 2001. "Carer Break or Carer-Blind? Policies for Informal Carers in the UK." *Social Policy and Administration* 35 (4): 441–58.

Pinquart, M., and S. Sörensen. 2003. "Differences between Caregivers and Noncaregivers in Psychological Health and Physical Health: A Meta-analysis." *Psychology and Aging* 18 (2): 250–67.

Prince, M.J. 1996. "At the Edge of Canada's Welfare State: Social Policy-Making in British Columbia." In *Politics, Policy, and Government in British Columbia*, edited by R.K. Carty. 236–71. Vancouver: University of British Columbia Press.

Public Health Agency of Canada. 2009. *Injury Prevention for Seniors.* Available online.

Puntis, J.W.L. 1998. The Economics of Home Parental Nutrition. *Nutrition* 14 (10): 809–12.

Pyke, K. 2000. "'The Normal American Family' as an Interpretive Structure of Family Life among Grown Children of Korean and Vietnamese Immigrants." *Journal of Marriage and Family* 62 (1): 240–55.

Ramage-Morin, P.L. 2008. "Chronic Pain in Canadian Seniors." *Health Reports* 19 (1): 37–52. Statistics Canada Catalogue no. 82-003-X. Ottawa: Statistics Canada. Available online.

Ramage-Morin, P.L., M. Shields, and L. Martel. 2010. "Health-Promoting Factors and Good Health among Canadians in Mid- to Late Life." *Health Reports* 21(3). Statistics Canada Catalogue no. 82-003-X. Ottawa: Statistics Canada. Available online.

Reid, R.C., K. Stajduhar, and N.L. Chappell. 2010. "The Impact of Work Interferences on Family Caregiver Outcomes." *Journal of Applied Gerontology* 29 (3): 267–89.

Research on Aging, Policies and Practice (RAPP). 2010. "Gender Differences in Family/ Friend Caregiving in Canada." *RAPP Fact Sheet.* December 2010.

Rich, M.W., et al. 1993. "Prevention of Readmission in Elderly Patients with Congestive Heart Failure: Results of a Prospective, Randomized Pilot Study." *Journal of General Internal Medicine* 8 (11): 585–90.

———. 1995. "A Multidisciplinary Intervention to Prevent the Readmission of Elderly Patients with Congestive Heart Failure." *New England Journal of Medicine* 333 (18): 1190–95.

Richards, D.M., and M.H. Irving. 1996. "Cost-Utility Analysis of Home Parenteral Nutrition." *British Journal of Surgery* 83 (9): 1226–29.

Rischin, D., M.A. White, J.P. Matthews, G.C. Toner, K. Watty, A.J. Sulkowski, J.L. Clarke, and L. Buchanan. 2000. "A Randomized Crossover Trial of Chemotherapy in the Home: Patient Preferences and Cost Analysis." *Medical Journal of Australia* 173 (3): 125–27.

Rizzi, M., M. Grassi, M. Pecis, A. Andreoli, A.E. Taurino, M. Sergi, and F. Fanfulla. 2009. "A Specific Home Care Program Improves the Survival of Patients with Chronic Obstructive Pulmonary Disease Receiving Long Term Oxygen Therapy." *Archives of Physical Medicine & Rehabilitation* 90 (3): 395–401.

Rizzo, J.A., D.I. Baker, G. McAvay, M.E. Tinetti. 1996. "The Cost-Effectiveness of a Multifactorial Targeted Prevention Program for Falls Among Community Elderly Persons." *Medical Care* 34 (9): 954–69.

Robb, N. 1994. "New Brunswick's Unique Extra-Mural Hospital Tries to Return Control of Health Care to Families." *Canadian Medical Association Journal* 150 (10): 1662–66.

Roberts, D. 2001. "Home Supported Discharge Was as Effective and Safe as Standard Hospital Admission in Patients with Chronic Obstructive Pulmonary Disease." . . . Commentary on E. Skwarska, G. Choen, K.M. Skwarski, et al., "Randomised

Controlled Trial of Supported Discharge in Patients with Exacerbations of Chronic Obstructive Pulmonary Disease." *Evidence-Based Nursing* 4 (3): 88–89.

Roberts, R.E.L., and V.L. Bengston. 1996. "Affective Ties to Parents in Early Adulthood and Self-Esteem Across 20 Years." *Social Psychology Quarterly* 59 (1): 96–106.

Robertson, K.A., and K. Kayhko. 2001. "Cost Analysis of an Intensive Home Follow-Up Program for First-Time Post-Myocardial Infarction Patients and Their Families." *Dynamics* 12 (4): 25–31.

Robinson, B.E., and H. Pham. 1996. "Cost-Effectiveness of Hospice Care." *Clinics in Geriatric Medicine* 12 (2): 417–28.

Robinson, J., R. Fortinsky, A. Kleppinger, N. Shugrue, and M. Porter. 2009. "A Broader View of Family Caregiving: Effects of Caregiving and Caregiver Conditions on Depressive Symptoms, Health, Work and Social Isolation." *The Journals of Gerontology, Series B* 64B (6): 788–98.

Robson, W.B.P. 2001. *Aging Populations and the Workforce: Challenges for Employers.* Final draft of the paper prepared for the Working Group on Business and the Challenge of Aging in the Western World, approved for publication at the British-North American Committee (BNAC) meeting in London, 12 May 2001. Available online.

———. 2009. *Boomer Bulge: Dealing with the Stress of Demographic Change on Government Budgets in Canada.* Toronto: C.D. Howe Institute. 13 January.

Rockwood, K., and A. Mitnitski. 2007. "Frailty in Relation to the Accumulation of Deficits." *Journal of Gerontology* 62A (7): 722–27.

Rockwood, K., X. Song, and A. Mitniski. 2011. "Changes in Relative Fitness and Frailty across the Adult Lifespan: Evidence from the Canadian National Population Health Survey." *Canadian Medical Association Journal* 183 (8): E487–94.

Romanow, R. 2002. *Building on Values: The Future of Health Care in Canada.* Ottawa: Commission on the Future of Health Care in Canada.

Rosenmayr, L., and E. Kockeis. 1963. "Propositions for a Sociological Theory of Aging and the Family." *International Social Science Journal* 15: 410–26.

Rosenthal, C.J., A. Martin-Matthews, and J.M. Keefe. 2007. "Care Management and Care Provision for Older Relatives Amongst Employed Informal Caregivers." *Ageing and Society* 27 (5): 755–78.

Rowe, J.W., and R.L. Kahn. 1998. *Successful Aging.* NY: Pantheon Books.

Ruggeri, G.C. 2002. *Population Aging, Health Care Spending and Sustainability: Do We Really Have a Crisis?* Ottawa: Caledon Institute of Social Policy.

Salisbury, C., N. Bosanquet, E.K. Wilkinson, P.J. Franks, S. Kite, et al. 1999. "The Impact of Different Models of Specialist Palliative Care on Patients' Quality of Life: A Systematic Literature Review." [Review]. *Palliative Medicine* 13 (1): 3–17.

Salkeld, G., R.G. Cumming, E. O'Neill, M. Thomas, G. Szonyi, and C. Westbury. 2000. "The Cost Effectiveness of a Home Hazard Reduction Program to Reduce Falls among Older Persons." *Australian & New Zealand Journal of Public Health* 24 (3): 265–71.

Sanderson, W.C., and S. Scherbov. 2010. "Remeasuring Aging." *Science* 329 (5997): 1287–88.

Saskatchewan. 2000. *The Impact of Preventive Home Care and Seniors Housing on Health Outcomes.* Saskatoon: Health Services Utilization and Research Commission.

Saskatchewan Commission on Directions in Health Care. 1990. *Future Directions for Health Care in Saskatchewan.* Regina: The Commission: Public Affairs Branch, Saskatchewan Department of Health.

Saskatchewan Health Services Utilization and Research Commission. 1998. *Hospital and Home Care Study (Report No. 10).* Saskatoon: Saskatchewan Health Services Utilization and Research Commission.

Schaefer, J., and C. Davis. 2004. "Care Management and the Chronic Care Model: A Multidisciplinary Role." *Lippincott's Case Management* 9 (2): 96–103.

Schellenberg, G., and Y. Ostrovksy. 2007. General Social Survey Report. *The Retirement Plans and Expectations of Older Worker.* Statistics Canada Catalogue no. 11-008-X Nov. 86 2008002. Ottawa: Statistics Canada. Available online.

Schinka, J.A., E. Francis, P. Hughes, L. LaLone, and C. Flynn. 1998. "Comparative Outcomes and Costs of Inpatient Care and Supportive Housing for Substance-Dependent Veterans." *Psychiatric Services* 49 (7): 946.

Schulz, R., and S. Beach. 1999. "Caregiving as a Risk Factor for Mortality: The Caregiver Health Effects Study." *JAMA Journal of the American Medical Association* 282 (23): 2215–19.

Scott, V.J., K. Votova, and E. Gallagher. 2006. "Falls Prevention Training for Community Health Workers: Strategies and Actions for Independent Living (SAIL)." *Journal of Gerontological Nursing* 32 (10): 48–56.

Scuvee-Moreau, J., X. Kurz, A. Dresse, and National Dementia Economic Study Group. 2002. "The Economic Impact of Dementia in Belgium: Results of the National Dementia Economic Study (NADES)." *Acta neurologica Belgica* 102 (3): 104–13.

Selig, S., T. Tomlinson, and T. Hickey. 1991. "Ethical Dimensions of Intergenerational Reciprocity: Implications for Practice." *The Gerontologist* 31 (5): 624–30.

Shapiro, E. 1993. "Manitoba's Single-Entry System to Long-Term Care." *Journal of Ambulatory Care Management* 16 (3): 69–74.

Sherman, C., and P. Boss. 2007. "Spousal Dementia Caregiving in the Context of Late-Life Remarriage." *Dementia: International Journal of Social Research and Practice* 6 (2): 245–70.

Sherwood, P.R., C.W. Given, B.A. Given, and A. von Eye. 2005. "Caregiver Burden and Depressive Symptoms: Analysis of Common Outcomes in Caregivers of Elderly Patients." *Journal of Aging and Health* 17 (2): 125–47.

Silverstein, M., and V.L. Bengtson. 1997. "Intergenerational Solidarity and the Structure of Adult Child-Parent Relationships in American Families." *American Journal of Sociology* 103 (2): 429–60.

Skellie, A., F. Favor, C. Tudor, and R. Strauss. 1984. "The Georgia Alternative Health Services Project: Cost-effectiveness Depends on Population Selection." *Home Health Care Service Quarterly* 4 (3–4): 49–72.

Smiley, D.V. 1963. *The Rowell-Sirois Report: Book 1.* Toronto: McClelland and Stewart Ltd.

Snowdon, A., K. Kellie Leitch, and J. Shell. 2010. *Innovation Takes Leadership: Opportunities and Challenges for Canada's Health Care System.* London, ON: Ivey Centre for Health Innovation and Leadership.

Song, X., A. Mitniski, and K. Rockwood. 2010. "Prevalence and 10-Year Outcomes of Frailty in Older Adults in Relation to Deficit Accumulation." *Journal of the American Geriatrics Society* 58 (4): 681–87.

Spitzer, D., A. Neufeld, M. Harrison, K. Hughes, and M. Stewart. 2003. "Caregiving in Transnational Context: 'My Wings Have Been Cut; Where Can I Fly?'" *Gender and Society* 17 (2): 267–86.

Statistics Canada. 2000–2001. *Canadian Community Health Survey (Cycle 1.1).* Statistics Canada Record no. 3226. Ottawa: Statistics Canada. Available online.

———. 2001. *Census in Brief, no. 4. Living Arrangements of Seniors Aged 65 and Over by Sex and Age Group, Canada, 2001.* Statistics Canada Catalogue no. 98-312-X2011003. Ottawa: Statistics Canada. Available online.

———. 2006. *2006 Census: Family Portrait: Continuity and Change in Canadian Families and Households in 2006: National Portrait: Individuals.* Statistics Canada Catalogue no. 97-553-XWE2006001. Ottawa: Statistics Canada. Available online.

———. 2008a. *Canadian Demographics at a Glance.* Statistics Canada Catalogue no. 91-003-XWE. Ottawa: Statistics Canada. Available online.

———. 2008b. *Canadian Survey of Experiences with Primary Health Care (CSE-PHC).* Statistics Canada Record no. 5138. Ottawa: Statistics Canada. Available online.

———. 2009. CANSIM Tables 051-0001 ("Estimates of Population by Age Group and Sex for July 1, Canada, Provinces and Territories, Annual—1971 to 2008") and 052-0004 ("Projected Population, by Projection Scenario, Sex and Age Group as at July 1, Canada, Provinces and Territories, Annual—2009 to 2056"). Ottawa: Statistics Canada. Available online.

———. 2010a. "Canadian Community Health Survey: Rapid Response on Stigma and Mental Health Experiences." *The Daily* 4 November. Available online.

———. 2010b. "Health Promoting Factors and Good Health among Canadians in Mid-to Late-Life." *Health Reports* 21, no. 3. Statistics Canada Catalogue no. 82-003-XWE. Available online.

———. 2010c. "Life Expectancy." In *Healthy People, Healthy Places.* Statistics Canada Catalogue no. 82-229-X. Ottawa: Statistics Canada. Available online.

———. 2010d. *Perceived Mental Health.* Statistics Canada Catalogue no. 82-229-X. Ottawa: Statistics Canada. Available online.

———. 2010e. "Population Projections for Canada, Provinces and Territories, 2009-2036." *Population Projections for Canada, Provinces and Territories.* Statistics Canada Catalogue no. 91-520-X. Ottawa: Statistics Canada. Available online.

Stevens, B., P. McKeever, P.C. Coyte, M. Daub, S. Gibbins, et al. 2001. *Substudy 12: Cost-Effectiveness of Home Versus Hospital Support of Breast Feeding in Neonates.* Victoria: National Evaluation of the Cost-Effectiveness of Home Care.

Stewart, S., J.E. Marley, and J.D. Horowitz. 1999. "Effects of a Multidisciplinary, Home-Based Intervention on Unplanned Readmissions and Survival among Patients with Chronic Congestive Heart Failure: A Randomised Controlled Study." *Lancet* 354 (9184): 1077–83.

Stones, M.J., and L. Stones. 1997. "Ageism: The Quiet Epidemic." *Canadian Journal of Public Health* 88 (5): 293–96.

Stuart, M., and M. Weinrich. 2001. "Home- and Community-Based Long-Term Care: Lessons from Denmark." *Gerontologist* 41 (4): 474–80.

———. 2004. "Integrated Health System for Chronic Disease Management: Lessons Learned from France." *Chest* 125: 695–703.

Tang, S.T., C.Y. Li, and Y-C. Liao. 2007. "Factors Associated with Depressive Distress among Taiwanese Family Caregivers of Cancer Patients at the End of Life." *Palliative Medicine* 21 (3): 249–57.

Tarlow, B.J., S.R. Wisniewski, S.H. Belle, M. Rubert, M.G. Ory, and D. Gallagher-Thompson. 2004. "Positive Aspects of Caregiving: Contributions of the REACH Project to the Development of New Measures for Alzheimer's Caregiving." *Research on Aging* 26 (4): 429–53.

Taylor, M.G. 1978. *Health Insurance and Canadian Public Policy: The Seven Decisions that Created the Canadian Health Insurance System.* Montreal and Kingston: McGill-Queen's University Press.

———. 1987. *Health Insurance and Canadian Public Policy: The Seven Decisions that Created the Canadian Health Insurance System and their Outcomes.* Montreal: McGill-Queen's University Press.

Teng, J., N.E. Mayo, E. Latimer, J. Hanley, S. Wood-Dauphinee, R. Côté, and S. Scott. 2003. "Costs and Caregiver Consequences of Early Supported Discharge for Stroke Patients." *Stroke* 34 (2): 528–36.

Thompson, V.D. 2010. *Health and Health Care Delivery in Canada.* Toronto: Mosby/ Elsevier Canada.

Titmuss, R.M. 1976. *Essays on "the Welfare State."* 3rd ed. London: Allen and Unwin.

Torjman, S. 1995. *CHST Spells COST for Disabled.* Ottawa: Caledon Institute for Social Policy. Available online.

Tousignant, M., R. Hébert, N. Dubuc, F. Simoneau, and L. Dieleman. 2003. "Application of a Case-Mix Classification Based on the Functional Autonomy of the Residents for Funding Long-Term Care Facilities." *Age and Ageing* 32 (1): 60–66.

Townsend, J., M. Piper, A.O. Frank, S. Dyer, W. North, et al. 1998. "Reduction in Hospital Readmission Stay of Elderly Patients by a Community-based Hospital Discharge Scheme: A Randomised Controlled Trial." *British Medical Journal* 297 (6647): 544–47.

Traphagen, J.W. 2008. "Constraint, Power and Intergenerational Discontinuity in Japan." *Journal of Intergenerational Relationships* 6 (2): 211–29.

Tuggey, J.M., P.K. Plant, and M.W. Elliott. 2003. "Domiciliary Non-Invasive Ventilation for Recurrent Acidotic Exacerbations of COPD: An Economic Analysis." *Thorax* 58 (10): 867–71.

Turcotte, M., and G. Schellenberg. 2006. *A Portrait of Seniors in Canada.* Statistics Canada Catalogue no. 89-519-XIE. Ottawa: Statistics Canada. Available online.

United Nations. Population Division. 1999. *World Population Prospects: The 1998 Revision. Volume 1: Comprehensive Tables.* ST/ESA/SER.A/177. Department of Economic and Social Affairs. NY: United Nations.

———. Statistics Bureau. 2008. *Population by Age, Sex and Urban/Rural Residence: Latest Available Year, 1997–2006.* NY: United Nations. Available online.

Van Dalen, H.P., K. Henkens, and J. Schippers. 2009. "Dealing with Older Workers in Europe: A Comparative Survey of Employers' Attitudes and Actions." *Journal of European Social Policy* 19 (1): 47–60.

Van Houtven, C.H., and E.C. Norton. 2008. "Informal Care and Medicare Expenditures: Testing for Heterogeneous Treatment Effects." *Journal of Health Economics* 27 (1): 134–56.

Van Loon, R.J. 1978. "From Shared Cost to Block Funding and Beyond: The Politics of Health Insurance in Canada." *Journal of Health Politics, Policy and Law* 2 (4): 454–78.

Veenhoven, R. 1991. "Is Happiness Relative?" *Social Indicators Research* 24 (1): 1–34.

Verma, J., and S. Samis. 2011. [Guest Editorial]. *HealthcarePapers.* 11 (1): 3–5.

Vinciguerra, V., T.J. Degnan, D.R Budman, R.S. Brody, T. Moore, et al. 1986. "Comparative Cost Analysis of Home and Hospital Treatment." In *Advances in Cancer Control: Health Care Financing and Research,* edited by L.E. Mortensen, P.N. Anderson, and P.F. Engstrom, 155–164. New York: Liss.

Vitaliano, P.P., J. Zhang, and J.M. Scanlan. 2003. "Is Caregiving Hazardous to One's Physical Health? A Meta-Analysis." *Psychological Bulletin* 129 (6): 946–72.

Wagner, E.H., C. Davis, J. Schaefer, M. Von Korff, and B. Austin. 2002. "A Survey of Leading Chronic Disease Management Programs: Are They Consistent with the Literature?" *Journal of Nursing Care Quality* 16 (2): 67–80.

Walker, A. 2002. "Growing Older: An ESRC Research Programme." *Quality in Ageing and Older Adults* 3 (1): 4–12.

Walker, B.L., N.J. Osgood, J.P. Richardson, and P.H. Ephross. 1998. "Staff and Elderly Knowledge and Attitudes Toward Elderly Sexuality." *Educational Gerontology* 24 (5): 471–89.

Ward-Griffin, C., and V. Marshall. 2003. "Reconceptualizing the Relationship Between 'Public' and 'Private' Eldercare." *Journal of Aging Studies* 17 (2): 189–208.

Weissert, W.G. 1985. "Seven Reasons Why It Is So Difficult to Make Community-Based Long Term Care Cost-Effective." *Health Services Research* 20 (4): 423–33.

Weissert, W.G., C.M. Cready, and J.E. Pawelak. 1988. "The Past and Future of Home- and Community-Based Long Term Care." *The Milbank Quarterly* 66 (2): 309–88

Weissert, W.G., T. Lesnick, M. Musliner, and K.A. Foley. 1997. "Cost Savings from Home and Community-Based Services: Arizona's Capitated Medicaid Long Term Care Program." *Journal of Health Politics, Policy and Law* 22 (6): 1329–57.

Whyte, M.K. 2004. "Filial Obligations in Chinese Families: Paradoxes of Modernization." In *Filial Piety: Practice and Discourse in Contemporary East Asia*, edited by Charlotte Ikels, 106–27. Palo Alto: Stanford University Press.

Wilensky, H.L., and C.N. Lebeaux. 1965. *Industrial Society and Social Welfare: The Impact of Industrialization on the Supply and Organization of Welfare Services in the United States.* NY: Free Press.

Wilkins, R., S. Uppal, P. Finés, S. Senécal, E. Guimond, and R. Dion. 2008. "Life Expectancy in the Inuit-Inhabited Areas of Canada, 1989 to 2003." *Health Reports* 19 (1): 1–14. Statistics Canada Catalogue No. 82-003-X. Ottawa: Statistics Canada. Available online.

Williams, C. 2005. "The Sandwich Generation." *Canadian Social Trends* (summer 2005): 16–24. Statistics Canada Catalogue No. 11-008. Ottawa: Statistics Canada. Available online.

Williams, P., R. Deber, P. Baranek, and A. Gildiner. 2001. "From Medicare to Home Care: Globalization, State Retrenchment, and the Profitization of Canada's Health-care System." In *Unhealthy Times. Political Economy Perspectives on Health and Care in Canada*, edited by P. Armstrong, H. Armstrong, and D. Coburn, 7–30. Toronto: Oxford University Press.

Wimo, A., B. Mattson, I. Krakau, T. Eriksson, A. Nelvig, et al. 1995. "Cost-Utility Analysis of Group Living in Dementia Care." *International Journal of Technology Assessment in Health Care* 11 (1): 49–65.

Wister, A.V. 2005. *Baby Boomer Health Dynamics: How Are We Aging?* Toronto: University of Toronto Press.

Wood, G., A. Wilkinson, and M. Harcourt. 2008. "Age Discrimination and Working Life: Perspectives and Contestations—A Review of the Contemporary Literature." *International Journal of Management Reviews* 10 (4): 425–42.

World Health Organization (WHO). 2002. *Active Ageing: A Policy Framework.* (contribution of the WHO to the Second United Nations World Assembly on Ageing, Madrid, Spain, April 2002). Geneva: WHO. Available online.

———. 2003. *Social Determinants of Health: The Solid Facts.* Copenhagen, Denmark: WHO Regional Office for Europe. Available online.

———. 2011. *Facing the Facts: The Impact of Chronic Disease in Canada.* Available online.

Zhan, H.J. 2006. "Joy and Sorrow: Explaining Chinese Caregivers' Reward and Stress." *Journal of Aging Studies* 20 (1): 27–38.

Index